Elements of Literature

Second Course

The Holt Reader

- Respond to and Analyze Texts
- Apply Reading Skills
- Develop Vocabulary and Practice Fluency

HOLT, RINEHART AND WINSTON

A Harcourt Education Company

Orlando • Austin • New York • San Diego • Toronto • London

Staff Credits

Executive Editor: Juliana Koenig

Senior Editor: Amy E. Fleming

Project Editor: Steve Oelenberger

Copyediting: Michael Neibergall, *Copyediting Manager;* Kristen Azzara, Mary Malone, *Copyediting Supervisors;* Christine Altgelt, Elizabeth Dickson, Leora Harris, Anne Heausler, Kathleen Scheiner, *Senior Copyeditors;* Emily Force, Julia Thomas Hu, Nancy Shore, *Copyeditors*

Project Administration: Marie Price, *Managing Editor;* Elizabeth LaManna, *Associate Managing Editor;* Janet Jenkins, *Senior Editorial Coordinator;* Christine Degollado, Betty Gabriel, Mark Koenig, Erik Netcher, *Editorial Coordinators*

Permissions: Ann Farrar, *Senior Permissions Editor;* Sally Garland, Susan Lowrance, *Permissions Editors*

Design: Betty Mintz, Richard Metzger, *Design Directors;* Chris Smith, *Senior Designer*

Series Design: Proof Positive/Farrowlyne Associates, Inc.

Production: Beth Prevelige, *Senior Production Manager;* Carol Trammel, *Production Manager;* Dolores Keller, *Production Coordinator*

Photo Research: Proof Positive/Farrowlyne Associates, Inc.

Manufacturing: Shirley Cantrell, *Manufacturing Supervisor;* Mark McDonald, *Inventory Analyst;* Amy Borseth, *Manufacturing Coordinator*

Cover

Photo Credits: (inset) *The Rocket* (1909) by Edward Middleton Manigault. Oil on canvas. Collection of Columbus Museum of Art, Ohio, Museum Purchase, Howard Fund II (1981.009). (Background) Photograph of fireworks, © Brian Stablyk/Getty Images.

Printed in the United States of America
ISBN 0-03-068392-0

1 2 3 4 5 6 179 07 06 05 04 03

Contents

• PART ONE •
READING LITERATURE

COLLECTION 4   The Human Spirit

To the Student

A Book for You

A book is like a garden carried in the pocket.
—Chinese Proverb

The more you put into reading, the more you get out of it. This book is designed to do just that—help you interact with the selections you read by marking them up, asking your own questions, taking notes, recording your own ideas, and responding to the questions of others.

A Book Designed for Your Success

The Holt Reader goes hand in hand with *Elements of Literature.* It is designed to help you interact with the selections and master the language arts skills.

The book has two parts, each of which follows a simple format:

Part 1   Reading Literature

To help you master how to respond to, analyze, evaluate, and interpret literature, *The Holt Reader* provides—

For each collection:
- The academic vocabulary you need to know to master the literary skills for the collection, defined for ready reference and use.
- Two selections from the corresponding collection in *Elements of Literature,* reprinted in an interactive format to support and guide your reading.
- A new selection for you to read and respond to, enabling you to apply and extend your skills and build toward independence.

For each selection:
- A Before You Read page that preteaches the literary focus and provides a reading skill to help you understand the selection.
- A Vocabulary Development page or section that preteaches selection vocabulary and provides a vocabulary skill to use while reading the prose selections.
- Literature printed in an interactive format to guide your reading and help you respond to the text.
- A Skills Practice graphic organizer that helps you understand the literary focus of the selection.
- A Skills Review page that helps you practice vocabulary and assess your understanding of the selection you've just read.

Part 2   Reading Informational Texts

To help you master how to read informational texts, this book contains—

- The academic vocabulary you need to know to understand informational reading skills, defined for ready reference and use.
- New informational selections in interactive format to guide your reading and help you respond to the text.
- A Before You Read page that preteaches a reading skill to help you comprehend the selection. Selection vocabulary is also pretaught on this page.
- A Skills Practice graphic organizer that helps you understand the reading focus of the selection.
- A Skills Review page that helps you practice vocabulary and assess your understanding of the selection you've just read.

A Book for Your Own Thoughts and Feelings

Reading is about *you*. It is about connecting your thoughts and feelings to the thoughts and feelings of the writer. Make this book your own. The more you give of yourself to your reading, the more you will get out of it. We encourage you to write in it. Jot down how you feel about the selection. Question the text. Note details you think need to be cleared up or topics you would like to learn more about.

A Walk Through the Book

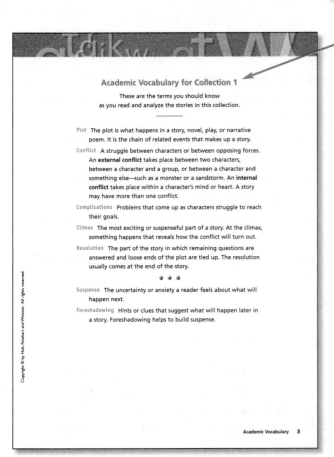

Academic Vocabulary for Collection 1

These are the terms you should know
as you read and analyze the stories in this collection.

Plot The plot is what happens in a story, novel, play, or narrative poem. It is the chain of related events that makes up a story.

Conflict A struggle between characters or between opposing forces. An **external conflict** takes place between two characters, between a character and a group, or between a character and something else—such as a monster or a sandstorm. An **internal conflict** takes place within a character's mind or heart. A story may have more than one conflict.

Complications Problems that come up as characters struggle to reach their goals.

Climax The most exciting or suspenseful part of a story. At the climax, something happens that reveals how the conflict will turn out.

Resolution The part of the story in which remaining questions are answered and loose ends of the plot are tied up. The resolution usually comes at the end of the story.

● ● ●

Suspense The uncertainty or anxiety a reader feels about what will happen next.

Foreshadowing Hints or clues that suggest what will happen later in a story. Foreshadowing helps to build suspense.

Academic Vocabulary   **3**

Academic Vocabulary
Academic vocabulary refers to the language of books, tests, and formal writing. Each collection begins with the terms, or academic language, you need to know to master the skills for that collection.

Before You Read

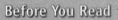

Broken Chain by Gary Soto

LITERARY FOCUS: CONFLICT

Plot is a series of related events that take place in a story. Through the plot we learn what happens to a story's characters. Most main characters in stories grapple with one or more conflicts as the action unfolds. **Conflict** is a character's struggle to get what he or she wants. An **external conflict** occurs when a character struggles against outside forces. An **internal conflict** occurs when a struggle takes place within a character's own mind. As the plot of a story unfolds, the character acts to resolve the conflicts. Here are some examples of external and internal conflicts:

External Conflict	Internal Conflict
A camper goes on a hike, loses her compass, and can't find her way back.	An athlete can't decide whether to try out for the swim team or for the soccer team.
Two friends in a spelling bee compete for the grand prize.	Someone who once nearly drowned has to overcome a fear of the water.
An office worker gets locked in a supply closet.	A young actor experiences stage fright.

READING SKILLS: SUMMARIZING A PLOT

When you **summarize a plot**, you retell the main events in a story. Summarizing a plot helps you clarify what's happened to whom and when it happened. As you read "Broken Chain," look for Summarize notes in the margins. Then, use your own words to explain what has taken place.

Literary Skills
Understand conflict.

Reading Skills
Summarize a story's plot.

Vocabulary Skills
Understand the history of English.

4 Part 1   Collection 1 / Telling Stories

Before You Read
Previewing what you will learn builds success. This page tells you what the selection is about and prepares you to read it.

Literary Focus
This feature introduces the literary focus for the selection.

Reading Skills
This feature provides a reading skill for you to apply to the selection. It ties into and supports the literary focus.

Language Arts Skills
The skills covered with the selection are listed here.

Vocabulary Development

Vocabulary words for the selection are pretaught. Each entry gives the pronunciation and definition of the word as well as a context sentence.

Vocabulary Skills

When you read, you not only have to recognize words but also decode them and determine meaning. This feature introduces a vocabulary skill to use to understand words in the selection.

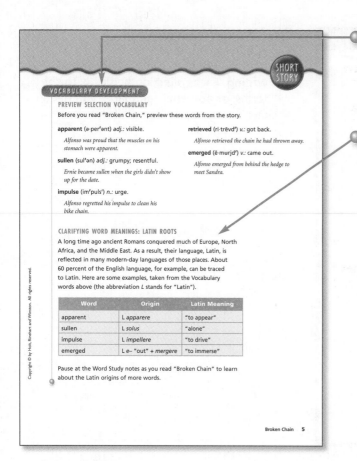

VOCABULARY DEVELOPMENT

PREVIEW SELECTION VOCABULARY

Before you read "Broken Chain," preview these words from the story.

apparent (ə·per'ənt) *adj.*: visible.

Alfonso was proud that the muscles on his stomach were apparent.

sullen (sul'ən) *adj.*: grumpy; resentful.

Ernie became sullen when the girls didn't show up for the date.

impulse (im'puls') *n.*: urge.

Alfonso regretted his impulse to clean his bike chain.

retrieved (ri·trēvd') *v.*: got back.

Alfonso retrieved the chain he had thrown away.

emerged (ē·murjd') *v.*: came out.

Alfonso emerged from behind the hedge to meet Sandra.

CLARIFYING WORD MEANINGS: LATIN ROOTS

A long time ago ancient Romans conquered much of Europe, North Africa, and the Middle East. As a result, their language, Latin, is reflected in many modern-day languages of those places. About 60 percent of the English language, for example, can be traced to Latin. Here are some examples, taken from the Vocabulary words above (the abbreviation *L* stands for "Latin").

Word	Origin	Latin Meaning
apparent	L *apparere*	"to appear"
sullen	L *solus*	"alone"
impulse	L *impellere*	"to drive"
emerged	L e– "out" + *mergere*	"to immerse"

Pause at the Word Study notes as you read "Broken Chain" to learn about the Latin origins of more words.

Broken Chain **5**

Side-Column Notes

Each selection is accompanied by notes in the side column that guide your interaction with the selection. Many notes ask you to underline or circle in the text itself. Others provide lines on which you can write your responses to questions.

Types of Notes

The different types of notes throughout the selection help you—
- Focus on literary elements
- Apply the reading skill
- Apply the vocabulary skill
- Think critically about the selection
- Develop word knowledge
- Build vocabulary
- Build fluency

Broken Chain

Gary Soto

Circle the name of the character introduced in the first paragraph. Underline two things he is doing to try to change the way he looks.

apparent (ə·per'ənt) *adj.*: visible; easily seen; obvious.

IDENTIFY

Why doesn't Alfonso da to color his hair (lines 15–21,

Alfonso sat on the porch trying to push his crooked teeth to where he thought they belonged. He hated the way he looked. Last week he did fifty sit-ups a day, thinking that he would burn those already **apparent** ripples on his stomach to even deeper ripples, dark ones, so when he went swimming at the canal next summer, girls in cut-offs would notice. And the guys would think he was tough, someone who could take a punch and give it back. He wanted "cuts" like those he had seen on a calendar of an Aztec[1] warrior
10 standing on a pyramid with a woman in his arms. (Even she had cuts he could see beneath her thin dress.) The calendar hung above the cash register at La Plaza. Orsua, the owner, said Alfonso could have the calendar at the end of the year if the waitress, Yolanda, didn't take it first.

Alfonso studied the magazine pictures of rock stars for a hairstyle. He liked the way Prince looked—and the bass player from Los Lobos. Alfonso thought he would look cool with his hair razored into a V in the back and streaked purple. But he knew his mother wouldn't go for it. And his

1. **Aztec:** member of an American Indian people of what is now Mexico.

6   Part 1   Collection 1 / Telling Stories

20   father, who was puro Mexicano, would sit in his chair after
work, **sullen** as a toad, and call him "sissy."

     Alfonso didn't dare color his hair. But one day he had
had it butched on the top, like in the magazines. His father
had come home that evening from a softball game, happy
that his team had drilled four homers in a thirteen-to-five
bashing of Color Tile. He'd swaggered into the living room
but had stopped cold when he saw Alfonso and asked, not
joking but with real concern, "Did you hurt your head at
school? ¿Qué pasó?"[2]

30   Alfonso had pretended not to hear his father and had
gone to his room, where he studied his hair from all angles
in the mirror. He liked what he saw until he smiled and
realized for the first time that his teeth were crooked, like
a pile of wrecked cars. He grew depressed and turned away
from the mirror. He sat on his bed and leafed through the
rock magazine until he came to the rock star with the
butched top. His mouth was closed, but Alfonso was sure
his teeth weren't crooked.

     Alfonso didn't want to be the handsomest kid at school,

40   but he was determined to be better looking than average.
The next day he spent his lawn-mowing money on a new
shirt and, with a pocketknife, scooped the moons of dirt
from under his fingernails.

     He spent hours in front of the mirror trying to herd
his teeth into place with his thumb. He asked his mother if
he could have braces, like Frankie Molina, her godson, but
he asked at the wrong time. She was at the kitchen table
licking the envelope to the house payment. She glared up
at him. "Do you think money grows on trees?"

50   His mother clipped coupons from magazines and
newspapers, kept a vegetable garden in the summer, and

2. **¿Qué pasó?** (kā′ pä-sō′): Spanish for "What happened?"

VOCABULARY

sullen (sul′ən) *adj.*: grumpy;
resentful.

IDENTIFY

What do you learn about
Alfonso's father in lines
22–29?

INFER

Re-read lines 44–55. Based on
these details, what inference
can you make about the
family's financial situation?

Vocabulary

The vocabulary words that were pretaught
are defined in the side column and set in
boldface in the selection, allowing you to
see them in context.

PREDICT

Pause at line 184. Will Ernie
let Alfonso borrow his bike?
Tell what you think will happen next.

FLUENCY

Re-read the boxed passage.
As each speaker changes,
think about who is speaking
and how he might say the
words. Then, read the passage aloud, trying to express
the different feelings of the
characters.

     his hands stuffed in his pockets. But when he looked back
over his shoulder, the wind raking through his butch,
Sandra wasn't even looking. She was already on her lawn,

180   heading for the porch.

     That night he took a bath, pampered his hair into
place, and did more than his usual set of exercises. In bed,
in between the push-and-rest on his teeth, he pestered his
brother to let him borrow his bike.

     "Come on, Ernie," he whined. "Just for an hour."

     "Chale,[8] I might want to use it."

     "Come on, man, I'll let you have my trick-or-treat
candy."

     "What you got?"

190   "Three baby Milky Ways and some Skittles."

     "Who's going to use it?"

     Alfonso hesitated, then risked the truth. "I met this
girl. She doesn't live too far."

     Ernie rolled over on his stomach and stared at the out-
line of his brother, whose head was resting on his elbow.
"*You* got a girlfriend?"

     "She ain't my girlfriend, just a girl."

     "What does she look like?"

     "Like a girl."

200   "Come on, what does she look like?"

     "She's got ponytails and a little brother."

     "Ponytails! Those girls who messed with Frostie and
me had ponytails. Is she cool?"

     "I think so."

     Ernie sat up in bed. "I bet you that's her."

     Alfonso felt his stomach knot up. "She's going to be my
girlfriend, not yours!"

     "I'm going to get even with her!"

8. **chale** (chä′lä): Spanish slang expression roughly meaning "it's
not possible."

Fluency

Successful readers are able to read
fluently—clearly, easily, quickly, and
without word identification problems.
In most selections, you'll be given an
opportunity to practice and improve
your fluency.

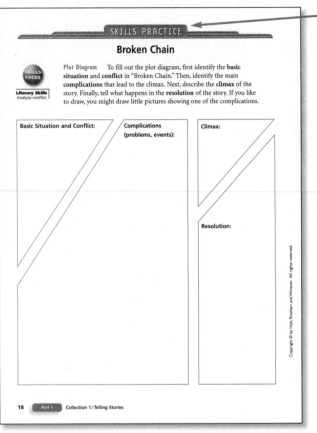

Skills Practice
Graphic organizers help reinforce your understanding of the literary focus in a highly visual and creative way.

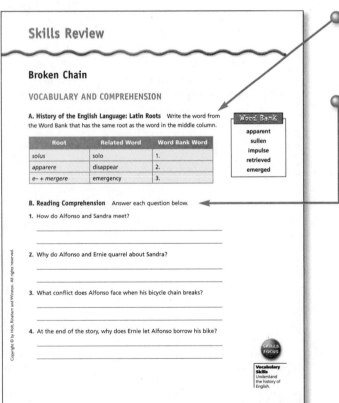

Skills Review: Vocabulary
Test your knowledge of the selection vocabulary and the vocabulary skill by completing this short activity.

Reading Comprehension
This feature allows you to see how well you've understood the selection you have just read.

Part One

Reading Literature

Telling Stories

Acomo Pueblo Storyteller: artist, Peggy Garcia;
Isleta Pueblo Corn Maiden: artist, Robin Teller.

Photo: Diane J. Ali.

Academic Vocabulary for Collection 1

These are the terms you should know
as you read and analyze the stories in this collection.

Plot The plot is what happens in a story, novel, play, or narrative poem. It is the chain of related events that makes up a story.

Conflict A struggle between characters or between opposing forces. An **external conflict** takes place between two characters, between a character and a group, or between a character and something else—such as a monster or a sandstorm. An **internal conflict** takes place within a character's mind or heart. A story may have more than one conflict.

Complications Problems that come up as characters struggle to reach their goals.

Climax The most exciting or suspenseful part of a story. At the climax, something happens that reveals how the conflict will turn out.

Resolution The part of the story in which remaining questions are answered and loose ends of the plot are tied up. The resolution usually comes at the end of the story.

● ● ●

Suspense The uncertainty or anxiety a reader feels about what will happen next.

Foreshadowing Hints or clues that suggest what will happen later in a story. Foreshadowing helps to build suspense.

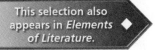

Broken Chain by Gary Soto

LITERARY FOCUS: CONFLICT

Plot is a series of related events that take place in a story. Through the plot we learn what happens to a story's characters. Most main characters in stories grapple with one or more conflicts as the action unfolds. **Conflict** is a character's struggle to get what he or she wants. An **external conflict** occurs when a character struggles against outside forces. An **internal conflict** occurs when a struggle takes place within a character's own mind. As the plot of a story unfolds, the character acts to resolve the conflicts. Here are some examples of external and internal conflicts:

External Conflict	Internal Conflict
A camper goes on a hike, loses her compass, and can't find her way back.	An athlete can't decide whether to try out for the swim team or for the soccer team.
Two friends in a spelling bee compete for the grand prize.	Someone who once nearly drowned has to overcome a fear of the water.
An office worker gets locked in a supply closet.	A young actor experiences stage fright.

READING SKILLS: SUMMARIZING A PLOT

When you **summarize a plot,** you retell the main events in a story. Summarizing a plot helps you clarify what's happened to whom and when it happened. As you read "Broken Chain," look for Summarize notes in the margins. Then, use your own words to explain what has taken place.

Literary Skills
Understand conflict.

Reading Skills
Summarize a story's plot.

Vocabulary Skills
Understand the history of English.

VOCABULARY DEVELOPMENT

PREVIEW SELECTION VOCABULARY

Before you read "Broken Chain," preview these words from the story.

apparent (ə·per'ənt) *adj.:* visible.

> *Alfonso was proud that the muscles on his stomach were apparent.*

sullen (sul'ən) *adj.:* grumpy; resentful.

> *Ernie became sullen when the girls didn't show up for the date.*

impulse (im'puls') *n.:* urge.

> *Alfonso regretted his impulse to clean his bike chain.*

retrieved (ri·trēvd') *v.:* got back.

> *Alfonso retrieved the chain he had thrown away.*

emerged (ē·murjd') *v.:* came out.

> *Alfonso emerged from behind the hedge to meet Sandra.*

CLARIFYING WORD MEANINGS: LATIN ROOTS

A long time ago ancient Romans conquered much of Europe, North Africa, and the Middle East. As a result, their language, Latin, is reflected in many modern-day languages of those places. About 60 percent of the English language, for example, can be traced to Latin. Here are some examples, taken from the Vocabulary words above (the abbreviation *L* stands for "Latin").

Word	Origin	Latin Meaning
apparent	L *apparere*	"to appear"
sullen	L *solus*	"alone"
impulse	L *impellere*	"to drive"
emerged	L e– "out" + *mergere*	"to immerse"

Pause at the Word Study notes as you read "Broken Chain" to learn about the Latin origins of more words.

Broken Chain

Gary Soto

© Michael Newman/Photo Edit, Inc.

Alfonso sat on the porch trying to push his crooked teeth to where he thought they belonged. He hated the way he looked. Last week he did fifty sit-ups a day, thinking that he would burn those already **apparent** ripples on his stomach to even deeper ripples, dark ones, so when he went swimming at the canal next summer, girls in cut-offs would notice. And the guys would think he was tough, someone who could take a punch and give it back. He wanted "cuts" like those he had seen on a calendar of an Aztec[1] warrior
10 standing on a pyramid with a woman in his arms. (Even she had cuts he could see beneath her thin dress.) The calendar hung above the cash register at La Plaza. Orsua, the owner, said Alfonso could have the calendar at the end of the year if the waitress, Yolanda, didn't take it first.

Alfonso studied the magazine pictures of rock stars for a hairstyle. He liked the way Prince looked—and the bass player from Los Lobos. Alfonso thought he would look cool with his hair razored into a V in the back and streaked purple. But he knew his mother wouldn't go for it. And his

---

1. **Aztec:** member of an American Indian people of what is now Mexico.

20 father, who was puro Mexicano, would sit in his chair after work, **sullen** as a toad, and call him "sissy."

Alfonso didn't dare color his hair. But one day he had had it butched on the top, like in the magazines. His father had come home that evening from a softball game, happy that his team had drilled four homers in a thirteen-to-five bashing of Color Tile. He'd swaggered into the living room but had stopped cold when he saw Alfonso and asked, not joking but with real concern, "Did you hurt your head at school? ¿Qué pasó?"[2]

30 Alfonso had pretended not to hear his father and had gone to his room, where he studied his hair from all angles in the mirror. He liked what he saw until he smiled and realized for the first time that his teeth were crooked, like a pile of wrecked cars. He grew depressed and turned away from the mirror. He sat on his bed and leafed through the rock magazine until he came to the rock star with the butched top. His mouth was closed, but Alfonso was sure his teeth weren't crooked.

Alfonso didn't want to be the handsomest kid at school,
40 but he was determined to be better looking than average. The next day he spent his lawn-mowing money on a new shirt and, with a pocketknife, scooped the moons of dirt from under his fingernails.

He spent hours in front of the mirror trying to herd his teeth into place with his thumb. He asked his mother if he could have braces, like Frankie Molina, her godson, but he asked at the wrong time. She was at the kitchen table licking the envelope to the house payment. She glared up at him. "Do you think money grows on trees?"

50 His mother clipped coupons from magazines and newspapers, kept a vegetable garden in the summer, and

VOCABULARY

sullen (sul′ən) *adj.:* grumpy; resentful.

IDENTIFY

What do you learn about Alfonso's father in lines 22–29?

_____

_____

_____

_____

_____

_____

_____

INFER

Re-read lines 44–55. Based on these details, what inference can you make about the family's financial situation?

_____

_____

_____

_____

_____

_____

_____

---

2. **¿Qué pasó?** (kā′ pä·sô′): Spanish for "What happened?"

Pause at line 68. List three
important things you've
learned about Alfonso so
far. What main idea about
Alfonso's **character** do these
details add up to? State
that main idea in a complete
sentence.

_____

_____

_____

_____

_____

_____

_____

_____

_____

_____

_____

_____

_____

_____

_____

WORD STUDY

Depressed (dē·prest′), in line
70, means "gloomy; sad." It
comes from the Latin roots
de–, meaning "down," and
premere, meaning "to press."

shopped at Penney's and K-Mart. Their family ate a lot of
frijoles,[3] which was OK because nothing else tasted so good,
though one time Alfonso had had Chinese pot stickers[4] and
thought they were the next best food in the world.

He didn't ask his mother for braces again, even when
she was in a better mood. He decided to fix his teeth by
pushing on them with his thumbs. After breakfast that
Saturday he went to his room, closed the door quietly,
turned the radio on, and pushed for three hours straight.

He pushed for ten minutes, rested for five, and every
half hour, during a radio commercial, checked to see if his
smile had improved. It hadn't.

Eventually he grew bored and went outside with an
old gym sock to wipe down his bike, a ten-speed from
Montgomery Ward. His thumbs were tired and wrinkled
and pink, the way they got when he stayed in the bathtub
too long.

Alfonso's older brother, Ernie, rode up on *his*
Montgomery Ward bicycle looking depressed. He parked his
bike against the peach tree and sat on the back steps, keeping his head down and stepping on ants that came too close.

Alfonso knew better than to say anything when Ernie
looked mad. He turned his bike over, balancing it on the
handlebars and seat, and flossed the spokes with the sock.
When he was finished, he pressed a knuckle to his teeth
until they tingled.

Ernie groaned and said, "Ah, man."

Alfonso waited a few minutes before asking, "What's the
matter?" He pretended not to be too interested. He picked up
a wad of steel wool and continued cleaning the spokes.

---

3. **frijoles** (frē·ḱhōl′ās): Spanish for "beans."
4. **pot stickers** *n.*: dumplings.

Ernie hesitated, not sure if Alfonso would laugh. But it came out. "Those girls didn't show up. And you better not laugh."

"What girls?"

Then Alfonso remembered his brother bragging about how he and Frostie met two girls from Kings Canyon Junior High last week on Halloween night. They were dressed as Gypsies, the costume for all poor Chicanas[5]—they just had to borrow scarves and gaudy red lipstick from their abuelitas.[6]

Alfonso walked over to his brother. He compared their two bikes: His gleamed like a handful of dimes, while Ernie's looked dirty.

"They said we were supposed to wait at the corner. But they didn't show up. Me and Frostie waited and waited. . . . They were playing games with us."

Alfonso thought that was a pretty dirty trick but sort of funny too. He would have to try that someday.

"Were they cute?" Alfonso asked.

"I guess so."

"Do you think you could recognize them?"

"If they were wearing red lipstick, maybe."

Alfonso sat with his brother in silence, both of them smearing ants with their floppy high tops. Girls could sure act weird, especially the ones you meet on Halloween.

Later that day, Alfonso sat on the porch pressing on his teeth. Press, relax; press, relax. His portable radio was on, but not loud enough to make Mr. Rojas come down the steps and wave his cane at him.

Alfonso's father drove up. Alfonso could tell by the way he sat in his truck, a Datsun with a different-colored front fender, that his team had lost their softball game. Alfonso got

5. **Chicanas** (chi·kä′nəz): Mexican American girls and women.
6. **abuelitas** (ä′bwä·lē′täs) *n.:* in Spanish, an affectionate term for "grandmothers," like *grandmas* in English.

SUMMARIZE

Re-read lines 69–96. Summarize what has happened in the story so far.

_____

_____

_____

_____

_____

_____

_____

_____

_____

_____

_____

_____

_____

_____

_____

_____

_____

_____

_____

_____

_____

CLARIFY

Re-read lines 110–117. Why does Alfonso go to the back yard?

_____

_____

_____

_____

_____

_____

INTERPRET

Underline Alfonso's good deed in lines 118–128. What does it show about his character?

_____

_____

_____

_____

_____

_____

_____

WORD STUDY

Observation (äb′zər·vā′shən), in line 142, means "a comment or remark based on something you've seen." It comes from Latin *observatio,* meaning "outward display."

off the porch in a hurry because he knew his father would be in a bad mood. He went to the back yard, where he unlocked his bike, sat on it with the kickstand down, and pressed on his teeth. He punched himself in the stomach, and growled, "Cuts." Then he patted his butch and whispered, "Fresh."

After a while Alfonso pedaled up the street, hands in his pockets, toward Foster's Freeze, where he was chased by
120 a ratlike Chihuahua.[7] At his old school, John Burroughs Elementary, he found a kid hanging upside down on the top of a barbed-wire fence with a girl looking up at him. Alfonso skidded to a stop and helped the kid untangle his pants from the barbed wire. The kid was grateful. He had been afraid he would have to stay up there all night. His sister, who was Alfonso's age, was also grateful. If she had to go home and tell her mother that Frankie was stuck on a fence and couldn't get down, she would get scolded.

"Thanks," she said. "What's your name?"
130 Alfonso remembered her from his school and noticed that she was kind of cute, with ponytails and straight teeth. "Alfonso. You go to my school, huh?"

"Yeah. I've seen you around. You live nearby?"

"Over on Madison."

"My uncle used to live on that street, but he moved to Stockton."

"Stockton's near Sacramento, isn't it?"

"You been there?"

"No." Alfonso looked down at his shoes. He wanted
140 to say something clever the way people do on TV. But the only thing he could think to say was that the governor lived in Sacramento. As soon as he shared this observation, he winced inside.

---

7. **Chihuahua** (chi·wä′wä): small dog with large pointed ears.

Alfonso walked with the girl and the boy as they started for home. They didn't talk much. Every few steps, the girl, whose name was Sandra, would look at him out of the corner of her eye, and Alfonso would look away. He learned that she was in seventh grade, just like him, and that she had a pet terrier named Queenie. Her father was a mechanic at Rudy's Speedy Repair, and her mother was a teacher's aide at Jefferson Elementary.

When they came to the street, Alfonso and Sandra stopped at her corner, but her brother ran home. Alfonso watched him stop in the front yard to talk to a lady he guessed was their mother. She was raking leaves into a pile.

"I live over there," she said, pointing.

Alfonso looked over her shoulder for a long time, trying to muster enough nerve to ask her if she'd like to go bike riding tomorrow.

Shyly, he asked, "You wanna go bike riding?"

"Maybe." She played with a ponytail and crossed one leg in front of the other. "But my bike has a flat."

"I can get my brother's bike. He won't mind."

She thought a moment before she said, "OK. But not tomorrow. I have to go to my aunt's."

"How about after school on Monday?"

"I have to take care of my brother until my mom comes home from work. How 'bout four-thirty?"

"OK," he said. "Four-thirty." Instead of parting immediately, they talked for a while, asking questions like "Who's your favorite group?" "Have you ever been on the Big Dipper at Santa Cruz?" and "Have you ever tasted pot stickers?" But the question-and-answer period ended when Sandra's mother called her home.

Alfonso took off as fast as he could on his bike, jumped the curb, and, cool as he could be, raced away with

Re-read lines 118–163. Summarize how Alfonso meets Sandra and how he goes about asking her to see him again.

PREDICT

Pause at line 184. Will Ernie let Alfonso borrow his bike? Tell what you think will happen next.

_____

_____

_____

_____

_____

_____

_____

_____

FLUENCY

Re-read the boxed passage. As each speaker changes, think about who is speaking and how he might say the words. Then, read the passage aloud, trying to express the different feelings of the characters.

_____

_____

_____

_____

_____

_____

_____

his hands stuffed in his pockets. But when he looked back over his shoulder, the wind raking through his butch, Sandra wasn't even looking. She was already on her lawn, 180 heading for the porch.

That night he took a bath, pampered his hair into place, and did more than his usual set of exercises. In bed, in between the push-and-rest on his teeth, he pestered his brother to let him borrow his bike.

"Come on, Ernie," he whined. "Just for an hour."

"Chale,[8] I might want to use it."

"Come on, man, I'll let you have my trick-or-treat candy."

"What you got?"

190 "Three baby Milky Ways and some Skittles."

"Who's going to use it?"

Alfonso hesitated, then risked the truth. "I met this girl. She doesn't live too far."

Ernie rolled over on his stomach and stared at the outline of his brother, whose head was resting on his elbow. "*You* got a girlfriend?"

"She ain't my girlfriend, just a girl."

"What does she look like?"

"Like a girl."

200 "Come on, what does she look like?"

"She's got ponytails and a little brother."

"Ponytails! Those girls who messed with Frostie and me had ponytails. Is she cool?"

"I think so."

Ernie sat up in bed. "I bet you that's her."

Alfonso felt his stomach knot up. "She's going to be my girlfriend, not yours!"

"I'm going to get even with her!"

---

8. **chale** (chä′lä): Spanish slang expression roughly meaning "it's not possible."

210 "You better not touch her," Alfonso snarled, throwing a wadded Kleenex at him. "I'll run you over with my bike."

For the next hour, until their mother threatened them from the living room to be quiet or else, they argued whether it was the same girl who had stood Ernie up. Alfonso said over and over that she was too nice to pull a stunt like that. But Ernie argued that she lived only two blocks from where those girls had told them to wait, that she was in the same grade, and, the clincher, that she had ponytails. Secretly, however, Ernie was jealous that his brother, two years younger than himself, might have found a girlfriend.

220 Sunday morning, Ernie and Alfonso stayed away from each other, though over breakfast they fought over the last tortilla. Their mother, sewing at the kitchen table, warned them to knock it off. At church they made faces at one another when the priest, Father Jerry, wasn't looking. Ernie punched Alfonso in the arm, and Alfonso, his eyes wide with anger, punched back.

Monday morning they hurried to school on their bikes, neither saying a word, though they rode side by side. In first period, Alfonso worried himself sick. How would he 230 borrow a bike for her? He considered asking his best friend, Raul, for his bike. But Alfonso knew Raul, a paperboy with dollar signs in his eyes, would charge him, and he had less than sixty cents, counting the soda bottles he could cash.

Between history and math, Alfonso saw Sandra and her girlfriend huddling at their lockers. He hurried by without being seen.

During lunch Alfonso hid in metal shop so he wouldn't run into Sandra. What would he say to her? If he weren't mad at his brother, he could ask Ernie what girls and guys 240 talk about. But he *was* mad, and anyway, Ernie was pitching nickels with his friends.

IDENTIFY

Re-read lines 181–210. Then, identify the **conflict** between the brothers. What two things are Alfonso and Ernie fighting over?

_____

_____

_____

_____

_____

_____

_____

_____

_____

INTERPRET

An **idiom** is a figure of speech—its actual meaning is different from its literal meaning. Underline the idiom in lines 231–232. Explain what it means.

_____

_____

_____

_____

_____

_____

Alfonso hurried home after school. He did the morning dishes as his mother had asked and raked the leaves. After finishing his chores, he did a hundred sit-ups, pushed on his teeth until they hurt, showered, and combed his hair into a perfect butch. He then stepped out to the patio to clean his bike. On an **impulse,** he removed the chain to wipe off the gritty oil. But while he was unhooking it from the back sprocket, it snapped. The chain lay in his hand like
250   a dead snake.

Alfonso couldn't believe his luck. Now, not only did he not have an extra bike for Sandra, he had no bike for himself. Frustrated and on the verge of tears, he flung the chain as far as he could. It landed with a hard slap against the back fence and spooked his sleeping cat, Benny. Benny looked around, blinking his soft gray eyes, and went back to sleep.

Alfonso **retrieved** the chain, which was hopelessly broken. He cursed himself for being stupid, yelled at his bike

IDENTIFY

Pause at line 256. When Sandra said she'd meet Alfonso and go bike riding with him, everything seemed to be going well. List the **complications** in the plot that have made Alfonso's situation increasingly desperate.

© Getty Images.

VOCABULARY

impulse (im′puls′) *n.:* urge.

retrieved (ri·trēvd′) *v.:* got back.

for being cheap, and slammed the chain onto the cement.

260 The chain snapped in another place and hit him when it popped up, slicing his hand like a snake's fang.

"Ow!" he cried, his mouth immediately going to his hand to suck on the wound.

After a dab of iodine, which only made his cut hurt more, and a lot of thought, he went to the bedroom to plead with Ernie, who was changing to his after-school clothes.

"Come on, man, let me use it," Alfonso pleaded. "Please, Ernie, I'll do anything."

Although Ernie could see Alfonso's desperation, he had

270 plans with his friend Raymundo. They were going to catch frogs at the Mayfair canal. He felt sorry for his brother and gave him a stick of gum to make him feel better, but there was nothing he could do. The canal was three miles away, and the frogs were waiting.

Alfonso took the stick of gum, placed it in his shirt pocket, and left the bedroom with his head down. He went outside, slamming the screen door behind him, and sat in the alley behind his house. A sparrow landed in the weeds, and when it tried to come close, Alfonso screamed for it to scram.

280 The sparrow responded with a squeaky chirp and flew away.

At four he decided to get it over with and started walking to Sandra's house, trudging slowly, as if he were waist-deep in water. Shame colored his face. How could he disappoint his first date? She would probably laugh. She might even call him menso.[9]

He stopped at the corner where they were supposed to meet and watched her house. But there was no one outside, only a rake leaning against the steps.

Why did he have to take the chain off? he scolded him-

290 self. He always messed things up when he tried to take them apart, like the time he tried to repad his baseball mitt. He

---

9. **menso** (men′sô) adj.: Spanish for "stupid."

EVALUATE

Pause at line 274. Why won't Ernie lend Alfonso his bike? What do you think of this reason?

_____

_____

_____

_____

_____

_____

WORD STUDY

The noun *desperation* (des′pər·ā′shən), in line 269, is from Latin *de–*, "without," and *sperare*, "to hope." What is a synonym for *desperation*?

_____

_____

_____

_____

_____

_____

_____

IDENTIFY

Underline the details in lines 275–285 that show that Alfonso is upset.

PREDICT

Pause at line 300 and tell what you think will happen in the rest of the story.

_____

_____

_____

_____

_____

_____

_____

_____

_____

_____

_____

_____

_____

_____

_____

_____

_____

IDENTIFY

The **climax** is the most exciting moment in the plot, when the outcome of the main **conflict** is decided. Underline the passage in lines 310–323 that describes the climax in this story.

had unlaced the mitt and filled the pocket with cotton balls. But when he tried to put it back together, he had forgotten how it laced up. Everything became tangled like kite string. When he showed the mess to his mother, who was at the stove cooking dinner, she scolded him but put it back together and didn't tell his father what a dumb thing he had done.

Now he had to face Sandra and say, "I broke my bike, and my stingy brother took off on his."

He waited at the corner a few minutes, hiding behind a hedge for what seemed like forever. Just as he was starting to think about going home, he heard footsteps and knew it was too late. His hands, moist from worry, hung at his sides and a thread of sweat raced down his armpit.

He peeked through the hedge. She was wearing a sweater with a checkerboard pattern. A red purse was slung over her shoulder. He could see her looking for him, standing on tiptoe to see if he was coming around the corner.

What have I done? Alfonso thought. He bit his lip, called himself menso, and pounded his palm against his forehead. Someone slapped the back of his head. He turned around and saw Ernie.

"We got the frogs, Alfonso," he said, holding up a wiggling plastic bag. "I'll show you later."

Ernie looked through the hedge, with one eye closed, at the girl. "She's not the one who messed with Frostie and me," he said finally. "You still wanna borrow my bike?"

Alfonso couldn't believe his luck. What a brother! What a pal! He promised to take Ernie's turn next time it was his turn to do the dishes. Ernie hopped on Raymundo's handlebars and said he would remember that promise. Then he was gone as they took off without looking back.

Free of worry now that his brother had come through, Alfonso **emerged** from behind the hedge with Ernie's bike, which was mud-splashed but better than nothing. Sandra waved.

"Hi," she said.

"Hi," he said back.

330 She looked cheerful. Alfonso told her his bike was broken and asked if she wanted to ride with him.

"Sounds good," she said, and jumped on the crossbar.

It took all of Alfonso's strength to steady the bike. He started off slowly, gritting his teeth, because she was heavier than he thought. But once he got going, it got easier. He pedaled smoothly, sometimes with only one hand on the handlebars, as they sped up one street and down another. Whenever he ran over a pothole, which was often, she screamed with delight, and once, when it looked like they

340 were going to crash, she placed her hand over his, and it felt like love.

VOCABULARY

emerged (ē·mʉrjd') v.: came out.

EXTEND

Suppose that Ernie had not brought the bike. Suggest two other ways of ending this story.

_____

_____

_____

_____

_____

_____

_____

_____

_____

_____

_____

_____

_____

_____

_____

_____

_____

_____

_____

_____

Broken Chain

SKILLS FOCUS

Literary Skills
Analyze conflict.

Plot Diagram   To fill out the plot diagram, first identify the **basic situation** and **conflict** in "Broken Chain." Then, identify the main **complications** that lead to the climax. Next, describe the **climax** of the story. Finally, tell what happens in the **resolution** of the story. If you like to draw, you might draw little pictures showing one of the complications.

Basic Situation and Conflict:

Complications (problems, events):

Climax:

Resolution:

Broken Chain

VOCABULARY AND COMPREHENSION

A. History of the English Language: Latin Roots   Write the word from the Word Bank that has the same root as the word in the middle column.

Root	Related Word	Word Bank Word
solus	solo	1.
apparere	disappear	2.
e– + mergere	emergency	3.

B. Reading Comprehension   Answer each question below.

1. How do Alfonso and Sandra meet?

_____

_____

2. Why do Alfonso and Ernie quarrel about Sandra?

_____

_____

3. What conflict does Alfonso face when his bicycle chain breaks?

_____

_____

4. At the end of the story, why does Ernie let Alfonso borrow his bike?

_____

_____

SKILLS FOCUS

Vocabulary Skills
Understand the history of English.

Before You Read

This selection also appears in *Elements of Literature.*

The Landlady by Roald Dahl

LITERARY FOCUS: FORESHADOWING

A wedding celebration comes to an abrupt end as a violent storm rages through a village. Is this occurrence just a weather event, or might it hint at trouble ahead? Writers sometimes use clues or hints like this to suggest events that will happen later in their stories. Using clues or hints this way is called **foreshadowing.** Foreshadowing helps to build a feeling of suspense in the reader. It is an important element in tales of mystery and danger such as "The Landlady."

READING SKILLS: PREDICTING

When you make a **prediction,** or guess, about a story, you take note of the details you're given and try to figure out what will happen later. As you read "The Landlady," you will discover that the writer has used fore-shadowing. Those clever clues will also help you make predictions. You may want to record your predictions in this chart as you read the story.

Clues	Predictions
Billy sees a notice in the window of a boardinghouse.	
When he presses the bell, a woman answers instantly.	
There are no hats or coats in the hall.	
The names in the guest book seem familiar to Billy.	
The parrot and the dog are stuffed.	
The tea has an unpleasant taste.	

SKILLS FOCUS

Literary Skills
Understand foreshadowing.

Reading Skills
Make predictions.

The Landlady

Roald Dahl

Illustration by Krysten Brooker.

Billy Weaver had traveled down from London on the slow afternoon train, with a change at Reading on the way, and by the time he got to Bath, it was about nine o'clock in the evening, and the moon was coming up out of a clear starry sky over the houses opposite the station entrance. But the air was deadly cold and the wind was like a flat blade of ice on his cheeks.

"Excuse me," he said, "but is there a fairly cheap hotel not too far away from here?"

10   "Try The Bell and Dragon," the porter[1] answered, pointing down the road. "They might take you in. It's about a quarter of a mile along on the other side."

"The Landlady" from *Kiss, Kiss* by Roald Dahl. Copyright © 1959 by Roald Dahl. Reproduced by permission of **David Higham Associates.**

---

1. porter *n.:* person hired to carry luggage.

IDENTIFY

Pause at line 7. Circle the name of the **character** who is introduced in this passage. Underline details that establish the **setting.**

Re-read lines 20–27. How
would you describe Billy's
mood?

_____

_____

_____

_____

_____

_____

_____

_____

_____

_____

Underline details in lines
37–58 that make the boardinghouse seem inviting and
comfortable.

Billy thanked him and picked up his suitcase and set
out to walk the quarter-mile to The Bell and Dragon. He
had never been to Bath before. He didn't know anyone who
lived there. But Mr. Greenslade at the head office in London
had told him it was a splendid town. "Find your own lodg-
ings," he had said, "and then go along and report to the
branch manager as soon as you've got yourself settled."

20   Billy was seventeen years old. He was wearing a new
navy-blue overcoat, a new brown trilby hat,[2] and a new
brown suit, and he was feeling fine. He walked briskly
down the street. He was trying to do everything briskly
these days. Briskness, he had decided, was the one common
characteristic of all successful businessmen. The big shots
up at the head office were absolutely fantastically brisk all
the time. They were amazing.

There were no shops on this wide street that he was
walking along, only a line of tall houses on each side, all of
30   them identical. They had porches and pillars and four or
five steps going up to their front doors, and it was obvious
that once upon a time they had been very swanky residences.
But now, even in the darkness, he could see that the paint
was peeling from the woodwork on their doors and windows
and that the handsome white facades[3] were cracked and
blotchy from neglect.

Suddenly, in a downstairs window that was brilliantly
illuminated by a street lamp not six yards away, Billy caught
sight of a printed notice propped up against the glass in
40   one of the upper panes. It said "Bed and Breakfast." There
was a vase of yellow chrysanthemums, tall and beautiful,
standing just underneath the notice.

He stopped walking. He moved a bit closer. Green
curtains (some sort of velvety material) were hanging down

---

2. **trilby hat:** soft hat with the top deeply indented.
3. **facades** (fə·sädz′) *n.:* fronts of buildings.

on either side of the window. The chrysanthemums looked wonderful beside them. He went right up and peered through the glass into the room, and the first thing he saw was a bright fire burning in the hearth. On the carpet in front of the fire, a pretty little dachshund was curled up

50 asleep with its nose tucked into its belly. The room itself, so far as he could see in the half darkness, was filled with pleasant furniture. There was a baby grand piano and a big sofa and several plump armchairs, and in one corner he spotted a large parrot in a cage. Animals were usually a good sign in a place like this, Billy told himself; and all in all, it looked to him as though it would be a pretty decent house to stay in. Certainly it would be more comfortable than The Bell and Dragon.

On the other hand, a pub would be more congenial[4]
60 than a boardinghouse. There would be beer and darts in the evenings, and lots of people to talk to, and it would probably be a good bit cheaper, too. He had stayed a couple of nights in a pub once before and he had liked it. He had never stayed in any boardinghouses, and, to be perfectly honest, he was a tiny bit frightened of them. The name itself conjured up[5] images of watery cabbage, rapacious[6] landladies, and a powerful smell of kippers[7] in the living room.

After dithering about[8] like this in the cold for two or three minutes, Billy decided that he would walk on and
70 take a look at The Bell and Dragon before making up his mind. He turned to go.

And now a queer thing happened to him. He was in the act of stepping back and turning away from the window when all at once his eye was caught and held in the most

---

4. **congenial** (kən·jēn′yəl) *adj.:* agreeable; pleasant.
5. **conjured** (kun′jərd) **up:** called to mind.
6. **rapacious** (rə·pā′shəs) *adj.:* greedy.
7. **kippers** *n.:* fish that have been salted and smoked. Kippers are commonly eaten for breakfast in Great Britain.
8. **dithering about:** acting nervous and confused.

WORD STUDY

A dachshund (line 49) is a breed of dog that has a long body, short legs, and droopy ears. The word *dachshund* comes from German and is pronounced (däks′hoont′).

IDENTIFY

In lines 59–67, Billy thinks about whether to stay at the pub or at the boardinghouse. Underline details that describe the benefits of staying at the pub.

PREDICT

Pause at line 71. Where will Billy decide to stay?

_____

_____

_____

_____

_____

_____

_____

_____

_____

_____

_____

_____

_____

What does the comparison of the landlady to a jack-in-the-box suggest about her (lines 90–91)?

_____

_____

_____

_____

_____

_____

_____

Re-read lines 103–106. What is strange about the landlady's responses to Billy's comments?

_____

_____

_____

_____

_____

_____

_____

peculiar manner by the small notice that was there. BED AND BREAKFAST, it said. BED AND BREAKFAST, BED AND BREAKFAST, BED AND BREAKFAST. Each word was like a large black eye staring at him through the glass, holding him, compelling him, forcing him to stay where he was and not to walk

80　away from that house, and the next thing he knew, he was actually moving across from the window to the front door of the house, climbing the steps that led up to it, and reaching for the bell.

He pressed the bell. Far away in a back room he heard it ringing, and then *at once*—it must have been at once because he hadn't even had time to take his finger from the bell button—the door swung open and a woman was standing there.

Normally you ring the bell and you have at least a

90　half-minute's wait before the door opens. But this dame was like a jack-in-the-box. He pressed the bell—and out she popped! It made him jump.

She was about forty-five or fifty years old, and the moment she saw him, she gave him a warm, welcoming smile.

"*Please* come in," she said pleasantly. She stepped aside, holding the door wide open, and Billy found himself automatically starting forward. The compulsion or, more accurately, the desire to follow after her into that house was

100　extraordinarily strong.

"I saw the notice in the window," he said, holding himself back.

"Yes, I know."

"I was wondering about a room."

"It's *all* ready for you, my dear," she said. She had a round pink face and very gentle blue eyes.

"I was on my way to The Bell and Dragon," Billy told her. "But the notice in your window just happened to catch my eye."

110 "My dear boy," she said, "why don't you come in out of the cold?"

"How much do you charge?"

"Five and sixpence a night, including breakfast."

It was fantastically cheap. It was less than half of what he had been willing to pay.

"If that is too much," she added, "then perhaps I can reduce it just a tiny bit. Do you desire an egg for breakfast? Eggs are expensive at the moment. It would be sixpence less without the egg."

120 "Five and sixpence is fine," he answered. "I should like very much to stay here."

"I knew you would. Do come in."

Illustration by Krysten Brooker.

INFER

The landlady tells Billy that she knew he would stay at her bed and breakfast (line 122). Why do you think the landlady is so certain about Billy's intentions?

Notes _____

She seemed terribly nice. She looked exactly like the mother of one's best school friend welcoming one into the house to stay for the Christmas holidays. Billy took off his hat and stepped over the threshold.

"Just hang it there," she said, "and let me help you with your coat."

There were no other hats or coats in the hall. There were no umbrellas, no walking sticks—nothing.

"We have it *all* to ourselves," she said, smiling at him over her shoulder as she led the way upstairs. "You see, it isn't very often I have the pleasure of taking a visitor into my little nest."

The old girl is slightly dotty,[9] Billy told himself. But at five and sixpence a night, who cares about that? "I should've thought you'd be simply swamped with applicants," he said politely.

"Oh, I am, my dear, I am, of course I am. But the trouble is that I'm inclined to be just a teeny-weeny bit choosy and particular—if you see what I mean."

"Ah, yes."

"But I'm always ready. Everything is always ready day and night in this house just on the off chance that an acceptable young gentleman will come along. And it is such a pleasure, my dear, such a very great pleasure when now and again I open the door and I see someone standing there who is just *exactly* right." She was halfway up the stairs, and she paused with one hand on the stair rail, turning her head and smiling down at him with pale lips. "Like you," she added, and her blue eyes traveled slowly all the way down the length of Billy's body, to his feet, and then up again.

On the second-floor landing she said to him, "This floor is mine."

9. **dotty** *adj.*: crazy.

They climbed up another flight. "And this one is *all* yours," she said. "Here's your room. I do hope you'll like it." She took him into a small but charming front bedroom, switching on the light as she went in.

"The morning sun comes right in the window, Mr. Perkins. It *is* Mr. Perkins, isn't it?"

"No," he said. "It's Weaver."

"Mr. Weaver. How nice. I've put a water bottle between the sheets to air them out, Mr. Weaver. It's such a comfort to have a hot-water bottle in a strange bed with clean sheets, don't you agree? And you may light the gas fire at any time if you feel chilly."

"Thank you," Billy said. "Thank you ever so much." He noticed that the bedspread had been taken off the bed and that the bedclothes had been neatly turned back on one side, all ready for someone to get in.

"I'm so glad you appeared," she said, looking earnestly into his face. "I was beginning to get worried."

"That's all right," Billy answered brightly. "You mustn't worry about me." He put his suitcase on the chair and started to open it.

"And what about supper, my dear? Did you manage to get anything to eat before you came here?"

"I'm not a bit hungry, thank you," he said. "I think I'll just go to bed as soon as possible because tomorrow I've got to get up rather early and report to the office."

"Very well, then. I'll leave you now so that you can unpack. But before you go to bed, would you be kind enough to pop into the sitting room on the ground floor and sign the book? Everyone has to do that because it's the law of the land, and we don't want to go breaking any laws at *this* stage in the proceedings, do we?" She gave him a little

Notes _____

_____

_____

_____

_____

_____

_____

_____

CONNECT

Pause at line 170. If you were Billy, would you be worried? Tell why or why not.

_____

_____

_____

_____

_____

_____

_____

_____

_____

_____

_____

_____

_____

IDENTIFY

Pause at line 188. How would you describe the landlady's personality? Explain.

_____

_____

_____

_____

_____

_____

_____

IDENTIFY

Circle the words in lines 189–194 that show what Billy thinks of the landlady.

INTERPRET

Pause at line 201. Do you agree that Billy is lucky? Explain.

_____

_____

_____

_____

_____

_____

_____

_____

wave of the hand and went quickly out of the room and closed the door.

190　　Now, the fact that his landlady appeared to be slightly off her rocker didn't worry Billy in the least. After all, she not only was harmless—there was no question about that—but she was also quite obviously a kind and generous soul. He guessed that she had probably lost a son in the war, or something like that, and had never gotten over it.

So a few minutes later, after unpacking his suitcase and washing his hands, he trotted downstairs to the ground floor and entered the living room. His landlady wasn't there, but the fire was glowing in the hearth, and the little dachshund was still sleeping soundly in front of it. The 200　room was wonderfully warm and cozy. I'm a lucky fellow, he thought, rubbing his hands. This is a bit of all right.

He found the guest book lying open on the piano, so he took out his pen and wrote down his name and address. There were only two other entries above his on the page, and as one always does with guest books, he started to read them. One was a Christopher Mulholland from Cardiff. The other was Gregory W. Temple from Bristol.

That's funny, he thought suddenly. Christopher Mulholland. It rings a bell.

210　　Now where on earth had he heard that rather unusual name before?

Was it a boy at school? No. Was it one of his sister's numerous young men, perhaps, or a friend of his father's? No, no, it wasn't any of those. He glanced down again at the book.

Christopher Mulholland
231 Cathedral Road, Cardiff

Gregory W. Temple
27 Sycamore Drive, Bristol

220   As a matter of fact, now he came to think of it, he wasn't at all sure that the second name didn't have almost as much of a familiar ring about it as the first.

"Gregory Temple?" he said aloud, searching his memory. "Christopher Mulholland? . . ."

"Such charming boys," a voice behind him answered, and he turned and saw his landlady sailing into the room with a large silver tea tray in her hands. She was holding it well out in front of her, and rather high up, as though the tray were a pair of reins on a frisky horse.

230   "They sound somehow familiar," he said.

"They do? How interesting."

"I'm almost positive I've heard those names before somewhere. Isn't that odd? Maybe it was in the newspapers. They weren't famous in any way, were they? I mean famous cricketers[10] or footballers or something like that?"

"Famous," she said, setting the tea tray down on the low table in front of the sofa. "Oh no, I don't think they were famous. But they were incredibly handsome, both of them, I can promise you that. They were tall and young and

240   handsome, my dear, just exactly like you."

Once more, Billy glanced down at the book. "Look here," he said, noticing the dates. "This last entry is over two years old."

"It is?"

"Yes, indeed. And Christopher Mulholland's is nearly a year before that—more than *three years* ago."

"Dear me," she said, shaking her head and heaving a dainty little sigh. "I would never have thought it. How time does fly away from us all, doesn't it, Mr. Wilkins?"

250   "It's Weaver," Billy said. "W-e-a-v-e-r."

IDENTIFY

What odd thing has Billy discovered in the guest book (lines 208–224)?

_____

_____

_____

_____

_____

_____

_____

_____

_____

COMPARE & CONTRAST

Pause at line 240. According to the landlady, how does Billy resemble the previous guests?

_____

_____

_____

_____

_____

_____

_____

_____

---

10. cricketers *n.:* people who play cricket, a game that is popular in Great Britain.

_____

_____

_____

_____

_____

_____

_____

_____

CLARIFY

Re-read lines 257–264. What is Billy trying to figure out? What does he reveal about the two guests' names?

_____

_____

_____

_____

_____

_____

_____

_____

"Oh, of course it is!" she cried, sitting down on the sofa. "How silly of me. I do apologize. In one ear and out the other, that's me, Mr. Weaver."

"You know something?" Billy said. "Something that's really quite extraordinary about all this?"

"No, dear, I don't."

"Well, you see, both of these names—Mulholland and Temple—I not only seem to remember each one of them separately, so to speak, but somehow or other, in some
260 peculiar way, they both appear to be sort of connected together as well. As though they were both famous for the same sort of thing, if you see what I mean—like . . . well . . . like Dempsey and Tunney, for example, or Churchill and Roosevelt."[11]

Illustration by Krysten Brooker.

11. **Dempsey and Tunney . . . Churchill and Roosevelt:** Jack Dempsey and Gene Tunney were American boxers who competed for the world heavyweight championship in 1926. Winston Churchill was prime minister of Great Britain, and Franklin D. Roosevelt was president of the United States, during World War II.

"How amusing," she said. "But come over here now, dear, and sit down beside me on the sofa and I'll give you a nice cup of tea and a ginger biscuit[12] before you go to bed."

"You really shouldn't bother," Billy said. "I didn't mean you to do anything like that." He stood by the piano, watching her as she fussed about with the cups and saucers. He noticed that she had small, white, quickly moving hands and red fingernails.

"I'm almost positive it was in the newspapers I saw them," Billy said. "I'll think of it in a second. I'm sure I will."

There is nothing more tantalizing[13] than a thing like this that lingers just outside the borders of one's memory. He hated to give up.

"Now wait a minute," he said. "Wait just a minute. Mulholland . . . Christopher Mulholland . . . wasn't *that* the name of the Eton[14] schoolboy who was on a walking tour through the West Country, and then all of a sudden . . ."

"Milk?" she said. "And sugar?"

"Yes, please. And then all of a sudden . . ."

"Eton schoolboy?" she said. "Oh no, my dear, that can't possibly be right, because *my* Mr. Mulholland was certainly not an Eton schoolboy when he came to me. He was a Cambridge[15] undergraduate. Come over here now and sit next to me and warm yourself in front of this lovely fire. Come on. Your tea's all ready for you." She patted the empty place beside her on the sofa, and she sat there smiling at Billy and waiting for him to come over.

---

12. **biscuit** (bis′kit) *n.*: British term meaning "cookie."
13. **tantalizing** (tan′tə·līz′iŋ) *adj.*: teasing by remaining unavailable or by withholding something desired by someone; tempting. (In Greek mythology, Tantalus was a king condemned after death to stand in water that moved away whenever he tried to drink it and to remain under branches of fruit that were just out of reach.)
14. **Eton:** boys' prep school near London.
15. **Cambridge:** famous university in England.

PREDICT

Billy seems about to remember why Christopher Mulholland's name was in the newspaper (line 283). What do you think he's about to say before he's interrupted by the landlady?

INFER

Pause at line 291. Why do you think the landlady keeps interrupting Billy?

INFER

Pause at line 306. What might the strange smell indicate?

_____

_____

_____

_____

_____

_____

_____

PREDICT

Re-read lines 307–315. What do you guess has happened to the two guests?

_____

_____

_____

_____

_____

_____

_____

IDENTIFY

Circle the words in lines 321–331 that indicate the landlady's interest in her guests' appearance.

He crossed the room slowly and sat down on the edge of the sofa. She placed his teacup on the table in front of him.

"*There* we are," she said. "How nice and cozy this is, isn't it?"

Billy started sipping his tea. She did the same. For half a minute or so, neither of them spoke. But Billy knew that she was looking at him. Her body was half turned toward 300 him, and he could feel her eyes resting on his face, watching him over the rim of her teacup. Now and again, he caught a whiff of a peculiar smell that seemed to emanate[16] directly from her person. It was not in the least unpleasant, and it reminded him—well, he wasn't quite sure what it reminded him of. Pickled walnuts? New leather? Or was it the corridors of a hospital?

At length, she said, "Mr. Mulholland was a great one for his tea. Never in my life have I seen anyone drink as much tea as dear, sweet Mr. Mulholland."

310 "I suppose he left fairly recently," Billy said. He was still puzzling his head about the two names. He was positive now that he had seen them in the newspapers—in the headlines.

"Left?" she said, arching her brows. "But my dear boy, he never left. He's still here. Mr. Temple is also here. They're on the fourth floor, both of them together."

Billy set his cup down slowly on the table and stared at his landlady. She smiled back at him, and then she put out one of her white hands and patted him comfortingly on the knee. "How old are you, my dear?" she asked.

320 "Seventeen."

"Seventeen!" she cried. "Oh, it's the perfect age! Mr. Mulholland was also seventeen. But I think he was a trifle shorter than you are; in fact I'm sure he was, and his teeth

---

16. **emanate** (em′ə·nāt′) *v.*: come forth.

weren't *quite* so white. You have the most beautiful teeth, Mr. Weaver, did you know that?"

"They're not as good as they look," Billy said. "They've got simply masses of fillings in them at the back."

"Mr. Temple, of course, was a little older," she said, ignoring his remark. "He was actually twenty-eight. And yet
330 I never would have guessed it if he hadn't told me, never in my whole life. There wasn't a *blemish* on his body."

"A what?" Billy said.

"His skin was *just* like a baby's."

There was a pause. Billy picked up his teacup and took another sip of his tea; then he set it down again gently in its saucer. He waited for her to say something else, but she seemed to have lapsed into another of her silences. He sat there staring straight ahead of him into the far corner of the room, biting his lower lip.

340 "That parrot," he said at last. "You know something? It had me completely fooled when I first saw it through the window. I could have sworn it was alive."

"Alas, no longer."

"It's most terribly clever the way it's been done," he said. "It doesn't look in the least bit dead. Who did it?"

"I did."

"*You* did?"

"Of course," she said. "And have you met my little Basil as well?" She nodded toward the dachshund curled up so
350 comfortably in front of the fire. Billy looked at it. And suddenly, he realized that this animal had all the time been just as silent and motionless as the parrot. He put out a hand and touched it gently on the top of its back. The back was hard and cold, and when he pushed the hair to one side with his fingers, he could see the skin underneath, grayish black and dry and perfectly preserved.

INFER

Pause at line 327. Why do you think Billy tells the landlady about his fillings?

_____

_____

_____

_____

_____

_____

PREDICT

Pause at line 339. Billy seems to be thunderstruck by a sudden realization about the landlady. What do you think Billy is going to do?

_____

_____

_____

_____

_____

_____

_____

IDENTIFY

Re-read lines 340–356. Underline the horrifying things the landlady reveals about her activities.

INTERPRET

In lines 357–359, we learn
that Billy looks at the landlady with admiration. Do
you think his admiration is
sincere or fake? Explain.

_____

_____

_____

_____

_____

_____

_____

_____

PREDICT

Pause at line 365. What do
you think will happen to
Billy?

_____

_____

_____

_____

_____

_____

_____

_____

_____

_____

"Good gracious me," he said. "How absolutely fascinating." He turned away from the dog and stared with deep
admiration at the little woman beside him on the sofa. "It
360 must be most awfully difficult to do a thing like that."

"Not in the least," she said. "I stuff all my little pets
myself when they pass away. Will you have another cup
of tea?"

"No, thank you," Billy said. The tea tasted faintly of
bitter almonds, and he didn't much care for it.

"You did sign the book, didn't you?"

"Oh, yes."

"That's good. Because later on, if I happen to forget
what you were called, then I could always come down here
370 and look it up. I still do that almost every day with Mr.
Mulholland and Mr. . . . Mr. . . ."

"Temple," Billy said, "Gregory Temple. Excuse my asking,
but haven't there been any other guests here except them in
the last two or three years?"

Holding her teacup high in one hand, inclining her
head slightly to the left, she looked up at him out of the
corners of her eyes and gave him another gentle little smile.

"No, my dear," she said. "Only you."

The Landlady

Prediction Chart   "The Landlady" is fun to read because it is full of **foreshadowing clues** that build suspense. In the chart below, read each clue from the story, and then explain what prediction you made based on each clue.

SKILLS FOCUS

Literary Skills
Analyze foreshadowing.

Clues	Prediction
"But the air was deadly cold and the wind was like a flat blade of ice on his cheeks." (lines 5–7)	
"Each word was like a large black eye staring at him . . . , holding him, compelling him, forcing him to stay where he was. . . ." (lines 77–79)	
"'You see, it isn't very often I have the pleasure of taking a visitor into my little nest.'" (lines 132–134)	
"Now where on earth had he heard that rather unusual name before?" (lines 210–211)	
"Now and again, he caught a whiff of a peculiar smell that seemed to emanate directly from her person." (lines 301–303)	
"'I stuff all my little pets myself when they pass away.'" (lines 361–363)	
"The tea tasted faintly of bitter almonds, and he didn't much care for it." (lines 364–365)	

The Landlady

COMPREHENSION

Reading Comprehension   Answer each question below.

1. Why is Billy drawn to the window of the boardinghouse?

   _____

   _____

2. Why does Billy decide to stay at the boardinghouse?

   _____

   _____

3. What makes Billy assume that the landlady is harmless?

   _____

   _____

4. How does Billy react to the names in the guest book?

   _____

   _____

5. What does Billy discover about the landlady's pets?

   _____

   _____

6. What does the taste of bitter almonds suggest about the tea?

   _____

   _____

Orpheus and the Underworld

retold by Mollie McLean and Anne Wiseman

LITERARY FOCUS: PLOT

Everyone likes good stories. The events that happen in a story make up its **plot.** The **exposition,** or introduction, of a story tells about the characters and their situation. The story's main character usually faces a **conflict,** a struggle to get what he or she wants. **Complications** arise as the character takes steps to resolve the conflict. The plot reaches a **climax** when we find out how the conflict is resolved. In the story's **resolution,** loose ends are tied up as the story comes to a close.

Here's an example of how plot elements fit together:

Sample Plot
Exposition (Characters and Basic Situation): Cinderella lives with her stepmother and stepsisters, who treat her very unfairly.
Major Problem or Conflict: The stepsisters go to the prince's ball but make Cinderella stay home.
Major Plot Events: 1. The fairy godmother allows Cinderella to go to the ball. **2.** Cinderella meets the prince but has to leave early. She leaves a glass slipper behind. **3.** The prince looks for the person who lost the slipper.
Climax: Cinderella tries on the slipper, and it fits.
Resolution: The prince and Cinderella live happily ever after.

READING SKILLS: RETELLING

When you explain to a friend what happened to you yesterday, you are **retelling** what happened. You use the same skill when you retell a story. By retelling a story, you make sure you've understood the main plot events and their importance. As you read "Orpheus and the Underworld," look for the Retell notes. Then, use your own words to explain who did what to whom.

SKILLS FOCUS

Literary Skills
Understand plot.

Reading Skills
Retell a story.

ORPHEUS AND THE UNDERWORLD

a Greek myth *retold by* Mollie McLean and Anne Wiseman

IDENTIFY

Pause at line 6. Circle the two different names given for the place being described.

WORD STUDY

Mercury (line 12) is the name of a Roman god (his Greek name is Hermes). *Mercury* is also the name of a planet and of a chemical element.

IDENTIFY

Pause at line 18. If somebody wanted to get across the river Styx to the Underworld, what would he or she need?

_____

_____

_____

_____

_____

The Underworld

Many times the Greeks told of a dark kingdom called Hades (hā′dēz′). They said people went to this place when they died. No one was sure where Hades was. Some said it was at the edge of the world. Others said it was under the very ground upon which men walked. That is why some people called it the Underworld.

The kingdom of Hades had two parts—one beautiful, one ugly. The beautiful part was filled with sunlight and happiness. Here lived those who had been good on earth.
10 The other part was dark and sad. Those who had been wicked lived here.

When a man died, Mercury came to take him to the Underworld. He led him down a dark road until they came to a great river. This river was called the Styx (stiks). Here Charon (ker′ən), an old boatman, was waiting. If the dead man had a penny in his mouth, Charon would take him across the river in his boat. He would not take him if the dead man's friends had forgotten the money.

"The Underworld" and "Orpheus Goes to the Underworld" from *Adventures of the Greek Heroes* by Mollie McLean and Anne Wiseman. Copyright © 1961 by Mollie McLean and Anne M. Wiseman; copyright renewed © 1989 by Anne Wiseman. Reproduced by permission of **Houghton Mifflin Company**.

Once across the river, they came to a dark palace. Here
20 lived Pluto, king of the Underworld, and his beautiful wife,
Proserpina. Outside the gate sat Cerberus (sʉr′bər·əs), a
fierce three-headed dog with a hissing snake for a tail. He
would let everyone pass into the palace. He would let no
one out.

Inside the palace, it was cold and dark. The king and
queen sat quietly on black chairs. Their pale faces were sad.
They were so still that they looked as if they were made
of stone.

Into this room, Mercury would lead the man who had
30 died. Pluto would ask Mercury if the man with him had led
a good life. If the messenger-god said yes, the king sent the
man to the beautiful part of Hades. If Mercury said no,
Pluto gave the man some terrible labor.

Pluto had given terrible labors to many wicked men.
One man had to roll a giant rock up a hill. Just as he came
to the top, a magic power pushed the rock away from him.
Down it would go, and the man would have to try once
more. He would push the rock to the top again and again.
Each time it would roll back.

40 Tantalus had been a cruel man on earth. In Hades, he
had to stand in water which came up to his shoulders. But
when he tried to take a drink, the water would run away.
He was always thirsty. Over his head grew apples and
oranges. But when he put his hand out for them, they
would fly away. He was always hungry.

Pluto had also given hard labors to cruel women.
Three sisters who had been wicked and mean had to carry
water from a well in a sieve.

The people of the world were afraid of Hades. They
50 did not want to go to this dark place until their time had

RETELL

Pause at line 33. What happens after a person dies, according to this story?

_____

_____

_____

_____

_____

_____

_____

_____

_____

_____

WORD STUDY

Tantalize means "to offer something desirable but keep it out of reach." Explain how the meaning of tantalize is related to the mythic character Tantalus (line 40).

_____

_____

_____

_____

_____

_____

come. Once in a long time a mighty hero had to go to the Underworld. The next story tells of one of these heroes.

Orpheus Goes to the Underworld

In all of Greece there was no better singer than Orpheus (ôr′fē·əs). When he sang and played his lyre,° people would stop their work and hurry to his side. Animals of the forest would come near. Fierce monsters would sit quietly at his feet. Even tall trees would bend their heads to hear his song.

Orpheus went from place to place singing his songs of love and battle. One day he saw a beautiful girl in the crowd. He fell in love with her at once. He stopped playing and walked over to her.

10 "What is your name?" he asked.

"I am called Eurydice (yoo·rid′i·sē′)," she said quietly.

"I shall sing my next song for you," said Orpheus.

He picked up his lyre and sang a beautiful song. When Eurydice heard the song, she fell in love with the singer.

For many days, Orpheus stayed in this place. No longer did he wish to go about the world singing. He wanted only to please Eurydice. Every day he sang her a new song of love.

Then one fine day, Orpheus and Eurydice were married. All their friends came to wish them happiness. There 20 was a great feast. There was dancing and singing. Everyone was very happy until an old man stepped out of the crowd and said, "Stop the dancing! Stop the singing! There is something I must say!"

"What is it, old man?" asked Orpheus.

"I have seen a bad sign in the sky. There is sadness ahead for you and your wife," he answered.

° **lyre** (līr) *n.:* small stringed instrument of the harp family.

IDENTIFY

Pause at line 17. What does Orpheus want?

FLUENCY

Imagine you are an ancient storyteller telling this story to a crowd gathered around a campfire. Read the boxed passage aloud with expression.

"How can there be sadness for us?" laughed Orpheus. "We love each other too much to be unhappy."

"We shall see. We shall see," said the old man as he walked quietly away.

After the old man had gone, a dark shadow fell on the feast. Soon everyone went home.

The next day, Orpheus and Eurydice took a walk beside the river. As they came near a field, Eurydice saw some beautiful red flowers. She ran to pick them. All at once, she fell. Orpheus raced to her side. Just as he came near, he saw a snake moving away in the grass.

"My foot! My foot!" cried Eurydice. "Something has hurt my foot!"

Orpheus picked her up in his powerful arms. He ran as fast as he could. He wanted to get to the river to wash her foot. As soon as he put her down on the ground, he knew she was dead.

For a long time after this, Orpheus went about the world singing and playing his lyre. No more did he sing of love and battle. His songs now told of the great sadness he felt in his heart. Each song asked how he might get Eurydice back. He sang to the people of the world. He sang to the gods on Mount Olympus. No one could help him.

At last, Orpheus knew he must go to Hades. He went at once to the black cave which led to the Underworld. Down, down the dark road he went, singing his song of sadness all the way. Soon he was at the River Styx. Here stood the fierce old boatman. He had heard Orpheus coming. He, too, had felt the magic power of the hero's song. He took him across the river without a word.

On into the kingdom of Hades walked Orpheus. At the sound of his singing, Tantalus forgot how hungry and

RETELL

Pause at line 43. Retell what has happened to Eurydice.

_____
_____
_____
_____
_____
_____
_____
_____

IDENTIFY

What does Orpheus do after Eurydice dies (lines 44–49)?

_____
_____
_____
_____
_____
_____
_____
_____

Re-read lines 57–66. Circle the part that tells what Orpheus wants and his reason for wanting it.

Pause at line 76. What condition does Pluto make in order for Orpheus to get what he wants?

_____

_____

_____

_____

_____

_____

_____

Pause at line 76. What do you think is going to happen?

_____

_____

_____

_____

_____

_____

_____

_____

_____

60 thirsty he was. The man pushing the rock stopped his hard labor. The three sisters put their sieves on the ground and listened to the beautiful music. Orpheus walked on. He passed the cruel three-headed dog and went into the palace of Pluto. Here he saw the king and queen. He fell on his knees before them. Looking up, he said, "I have come to ask you to give me back my beautiful Eurydice. I cannot live without her."

The king and queen had heard the young hero's song. Their hearts had been moved by its sadness. Pluto said, "No one has ever left Hades before. We will let Eurydice go 70 because of your beautiful singing."

"You are very kind, Pluto," said Orpheus. "Where shall I look for her?"

"Do not look for her," said the king. "Go back the way you have come. She will follow you. Do not look back at her until you can see the light of the sun. If you once turn, she will be lost forever. Now, go! Remember my words!"

Orpheus started the long trip back. Out of the palace he went. He passed the three-headed dog. He went over the river. Soon he was on the dark road which led up to the 80 world. As he walked, he listened for footsteps behind him. He heard nothing. He began to wonder if Pluto had played some terrible trick on him. He walked on. Still he could hear nothing. Orpheus could stand it no longer. Just as he reached the end of the road, he turned around.

"Eurydice!" he called.

There before him, he saw a gray shadow. It was his beautiful wife.

"Orpheus!" she cried. "You should not have turned so soon! We were almost free! Goodbye! Goodbye!"

90   With a sad smile, she went back to the Underworld. Orpheus followed her, but this time no one would listen to his song. He knew she was lost forever.

After a time, Orpheus went back to the world. Never again did he sing a song of love!

© Mimmo Jodice/CORBIS.

Orpheus (detail) by Antonio Canova. Marble sculpture.

RETELL

Do Orpheus and Eurydice live happily ever after? Retell what happens after Pluto grants Orpheus's request.

_____
_____
_____
_____
_____
_____
_____
_____
_____
_____
_____
_____
_____
_____
_____
_____
_____
_____
_____
_____
_____

Orpheus and the Underworld

SKILLS FOCUS

Literary Skills
Analyze plot.

Plot Chart   Several elements make up a story's plot. In the **exposition** we are introduced to the story's characters and basic situation. We also learn of the main character's **conflict,** or struggle. At the story's **climax,** we learn whether or not the main character has succeeded in overcoming the conflict. Then in the **resolution** we learn what has become of the characters as the story ends.

The following chart contains an outline of a typical plot. Fill in the chart with details from "Orpheus Goes to the Underworld" (pages 40–43).

Exposition (Characters and Basic Situation):
Major Problem or Conflict:
Major Plot Events:
1.
2.
3.
4.
Climax:
Resolution:

Skills Review

Orpheus and the Underworld

COMPREHENSION

Reading Comprehension   Answer each question below.

1. What magical power does Orpheus's song have on all things? _____

_____

_____

2. Does the old man's prediction come true? Explain. _____

_____

_____

3. How does Orpheus's music change after Eurydice dies? _____

_____

_____

4. Why does Pluto allow Eurydice to return with Orpheus? _____

_____

_____

5. What complication is created by Pluto's instructions? _____

_____

_____

6. What happens at the end of the story? Do Orpheus and Eurydice live happily

ever after? Explain. _____

_____

_____

SKILLS FOCUS

Reading Skills
Retell a story.

Do the Right Thing

Marchers gather in front of the Lincoln Memorial
in Washington, D.C., with the Washington
Monument in the distance.

Don Uhrbrock/TimePix.

Academic Vocabulary for Collection 2

These are the terms you should know
as you read and analyze the selections in this collection.

————

Character A person in a story, a play, or other literary work. A character may also be an animal, a thing, or a natural force such as a flood or blizzard.

Characterization The ways in which a writer reveals the personality of a character. Writers reveal characters in two different ways: **direct characterization** and **indirect characterization.**

Direct Characterization A method in which the writer *tells* readers directly what a character is like. Example: "Teddy was the smartest person I ever knew."

Indirect Characterization A method in which the writer *shows* what a character is like and lets readers draw their own conclusions. There are five basic ways that a writer can show characterization indirectly:
- Describing the character's appearance
- Showing the character in action
- Allowing us to hear the character's words
- Revealing the character's thoughts and feelings
- Showing how others react to the character

Motivation The reasons a character behaves in a certain way. A character's motives may arise from feelings, experiences, or others' actions.

This selection also appears in *Elements of Literature.*

from Harriet Tubman: Conductor on the Underground Railroad

by Ann Petry

LITERARY FOCUS: CHARACTERS IN BIOGRAPHY

A **biography** is the story of someone's life written by another person. A biography deals with real people, yet the people are presented as if they were characters in a fictional work. We learn about biographical characters, or subjects, through their words, thoughts, feelings, actions, the reactions of others, and the narrator's descriptions. We also learn about their **motivations,** or the reasons for their actions. In the following excerpt from a biography of Harriet Tubman, you will learn about a fascinating person and her heroic deeds.

READING SKILLS: MAKING INFERENCES

You have probably heard the phrase "reading between the lines." This means figuring out what has been implied but not directly stated in words. When you read, you often make guesses about what has been hinted at in a text. This type of guess, called an **inference,** is based both on what you've read and what you already know.

Reading between the lines gives you more than just details. It helps you understand characters and ideas. Here is an example:

Text Passage	Sample Inference
Melinda Alice had left for school early. She wanted to study alone in a quiet spot because there was going to be a big math test.	Melinda Alice is a thoughtful, serious student.

As you read the following excerpt from a biography of Harriet Tubman, use details from the text to draw inferences about Tubman's character.

SKILLS FOCUS

Literary Skills
Understand characterization.

Reading Skills
Make inferences.

Vocabulary Skills
Understand word origins.

VOCABULARY DEVELOPMENT

PREVIEW SELECTION VOCABULARY

Get to know the following words before you read the next selection.

fugitives (fyōō′ji·tivz) *n.*: people fleeing from danger.

The fugitives escaped to the North, traveling by night.

incomprehensible (in·käm′prē·hen′sə·bəl) *adj.*: impossible to understand.

The Fugitive Slave Law had once been an incomprehensible set of words.

incentive (in·sent′iv) *n.*: reason to do something; motivation.

The incentive of a warm house and good food kept the fugitives going.

dispel (di·spel′) *v.*: scatter; drive away.

Harriet tried to dispel the fugitives' fear of capture.

eloquence (el′ə·kwəns) *n.*: ability to write or speak gracefully and convincingly.

Frederick Douglass was known for his eloquence in writing and speaking.

INFLUENCES ON ENGLISH: WORD ORIGINS

Thousands of words that we use in our everyday speech have come into English from other languages. All of the Vocabulary words from this selection come from Latin, an ancient language that is no longer spoken. Here are the origins of the Vocabulary words (the abbreviation *L* stands for "Latin").

Vocabulary Word	Latin Root Word	Meaning
fugitives	L *fugere*	"to flee"
incomprehensible	L *prehendere*	"to seize, grasp, get hold of"
incentive	L *canere*	"to sing"
dispel	L *pellere*	"to drive, beat"
eloquence	L *loqui*	"to speak or talk"

from
Harriet Tubman: Conductor on the Underground Railroad

Ann Petry

BACKGROUND: Literature and Religion

In the biblical Book of Exodus, God chooses Moses to lead the people of Israel out of slavery in Egypt. Pursued by the Egyptians, Moses takes his people on a long, perilous desert journey and leads them to the Promised Land. As you read about Harriet Tubman, ask yourself why she was called the Moses of her people.

IDENTIFY

Pause at line 6. Circle the name of the "man" who was "running off slaves."

The Railroad Runs to Canada

Along the Eastern Shore of Maryland, in Dorchester County, in Caroline County, the masters kept hearing whispers about the man named Moses, who was running off slaves. At first they did not believe in his existence. The stories about him were fantastic, unbelievable. Yet they watched for him. They offered rewards for his capture.

They never saw him. Now and then they heard whispered rumors to the effect that he was in the neighborhood. The woods were searched. The roads were watched. There
10 was never anything to indicate his whereabouts. But a few days afterward, a goodly number of slaves would be gone from the plantation. Neither the master nor the overseer had

heard or seen anything unusual in the quarter.[1] Sometimes one or the other would vaguely remember having heard a whippoorwill call somewhere in the woods, close by, late at night. Though it was the wrong season for whippoorwills.

Sometimes the masters thought they had heard the cry of a hoot owl, repeated, and would remember having thought that the intervals between the low moaning cry

20 were wrong, that it had been repeated four times in succession instead of three. There was never anything more than that to suggest that all was not well in the quarter. Yet, when morning came, they invariably discovered that a group of the finest slaves had taken to their heels.

Unfortunately, the discovery was almost always made on a Sunday. Thus a whole day was lost before the machinery of pursuit could be set in motion. The posters offering rewards for the **fugitives** could not be printed until Monday. The men who made a living hunting for runaway slaves were out of reach, off

CAUTION!!
COLORED PEOPLE
OF BOSTON, ONE & ALL,
You are hereby respectfully CAUTIONED and advised, to avoid conversing with the
Watchmen and Police Officers of Boston,
For since the recent ORDER OF THE MAYOR & ALDERMEN, they are empowered to act as
KIDNAPPERS
AND
Slave Catchers,
And they have already been actually employed in KIDNAPPING, CATCHING, AND KEEPING SLAVES. Therefore, if you value your LIBERTY, and the *Welfare of the Fugitives* among you, *Shun* them in every possible manner, as so many *HOUNDS* on the track of the most unfortunate of your race.
Keep a Sharp Look Out for KIDNAPPERS, and have TOP EYE open.
APRIL 24, 1851.

---

1. **quarter** *n.:* area in a plantation where enslaved blacks lived. It consisted of windowless, one-room cabins made of logs and mud.

INFER

Who or what do you think was making bird sounds? Underline the details in lines 17–21 that support your **inference**.

_____

_____

_____

_____

_____

_____

_____

IDENTIFY

On what day were runaway slaves usually missed? Underline the reasons slaves usually left on that day (lines 25–32).

_____

_____

_____

_____

_____

_____

VOCABULARY

fugitives (fyo͞o′ji·tivz) *n.:* people fleeing from danger.

_____

_____

_____

_____

_____

_____

_____

_____

IDENTIFY

Re-read lines 33–50. What was the real name of "the man named Moses, who was running off slaves"?

_____

_____

_____

_____

_____

_____

_____

_____

_____

30 in the woods with their dogs and their guns, in pursuit of four-footed game, or they were in camp meetings saying their prayers with their wives and families beside them.

Harriet Tubman could have told them that there was far more involved in this matter of running off slaves than signaling the would-be runaways by imitating the call of a whippoorwill, or a hoot owl, far more involved than a matter of waiting for a clear night when the North Star[2] was visible.

In December 1851, when she started out with the band of fugitives that she planned to take to Canada, she had been

40 in the vicinity of the plantation for days, planning the trip, carefully selecting the slaves that she would take with her.

She had announced her arrival in the quarter by singing the forbidden spiritual[3]—"Go down, Moses, 'way down to Egypt Land"—singing it softly outside the door of a slave cabin, late at night. The husky voice was beautiful even when it was barely more than a murmur borne on the wind.

Once she had made her presence known, word of her coming spread from cabin to cabin. The slaves whispered to each other, ear to mouth, mouth to ear, "Moses is here."

50 "Moses has come." "Get ready. Moses is back again." The ones who had agreed to go North with her put ashcake[4] and salt herring in an old bandanna, hastily tied it into a bundle, and then waited patiently for the signal that meant it was time to start.

There were eleven in this party, including one of her brothers and his wife. It was the largest group that she had ever conducted, but she was determined that more and more slaves should know what freedom was like.

---

2. **North Star:** Runaways fleeing north used the North Star (Polaris) to help them stay on course.
3. **forbidden spiritual:** Spirituals are religious songs, some of which are based on the biblical story of the Israelites' escape from slavery in Egypt. Plantation owners feared that the singing of spirituals might lead to rebellion.
4. **ashcake** _n.:_ cornmeal bread baked in hot ashes.

She had to take them all the way to Canada. The Fugitive
60 Slave Law[5] was no longer a great many **incomprehensible**
words written down on the country's lawbooks. The new
law had become a reality. It was Thomas Sims, a boy, picked
up on the streets of Boston at night and shipped back to
Georgia. It was Jerry and Shadrach, arrested and jailed with
no warning.

She had never been in Canada. The route beyond
Philadelphia was strange to her. But she could not let the
runaways who accompanied her know this. As they walked
along, she told them stories of her own first flight; she kept
70 painting vivid word pictures of what it would be like to
be free.

But there were so many of them this time. She knew
moments of doubt, when she was half afraid and kept looking back over her shoulder, imagining that she heard the
sound of pursuit. They would certainly be pursued. Eleven
of them. Eleven thousand dollars' worth of flesh and bone
and muscle that belonged to Maryland planters. If they
were caught, the eleven runaways would be whipped and
sold South, but she—she would probably be hanged.

80 They tried to sleep during the day but they never could
wholly relax into sleep. She could tell by the positions they
assumed, by their restless movements. And they walked at
night. Their progress was slow. It took them three nights of
walking to reach the first stop. She had told them about the
place where they would stay, promising warmth and good
food, holding these things out to them as an **incentive** to
keep going.

---

5. **Fugitive Slave Law:** harsh federal law passed in 1850 stating that
   slaves who escaped from slavery to free states could be forced to
   return to their owners. As a result, those who escaped were safe only
   in Canada. The law also made it a crime for a free person to help
   slaves escape or to prevent their return.

VOCABULARY

incomprehensible
(in·käm′prē·hen′sə·bəl) *adj.:*
impossible to understand.

IDENTIFY

Re-read lines 66–79. Underline the details that tell you
why this trip was different—
and more difficult—for
Tubman.

INFER

Pause at line 79. How would
Tubman be punished if she
was caught? What inference
can you make about Tubman's
character from the information you have read so far?

_____

_____

_____

_____

_____

_____

_____

_____

_____

VOCABULARY

incentive (in·sent′iv) *n.:*
reason to do something;
motivation.

IDENTIFY

Re-read lines 88–101. Underline the details that tell you the runaways will not be welcomed at their first stop. Circle the two reasons the farmer turns them away.

INTERPRET

How does Tubman keep up the runaways' courage? What does the narrator mean when she says that Tubman had to "bring some of the fear back" (line 116)?

_____

_____

_____

_____

_____

_____

_____

_____

_____

_____

_____

VOCABULARY

dispel (di·spel') *v.*: scatter; drive away.

When she knocked on the door of a farmhouse, a place where she and her parties of runaways had always been welcome, always been given shelter and plenty to eat, there was no answer. She knocked again, softly. A voice from within said, "Who is it?" There was fear in the voice.

She knew instantly from the sound of the voice that there was something wrong. She said, "A friend with friends," the password on the Underground Railroad.

The door opened, slowly. The man who stood in the doorway looked at her coldly, looked with unconcealed astonishment and fear at the eleven disheveled[6] runaways who were standing near her. Then he shouted, "Too many, too many. It's not safe. My place was searched last week. It's not safe!" and slammed the door in her face.

She turned away from the house, frowning. She had promised her passengers food and rest and warmth, and instead of that, there would be hunger and cold and more walking over the frozen ground. Somehow she would have to instill courage into these eleven people, most of them strangers, would have to feed them on hope and bright dreams of freedom instead of the fried pork and corn bread and milk she had promised them.

They stumbled along behind her, half dead for sleep, and she urged them on, though she was as tired and as discouraged as they were. She had never been in Canada, but she kept painting wondrous word pictures of what it would be like. She managed to **dispel** their fear of pursuit so that they would not become hysterical, panic-stricken. Then she had to bring some of the fear back, so that they would stay awake and keep walking though they drooped with sleep.

Yet, during the day, when they lay down deep in a thicket, they never really slept, because if a twig snapped or the wind sighed in the branches of a pine tree, they jumped

---

6. **disheveled** (di·shev'əld) *adj.*: untidy; rumpled.

to their feet, afraid of their own shadows, shivering and shaking. It was very cold, but they dared not make fires because someone would see the smoke and wonder about it.

She kept thinking, eleven of them. Eleven thousand dollars' worth of slaves. And she had to take them all the way to Canada. Sometimes she told them about Thomas Garrett, in Wilmington.[7] She said he was their friend even though he did not know them. He was the friend of all fugitives. He called them God's poor. He was a Quaker[8] and

130 his speech was a little different from that of other people. His clothing was different, too. He wore the wide-brimmed hat that the Quakers wear.

She said that he had thick white hair, soft, almost like a baby's, and the kindest eyes she had ever seen. He was a big man and strong, but he had never used his strength to harm anyone, always to help people. He would give all of them a new pair of shoes. Everybody. He always did. Once they reached his house in Wilmington, they would be safe. He would see to it that they were.

140 She described the house where he lived, told them about the store where he sold shoes. She said he kept a pail of milk and a loaf of bread in the drawer of his desk so that he would have food ready at hand for any of God's poor who should suddenly appear before him, fainting with hunger. There was a hidden room in the store. A whole wall swung open, and behind it was a room where he could hide fugitives. On the wall there were shelves filled with small boxes—boxes of shoes—so that you would never guess that the wall actually opened.

150 While she talked, she kept watching them. They did not believe her. She could tell by their expressions. They

7. **Wilmington:** city in Delaware.
8. **Quaker:** member of the Society of Friends, a religious group active in the movement to end slavery.

PREDICT

Pause at line 123. Things don't look good for the runaways. What do you think will happen to them?

_____

_____

_____

_____

_____

_____

_____

_____

_____

_____

IDENTIFY

Circle details from the text that tell you what Thomas Garrett does to help the fugitives (lines 133–149).

_____

_____

_____

_____

_____

_____

_____

_____

were thinking. New shoes, Thomas Garrett, Quaker, Wilmington—what foolishness was this? Who knew if she told the truth? Where was she taking them anyway?

That night they reached the next stop—a farm that belonged to a German. She made the runaways take shelter behind trees at the edge of the fields before she knocked at the door. She hesitated before she approached the door, thinking, suppose that he too should refuse shelter, 160 suppose—Then she thought, *Lord, I'm going to hold steady on to You and You've got to see me through*—and knocked softly.

She heard the familiar guttural voice say, "Who's there?"

She answered quickly, "A friend with friends."

He opened the door and greeted her warmly. "How many this time?" he asked.

"Eleven," she said and waited, doubting, wondering.

He said, "Good. Bring them in."

He and his wife fed them in the lamp-lit kitchen, their 170 faces glowing as they offered food and more food, urging them to eat, saying there was plenty for everybody, have more milk, have more bread, have more meat.

They spent the night in the warm kitchen. They really slept, all that night and until dusk the next day. When they left, it was with reluctance. They had all been warm and safe and well-fed. It was hard to exchange the security offered by that clean, warm kitchen for the darkness and the cold of a December night.

"Go On or Die"

Harriet had found it hard to leave the warmth and friend-
180 liness, too. But she urged them on. For a while, as they

walked, they seemed to carry in them a measure of contentment; some of the serenity and the cleanliness of that big, warm kitchen lingered on inside them. But as they walked farther and farther away from the warmth and the light, the cold and the darkness entered into them. They fell silent, sullen, suspicious. She waited for the moment when some one of them would turn mutinous.[9] It did not happen that night.

Two nights later, she was aware that the feet behind her were moving slower and slower. She heard the irritability in their voices, knew that soon someone would refuse to go on.

She started talking about William Still and the Philadelphia Vigilance Committee.[10] No one commented. No one asked any questions. She told them the story of William and Ellen Craft and how they escaped from Georgia. Ellen was so fair that she looked as though she were white, and so she dressed up in a man's clothing and she looked like a wealthy young planter. Her husband, William, who was dark, played the role of her slave. Thus they traveled from Macon, Georgia, to Philadelphia, riding on the trains, staying at the finest hotels. Ellen pretended to be very ill—her right arm was in a sling and her right hand was bandaged because she was supposed to have rheumatism.[11] Thus she avoided having to sign the register at the hotels, for she could not read or write. They finally arrived safely in Philadelphia and then went on to Boston.

No one said anything. Not one of them seemed to have heard her.

---

9. **mutinous** (my$\overline{oo}$t″n·əs) *adj.:* rebellious. *Mutiny* usually refers to a revolt of sailors against their officer.
10. **Philadelphia Vigilance Committee:** group that offered help to people escaping slavery. **William Still,** a free African American, was chairman of the committee.
11. **rheumatism** (r$\overline{oo}$′mə·tiz′əm) *n.:* painful swelling and stiffness of the joints or muscles.

INTERPRET

Why does Tubman tell stories
to the fugitives (lines
192–214)?

_____

_____

_____

_____

_____

_____

_____

_____

_____

_____

_____

_____

_____

_____

IDENTIFY

Re-read lines 232–242. Circle
the reason Tubman says no
slave can return to the plantation. Then, underline the
details that tell how one
returned slave might ruin the
whole operation for helping
runaways.

210 She told them about Frederick Douglass, the most
famous of the escaped slaves, of his **eloquence,** of his
magnificent appearance. Then she told them of her own
first, vain effort at running away, evoking the memory of
that miserable life she had led as a child, reliving it for a
moment in the telling.

But they had been tired too long, hungry too long,
afraid too long, footsore too long. One of them suddenly
cried out in despair, "Let me go back. It is better to be a
slave than to suffer like this in order to be free."

She carried a gun with her on these trips. She had
220 never used it—except as a threat. Now, as she aimed it, she
experienced a feeling of guilt, remembering that time, years
ago, when she had prayed for the death of Edward Brodas,
the Master, and then, not too long afterward, had heard that
great wailing cry that came from the throats of the field
hands, and knew from the sound that the Master was dead.

One of the runaways said again, "Let me go back. Let
me go back," and stood still, and then turned around and
said, over his shoulder, "I am going back."

She lifted the gun, aimed it at the despairing slave. She
230 said, "Go on with us or die." The husky, low-pitched voice
was grim.

He hesitated for a moment and then he joined the
others. They started walking again. She tried to explain to
them why none of them could go back to the plantation. If
a runaway returned, he would turn traitor; the master and
the overseer would force him to turn traitor. The returned
slave would disclose the stopping places, the hiding places,
the corn stacks they had used with the full knowledge of
the owner of the farm, the name of the German farmer
240 who had fed them and sheltered them. These people who
had risked their own security to help runaways would be
ruined, fined, imprisoned.

She said, "We got to go free or die. And freedom's not bought with dust."

This time she told them about the long agony of the Middle Passage[12] on the old slave ships, about the black horror of the holds, about the chains and the whips. They too knew these stories. But she wanted to remind them of the long, hard way they had come, about the long, hard way they had yet to go. She told them about Thomas Sims, the boy picked up on the streets of Boston and sent back to Georgia. She said when they got him back to Savannah, got him in prison there, they whipped him until a doctor who was standing by watching said, "You will kill him if you strike him again!" His master said, "Let him die!"

Thus she forced them to go on. Sometimes she thought she had become nothing but a voice speaking in the darkness, cajoling,[13] urging, threatening. Sometimes she told them things to make them laugh; sometimes she sang to them and heard the eleven voices behind her blending softly with hers, and then she knew that for the moment all was well with them.

She gave the impression of being a short, muscular, indomitable woman who could never be defeated. Yet at any moment she was liable to be seized by one of those curious fits of sleep, which might last for a few minutes or for hours.[14]

Even on this trip, she suddenly fell asleep in the woods. The runaways, ragged, dirty, hungry, cold, did not steal the gun as they might have and set off by themselves or turn

250

260

270

---

12. **Middle Passage:** route traveled by ships carrying captured Africans across the Atlantic Ocean to the Americas. The captives endured the horrors of the Middle Passage crammed into **holds,** airless cargo areas below decks.
13. **cajoling** (kə·jōl'iŋ) *v.* used as *adj.*: coaxing; persuading.
14. Harriet's losses of consciousness were caused by a serious head injury that she had suffered as a teenager. Harriet had tried to protect another slave from punishment, and an enraged overseer threw a two-pound weight at her head.

Explain what Tubman means when she says in lines 243–244, "We got to go free or die. And freedom's not bought with dust."

_____

_____

_____

_____

_____

_____

_____

_____

_____

FLUENCY

Read the boxed passage aloud twice. See if you can read it more smoothly each time. Try to use a voice that will show Tubman's strong character.

WORD STUDY

The word *indomitable* (in·däm'i·tə·bəl), in line 264, is defined in context. Underline the context clue you find.

WORD STUDY

The word *liable* (lī'ə·bəl), in line 265, means "likely to suffer from."

from **Harriet Tubman: Conductor on the Underground Railroad** 59

IDENTIFY

Underline the words in lines 268–275 that tell you that the runaways' attitude toward Tubman has changed.

INFER

William Still kept a record book of the fugitives he had met so that the fugitives and their families would have a way to find each other. Why did Still's book become even more important than he realized at the time that he kept it (lines 280–292)?

_____

_____

_____

_____

_____

_____

_____

_____

_____

_____

_____

_____

_____

_____

_____

back. They sat on the ground near her and waited patiently until she awakened. They had come to trust her implicitly, totally. They, too, had come to believe her repeated statement, "We got to go free or die." She was leading them into freedom, and so they waited until she was ready to go on.

Finally, they reached Thomas Garrett's house in Wilmington, Delaware. Just as Harriet had promised, Garrett gave them all new shoes, and provided carriages to take them on to the next stop.

280　By slow stages they reached Philadelphia, where William Still hastily recorded their names, and the plantations whence they had come, and something of the life they had led in slavery. Then he carefully hid what he had written, for fear it might be discovered. In 1872 he published this record in book form and called it *The Underground Railroad.* In the foreword to his book he said: "While I knew the danger of keeping strict records, and while I did not then dream that in my day slavery would be blotted out, or that the time would come when I could publish
290　these records, it used to afford me great satisfaction to take them down, fresh from the lips of fugitives on the way to freedom, and to preserve them as they had given them."

William Still, who was familiar with all the station stops on the Underground Railroad, supplied Harriet with money and sent her and her eleven fugitives on to Burlington, New Jersey.

Harriet felt safer now, though there were danger spots ahead. But the biggest part of her job was over. As they went farther and farther north, it grew colder; she was
300　aware of the wind on the Jersey ferry and aware of the cold damp in New York. From New York they went on to Syracuse,[15] where the temperature was even lower.

_____

15. **Syracuse:** city in central New York.

In Syracuse she met the Reverend J. W. Loguen, known as "Jarm" Loguen. This was the beginning of a lifelong friendship. Both Harriet and Jarm Loguen were to become friends and supporters of Old John Brown.[16]

From Syracuse they went north again, into a colder, snowier city—Rochester. Here they almost certainly stayed with Frederick Douglass, for he wrote in his autobiography:

310 "On one occasion I had eleven fugitives at the same time under my roof, and it was necessary for them to remain with me until I could collect sufficient money to get them to Canada. It was the largest number I ever had at any one time, and I had some difficulty in providing so many with food and shelter, but, as may well be imagined, they were not very fastidious[17] in either direction, and were well content with very plain food, and a strip of carpet on the floor for a bed, or a place on the straw in the barn loft."

Late in December 1851, Harriet arrived in St. Catharines,
320 Canada West (now Ontario), with the eleven fugitives. It had taken almost a month to complete this journey.

Arvis Stewart.

The Underground Railroad runs to Canada.

---

16. **Old John Brown** (1800–1859): abolitionist (opponent of slavery) who was active in the Railroad. In 1859, Brown led a raid on the federal arsenal at Harpers Ferry, then in Virginia, in hopes of inspiring a slave uprising. Federal troops overpowered Brown and his followers, and Brown was convicted of treason and was hanged.
17. **fastidious** (fa·stid′ē·əs) *adj.:* fussy; hard to please.

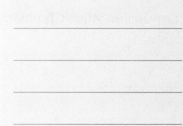

EVALUATE

Think over what you've learned about Harriet Tubman. Was she a good leader? Explain, using details from the text to support your response.

_____

_____

_____

_____

_____

_____

_____

_____

_____

_____

_____

_____

_____

_____

_____

_____

_____

_____

_____

_____

_____

_____

from Harriet Tubman: Conductor on the Underground Railroad

SKILLS FOCUS

Literary Skills
Analyze characterization.

Motivations Web   Characters have reasons, or motivations, for acting as they do. To learn more about why Harriet Tubman made the choices she made, fill in this motivations web. On the lines provided describe Tubman's actions and motivations. Then, review Tubman's actions and motivations to come up with a conclusion about her character.

Character: Harriet Tubman

Action/Motivation	_____
	_____
	_____

↓

Action/Motivation	_____
	_____
	_____

↓

Action/Motivation	_____
	_____
	_____

Conclusion About Tubman's Character:

_____

_____

_____

_____

Skills Review

from Harriet Tubman: Conductor on the Underground Railroad

VOCABULARY AND COMPREHENSION

A. Influences on English: Latin Roots   Write the word from the Word Bank that shares the root listed in the first column.

Latin Root Word	Meaning	Word Bank Word
fugere	"to flee"	
pellere	"to drive, beat"	
loqui	"to speak or talk"	
canere	"to sing"	
prehendere	"to seize, grasp, get hold of"	

Word Bank

fugitives
incomprehensible
incentive
dispel
eloquence

B. Reading Comprehension   Answer each question below.

1. What signals tell the slaves that Harriet is nearby? _____

_____

2. Why is it necessary for Harriet to take the fugitives into Canada?

_____

3. What password is used on the Underground Railroad? _____

_____

4. What does Harriet do to keep runaways from returning to their

plantations? _____

_____

5. How does William Still help Harriet and the fugitives? _____

_____

SKILLS FOCUS

Vocabulary Skills
Understand word origins.

Before You Read

This selection also appears in *Elements of Literature.*

Barbara Frietchie by John Greenleaf Whittier

LITERARY FOCUS: A CHARACTER'S CHARACTER

Suppose you heard someone described as a "good soldier." What qualities do you think the person would have? In literature a character's qualities are called the character's **character**. That's right. The word *character* also means "a person's essential quality or personality." Characters often reveal their characters best when they face a challenge. In the poem that follows, you'll meet quite a character, one whose character has become part of legend.

READING SKILLS: PARAPHRASING

You are **paraphrasing** when you restate a writer's text in your own words. You can use paraphrasing when you want to clarify the lines of a poem or a difficult passage in a prose work. A paraphrase is not a summary. In a summary you retell only the most important points in a text. In a paraphrase you reword all of the original text in simpler or clearer language.

To paraphrase a line of a poem, you'll find it helpful to first identify the subject and verb. Then, reword the sentence in normal word order. Here's how you might paraphrase line 23 of "Barbara Frietchie":

Original: "Up the street came the rebel tread,"
Paraphrase: The rebel tread came up the street.

SKILLS FOCUS

Literary Skills
Understand character.

Reading Skills
Paraphrase a poem.

Vocabulary Skills
Use multiple-meaning words.

VOCABULARY DEVELOPMENT

PREVIEW SELECTION VOCABULARY

Get to know these words before you read "Barbara Frietchie."

staff (staf) *n.:* pole; stick.

Frietchie hung the flag from a staff outside her window.

tread (tred) *n.:* step.

The tread of the soldiers echoed through the town.

rent (rent) *v.:* tore; ripped.

The rifle blast rent a hole in the flag.

stirred (stŭrd) *v.:* woke up.

The old woman stirred Jackson's feelings.

host (hōst) *n.:* army; large number; crowd.

The rebel host moved into Frederick, Maryland.

MULTIPLE MEANINGS

Many common English words have **multiple meanings.** The Vocabulary word *staff,* for example, can mean "pole" or "a group of workers." Words with multiple meanings may also work as different parts of speech. *To staff an office,* for example, uses *staff* as a verb meaning "to provide with workers." When you come across a word that has multiple meanings, use **context clues** to figure out the intended meaning.

As you read "Barbara Frietchie," look for and be sure to read the Vocabulary sidenotes. You'll learn more about multiple meanings in those sidenotes.

BARBARA FRIETCHIE

John Greenleaf Whittier

BACKGROUND: Literature and Social Studies

"Barbara Frietchie" is set in 1862, during the Civil War. Led by Generals Robert E. Lee and "Stonewall" Jackson, the Confederate troops marched into the town of Frederick, Maryland, on September 6. Lee and his men expected a warm welcome, but the people of Frederick were loyal to the Union. According to the poem, as the Confederate forces came into town, one person dared to display the U.S. flag.

Notes

Up from the meadows rich with corn,
Clear in the cool September morn,

The clustered spires of Frederick stand
Green-walled by the hills of Maryland.

5   Round about them orchards sweep,
Apple and peach tree fruited deep,

Fair as the garden of the Lord
To the eyes of the famished rebel horde,[1]

On that pleasant morn of the early fall
10   When Lee marched over the mountain wall;

Over the mountains winding down,
Horse and foot, into Frederick town.

VISUALIZE

Read lines 1–12. Circle the details that help you see where the town of Frederick is located in relation to the meadows, hills, orchards, and mountains. Underline the details that help you picture what these same features look like.

---

1. **horde** (hôrd) *n.:* crowd.

A church tower rises above surrounding treetops at a town in Frederick, Maryland.

Forty flags with their silver stars,

Forty flags with their crimson bars,

15   Flapped in the morning wind: the sun

Of noon looked down, and saw not one.

Up rose old Barbara Frietchie then,

Bowed with her fourscore years and ten;

Bravest of all in Frederick town,

20   She took up the flag the men hauled down

In her attic window the **staff** she set,

To show that one heart was loyal yet.

Up the street came the rebel **tread,**

Stonewall Jackson riding ahead.

25   Under his slouched hat left and right

He glanced; the old flag met his sight.

INFER

Pause at line 16. What happened to the forty flags that had been displayed in the morning?

_____

_____

_____

IDENTIFY

Re-read lines 17–18. Underline the words that reveal Frietchie's age. How old is she? (A "score" equals twenty years.)

_____

VOCABULARY

staff (staf) *n.:* pole; stick. *Staff* also means "group of workers" and "lines on which musical notes are written."

tread (tred) *n.:* act of stepping or walking. *Tread* also means "the outer part of tires or of shoe soles."

PARAPHRASE

Re-state in your own words the events in lines 9–22.

_____

_____

_____

_____

_____

CLARIFY

Re-read lines 23–36. What has happened?

_____

_____

_____

_____

INTERPRET

"Barbara Frietchie" contains **dialogue,** the words that characters speak. Circle the dialogue in lines 35–42. What does this dialogue reveal about Frietchie's **character** and about Jackson's **character**?

_____

_____

_____

VOCABULARY

rent (rent) *v.* (past tense of *rend,* meaning "tear"): tore; ripped. *Rent* also means "pay money for use of a house or an apartment or of things such as bowling shoes or ice skates."

stirred (sturd) *v.:* arose; woke up. *Stirred* also means "mixed a liquid or loose ingredients, as in a recipe."

host (hōst) *n.:* army; large number; crowd. *Host* also means "someone who entertains guests, at home or on TV."

"Halt!"—the dust-brown ranks stood fast.
"Fire!"—out blazed the rifle blast.

It shivered the window, pane and sash;
30 It **rent** the banner with seam and gash.

Quick, as it fell, from the broken staff
Dame Barbara snatched the silken scarf.

She leaned far out on the windowsill,
And shook it forth with a royal will.

35 "Shoot, if you must, this old gray head,
But spare your country's flag," she said.

A shade of sadness, a blush of shame,
Over the face of the leader came;

The nobler nature within him **stirred**
40 To life at that woman's deed and word;

"Who touches a hair of yon gray head
Dies like a dog! March on!" he said.

All day long through Frederick street
Sounded the tread of marching feet:

45 All day long that free flag tossed
Over the heads of the rebel **host.**

Ever its torn folds rose and fell
On the loyal winds that loved it well;

And through the hill gaps sunset light

50   Shone over it with a warm good night.

Barbara Frietchie's work is o'er,

And the Rebel rides on his raids no more.

Honor to her! and let a tear

Fall, for her sake, on Stonewall's bier.[2]

55   Over Barbara Frietchie's grave,

Flag of Freedom and Union, wave!

Peace and order and beauty draw

Round thy symbol of light and law;

And ever the stars above look down

60   On thy stars below in Frederick town!

---

2. bier (bir) *n.:* coffin and the platform on which it rests. Stonewall Jackson died in 1863 after being wounded in battle.

FLUENCY

Re-read the boxed passage aloud until you can read it smoothly. Then, read the words of Frietchie, Jackson, and the narrator in the tone of voice they might have used.

PARAPHRASE

Re-read lines 55–60, and paraphrase them, line for line.

_____

_____

_____

_____

_____

_____

_____

_____

_____

_____

_____

_____

_____

_____

_____

IDENTIFY

In lines 55–60, circle the seven words that the narrator associates with the American flag.

Barbara Frietchie

Character Graph   You find out about a character's **character** in several
ways: through his or her appearance, speech, actions, thoughts, and by
how others react to him or her. Re-read "Barbara Frietchie," and fill out
the graph below with details from the poem. Then, write a brief
description of Frietchie's character, in the center box.

SKILLS FOCUS

Literary Skills
Analyze
character.

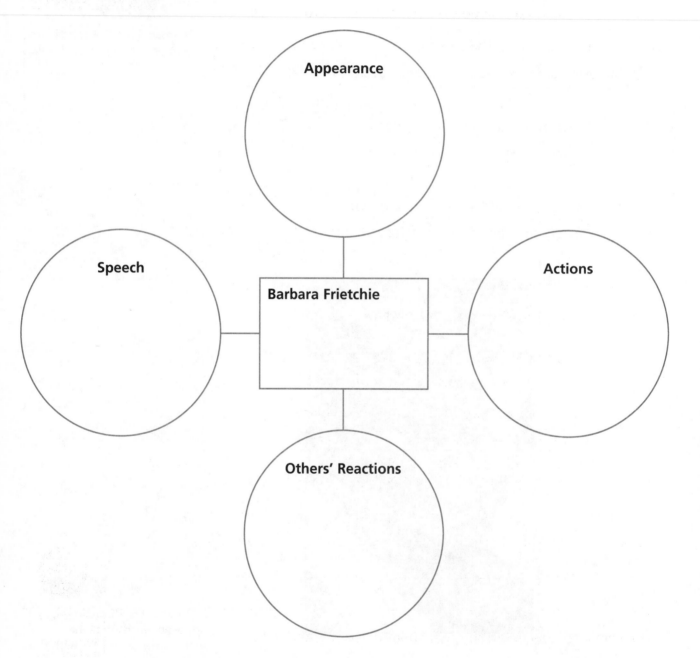

Appearance

Speech

Barbara Frietchie

Actions

Others' Reactions

Skills Review

Barbara Frietchie

VOCABULARY AND COMPREHENSION

A. Multiple Meanings Read each sentence. Circle the definition that matches the meaning of the boldface Word Bank word.

Word Bank

staff

tread

rent

stirred

host

1. The general praised his **staff** for their hard work and courage.

   (a) pole or stick

   (b) group of workers

2. The family decided to **rent** a car while on vacation.

   (a) tore

   (b) hire

3. The crops were destroyed by a **host** of locusts.

   (a) large group

   (b) person who throws a party

4. As the national anthem played, the crowd was **stirred.**

   (a) emotionally moved

   (b) mixed by hand

5. The disappointed child walked into his room with a heavy **tread.**

   (a) bottom sole of a shoe

   (b) step

B. Reading Comprehension Answer each question below.

1. When and where does "Barbara Frietchie" take place? _____

   _____

2. How do the townspeople react to the Confederate troops?

   _____

3. What does Barbara Frietchie dare to do when the Confederate troops

   march into town? _____

   _____

4. How does Stonewall Jackson feel about Barbara Frietchie? _____

   _____

Vocabulary Skills
Recognize multiple meanings.

Field Work by Rose Del Castillo Guilbault

LITERARY FOCUS: CHARACTER AND MOTIVATION

Motivation is the reason a character behaves a certain way. A character may, for example, behave a certain way because of feelings, experiences, and other people's actions. Without motivation, a character's behavior might not be believable. Sometimes a character's motivation is at first not clear, but as you become involved in the story, the character's actions begin to make sense.

As you read "Field Work," ask yourself these questions about its characters:

- What do the characters want or need?
- What fears and conflicts do the characters face?

READING SKILLS: READING FOR DETAILS

A **detail** is anything that is a part of something else. Your name and address, for example, are details about you. Writers use many different details to make a character vivid and interesting. These details may include the character's words, appearance, thoughts, feelings, actions, and the comments of other characters.

When you read a short story or a personal narrative such as "Field Work," pay attention to details that help explain why characters make certain choices.

Literary Skills
Understand character and motivation.

Reading Skills
Read for details.

Vocabulary Skills
Clarify word meanings through restatement.

VOCABULARY DEVELOPMENT

PREVIEW SELECTION VOCABULARY

Before you read "Field Work," study these words from the story.

despondent (di·spän′dənt) *adj.:* sad; dejected.

> *Rose was despondent because she wanted a vacation but had no money.*

stamina (stam′ə·nə) *n.:* endurance; resistance to fatigue, illness, hardship, and so on.

> *Working in the fields to harvest garlic required great stamina.*

insidious (in·sid′ē·əs) *adj.:* steadily treacherous; spreading slowly but with dangerous effects (like an insidious rumor or an insidious disease).

> *No amount of washing was able to remove the smell of the insidious garlic.*

CLARIFYING WORD MEANINGS: RESTATEMENT

When writers use difficult words, they sometimes give readers help by providing context clues. One type of context clue is a nearby word or group of words with the same meaning as the difficult word. Following are some examples. The words in italics have the same meaning as the boldface words.

- Our class was **despondent.** We were *sad* because the field trip had been cancelled.
- The athlete's **stamina** was amazing. No one would match his *powers of endurance.*
- The villain's comments were **insidious**—*crafty* and *sly.*

When you come across an unfamiliar word in your reading, check to see if nearby words restate the meaning of the unfamiliar word.

Field Work

Rose Del Castillo Guilbault

INTERPRET

What does the narrator mean when she says, "The fields were the stage where life's truths were played out. . . ." (lines 10–11)?

El fiel' was what my parents and their friends called it—their Anglicism[1] for the field. The first jobs I ever had were working el fiel'. I grew up in the Salinas Valley, where if you're young and Mexican, the only available summer jobs are agricultural work.

Although there is absolutely nothing romantic about working the fields, it did offer a fertile environment for learning important life lessons about work, family values, and what it means to grow up Mexican in the United States. The fields were the stage where life's truths were played out—the struggles, hardships, humiliations, the humor, friendships, and compassions. For many young Mexicans, field work is practically a rite of passage.[2]

I can remember with uncanny clarity the first time I worked in the fields. It was the summer of my eleventh year, and I was feeling **despondent** and bored. I wanted to go on vacation, as many of my classmates did, but my parents couldn't afford it.

My mother was sympathetic; she was yearning to see her family in Mexico. She came up with the idea that we

VOCABULARY

despondent (di·spän′dənt) *adj.:* sad; dejected.

---

1. **Anglicism** (aŋ′glə·siz′əm): here, word adapted from English for use in Spanish.
2. **rite of passage:** event marking an important change in a person's life, such as the movement from childhood to adulthood.

could earn the $50 we needed for Greyhound bus tickets to Mexicali[3] if we both worked the garlic harvest that was about to begin on the farm where we lived.

The first hurdle to earning the money was persuading my traditional Mexican father to let us do it. He had made it clear to my mother that he did not want her to work. To him, a working wife implied his inability to support his family.

To this day, I have no idea how she convinced him that it was all right. Maybe it was because the job was very short-term—five days—or maybe it was because we hadn't been to Mexico in more than a year. My father knew an annual visit to see relatives was my mother's lifeline. In any case, my father agreed to lobby his boss the next day to let us join the garlic-picking crew.

The boss was skeptical about employing us. Not because he was concerned about hiring a woman and a child; he worried more about our inexperience and **stamina.** After all, this was a man's job and he had a deadline. What if we slowed things down and he had to keep a worker for an extra day?

"Since when is picking garlic such an art?" my mother retorted when my father told her that night about the boss's reservations. But then he added that the boss had decided to take a chance on us.

We started immediately—at 6 A.M. the next day. The August morning was cold and gray, still shrouded in damp fog. We wore layers of clothes—a T-shirt, a sweat shirt, a windbreaker—to protect us from the early-morning chill and later discard when the afternoon sun got too hot. We wrapped scarves around our heads and topped them with knit caps. This was our field work uniform, and it is the

---

3. **Mexicali** (meks′i·kä′lē): city in northwestern Mexico, near the California border.

IDENTIFY

Pause at line 23. What do the narrator and her mother decide to do? What is their **motivation**—why do they decide to do it?

_____

_____

_____

_____

_____

_____

_____

_____

_____

_____

_____

_____

_____

_____

IDENTIFY

Why does the narrator's father decide to get work for his wife and daughter (lines 29–35)? Underline his reasons.

VOCABULARY

stamina (stam′ə·nə) n.: endurance; resistance to fatigue, illness, hardship, and so on.

© Royalty-Free/CORBIS.

INFER

Read on to line 75. What inferences do you make about the narrator based on the ways she tries to keep the bag around her waist?

same uniform you'll see men and women wearing today as you drive by California's valley fields.

A foreman showed us the proper way to pick garlic. "You hook your sack to this special belt. This frees your hands so you can pick the garlic and toss it into your sack."

We watched carefully as he hooked the bag to his waist and sauntered down the row, stooping slightly, while his

60   hands whirled like a harvester machine, making garlic bulbs fly from the ground into the sack.

"Easy!" he said, straightening his back.

And I learned it was easy—until the sack started getting full. Then it not only wouldn't stay on the belt hook, it became nearly impossible for a skinny eleven-year-old to budge.

I spent the morning engineering ways to keep the bag around my waist. I tried belting it and looping it on different parts of my body with my scarf. But it was hopeless;

70   at a certain level of fullness, the thing just couldn't be moved. So I resorted to a more laborious yet effective

method. I'd drag the sack with both my hands, then run back and forth, picking handfuls of garlic and depositing them in the stationary bag. I must have looked as silly as a Keystone Kop.[4]

I heard laughter echoing from the distant fields. I looked around, wondering what the joke was about, and slowly realized they were laughing at me! My stomach did a somersault when I heard the impatient crunch of the fore-man's boots behind me. Was I going to be told to go home?

"No, no, you don't do it right." He gestured wildly in front of me.

"But I can't do it the same way you do. The sack's too heavy," I explained.

Suddenly men's voices called out: "Déjala, hombre! Leave her alone, man. Let the kid do it her way."

The foreman shrugged, rolled his eyes upward, and walked away, muttering under his breath. My mother walked toward me, smiling. It was lunchtime.

After lunch, the afternoon sun slowed me down. Perspiration trickled down my back, making me itchy and sticky. It was discouraging to see everyone passing me, working row after row. Afternoon dragged on as heavy as the half-filled garlic sack I lugged.

By the end of the day, my shoulders felt as if someone had stuck a hot iron between them.

The following days became a blur of aching muscles and garlic bulbs. The rows seemed to stretch like rubber bands, expanding with each passing day. My mother's smile and words of encouragement—a salve the first few days—no longer soothed me.

Even at home I felt overpowered by the **insidious** garlic. It permeated my skin and clothes. No matter how

---

4. Keystone Kop: character in slapstick comedy films who does things in a clumsy, bumbling way.

WORD STUDY

What might "Déjala, hombre!" (line 85) mean? Circle the context clues you find.

_____

_____

_____

_____

_____

_____

WORD STUDY

Underline the three comparisons used in lines 95–101. Which are **similes** (those using a connecting word such as *like* or *as*)? Which is a **metaphor**?

_____

_____

_____

_____

_____

_____

_____

VOCABULARY

insidious (in·sid′ē·əs) *adj.:* steadily treacherous; spreading slowly but with dangerous effects (like an insidious rumor or an insidious disease).

INFER

Re-read lines 106–123. Underline the words that show that the narrator's motivation has changed. What does she *not* want to do?

_____

_____

_____

_____

_____

_____

_____

_____

PREDICT

Pause at line 135. What do you think the narrator will do?

_____

_____

_____

_____

_____

_____

_____

_____

_____

_____

_____

much I scrubbed, the garlic seemed to ooze from my pores, the odor suffocating me in my sleep.

On what was to be the last morning, I simply couldn't get out of bed. My body was so sore that the slightest move sent waves of pain through my muscles. My legs were wobbly from all the bending, and my shoulders felt as if they had been cleaved apart. My whole body was one throbbing ache. The field had defeated me.

"I just can't do it," I sobbed to my mother, the tears tasting like garlic.

"Anything worth having is worth working for," she said gently.

"I don't care about the vacation. I'm too tired. It's not worth it," I cried.

"There are only a few rows left. Are you sure you can't finish?" my mother persisted.

But to me the few rows might as well have been hundreds. I felt bad about giving up after working so hard, but it just didn't seem fair to pay such a high price to go on vacation. After all, my friends didn't have to.

My mother was very quiet all day. I'd forgotten it was to have been her vacation, too. My father was surprised to see us sitting neatly dressed when he came home. He listened quietly to my mother's explanation, and after a thoughtful pause said, "Well, if we all pitch in, we can still finish up the rows tonight, right on schedule."

As I looked at my father's dust-rimmed, bloodshot eyes, his dusty hair and mud-stained overalls, I was over-whelmed with a strange mixture of pity and gratitude. I knew by the slope of his shoulders he was very tired from his own grueling field work. And finishing up our leftover work was nothing short of an act of love.

I was torn. The thought of doing battle with the field again filled me with dread. But I said nothing, swallowing my reluctance until it formed a lump in my throat.

That summer evening, the three of us worked side by side, teasing, talking, laughing, as we completed the task. It was dark, and we had grown silent by the time the last of the garlic sacks were lined up. The rosy glow from the setting sun made me feel as warm as the relief of knowing the work was finally over and done.

I worked every summer thereafter, some in the fields (never again picking garlic!) and later in the vegetable-packing sheds, always alongside my mother. Working together created an unusual bond between us. And through this relationship, and relationships with other Mexican families thrust into this agricultural society, I got an education as solid and rich as the earth we worked.

Conklin/Monkmeyer.

Picking the crops.

IDENTIFY

Underline details in the final paragraph that tell what the narrator gains by working in the fields.

_____
_____
_____
_____
_____
_____
_____
_____
_____
_____

EVALUATE

Go back and underline the mother's statement in line 114. Do you agree with that statement? Explain.

_____
_____
_____
_____
_____
_____
_____

Field Work

SKILLS FOCUS

Literary Skills
Analyze character and motivation.

Motivation Map   The narrator, the mother, and the father in "Field Work" all have different motivations, or reasons for their actions. Read through the story again, and fill in the chart below with details from the story that help explain the motivations of one character.

Character's Name:

Action ◄———► Motivation

Action ◄———► Motivation

Action ◄———► Motivation

Skills Review

Field Work

VOCABULARY AND COMPREHENSION

A. Clarifying Word Meanings: Restatement   Fill in the blanks with the correct words from the Word Bank. Then, locate and underline the restatement of each Word Bank word that appears in the context.

Word Bank

despondent

stamina

insidious

Unless they kept up their (1) _____, the lost hikers would never have the endurance to make their way back to the lodge. Since they were all feeling (2) _____, the leader of the group suggested they sing in order to change their incredibly unhappy mood. The power of music helped chase away the (3) _____ gloom, which had spread slowly but surely and drained their energy.

B. Reading Comprehension   Answer each question below.

1. Why does the narrator decide to go to work in the fields?

   _____

2. What part of the field work does the narrator find most difficult?

   _____

3. Why does the foreman let the narrator pick garlic her own way?

   _____

4. Why does the narrator want to give up picking garlic?

   _____

5. How does the narrator's father solve their problem?

   _____

SKILLS FOCUS

Vocabulary Skills
Clarify word meanings through restatement.

Being There

Academic Vocabulary for Collection 3

These are the terms you should know
as you read and analyze the stories in this collection.

—————

Setting The time and place of a story, play, or narrative poem. The setting of a story includes such details as weather conditions and the time of year. Setting can also include the customs and language of characters in a certain place.

Atmosphere or **Mood** The overall feeling of a work of literature. A work's atmosphere can often be described in one or two adjectives, such as *dreamy* or *scary.* The setting of a story can greatly affect its atmosphere or mood.

Tone The writer's attitude toward his or her topic. Tone is conveyed by a writer's word choice and style. You can describe a writer's tone with an adjective such as *breezy, passionate,* or *scolding,* for example.

Before You Read

This selection also appears in *Elements of Literature.*

In Trouble by Gary Paulsen

LITERARY FOCUS: SETTING

Every story takes place in a particular time and place, or **setting.** Some stories take place on a desert island; others take place in the distant past; and some take place in the future or in places that are not real at all.

A writer uses many types of details to create a **setting.** Some details reveal the season, time of day, or historical period. Other details—those that describe a landscape, climate, and buildings—help develop a sense of place. Details of a setting may also include **customs**—the dress, occupations, and traditions of a people. You may also get information about setting from details about the language, dialects, and speech patterns of the characters.

In some stories, in fact, setting is like a **character,** complete with a personality. Setting also can play an important role in a **plot,** particularly when the main character is in conflict with a natural force such as a tornado or tidal wave. Often, setting affects a story's **mood,** or overall feeling.

READING SKILLS: VISUALIZING SETTING

When you read, don't just race through the words. Instead, let your mind form images based on details the writer has given you. This type of mental picturing is called **visualizing.** In the story that follows, Gary Paulsen has provided lots of details that create a vivid setting. Pause every so often as you read to visualize the time, place, and conditions present in the story.

SKILLS FOCUS

Literary Skills
Analyze setting and mood.

Reading Skills
Visualize setting.

Vocabulary Skills
Understand homophones and homographs.

VOCABULARY DEVELOPMENT

PREVIEW SELECTION VOCABULARY

Before you read "In Trouble," get to know these words from
the selection.

steeped (stēpt) *v.* used as *adj.:* filled with;
saturated; soaked.

> *The sky was steeped in brilliant colors.*

alleviate (ə·lē′vē·āt′) *v.:* relieve; reduce.

> *Dogs need activities to alleviate boredom.*

contention (kən·ten′shən) *n.:* conflict;
struggle.

> *There was contention among the dogs.*

exaltation (eg′zôl·tā′shən) *n.:* great joy.

> *Paulsen felt a sense of exaltation when he was
> with his dogs.*

chagrin (shə·grin′) *n.:* embarrassment and
annoyance caused by disappointment
or failure.

> *Paulsen felt chagrin over his mistake.*

SOUND-ALIKES AND LOOK-ALIKES

Words that sound the same but have different spellings and meanings
are called **homophones** (häm′ə·fōnz′). *Night* and *knight,* for example,
are homophones. **Homographs** (häm′ə·grafs′) are words that are
spelled the same but have different meanings and origins and sometimes different pronunciations. *Wind* (rhymes with *pinned*) and *wind*
(rhymes with *mind*) are homographs.

As you read "In Trouble," pause at Word Study notes to learn more
homophones and homographs.

from WOODSONG

IN TROUBLE

Gary Paulsen

> **BACKGROUND: Literature and Real Life**
> This selection is taken from *Woodsong,* a book Gary Paulsen wrote about his adventures with dogs. Earlier in the book, Paulsen tells about how he had been trapping coyotes and beavers in Minnesota. He had been covering the sixty miles of his route on foot or on skis until a friend gave him a team of four sled dogs. Those dogs would change his life. "In Trouble" is about some of these changes.

VISUALIZE

Re-read lines 1–14. Underline the details that help you see and feel "serious cold." Circle the **image,** the sensory detail, that makes you *hear* the cold.

_____

_____

_____

_____

_____

_____

VOCABULARY

steeped (stēpt) *v.* used as *adj.:* filled with; saturated; soaked.

Cold can be very strange. Not the cold felt running from the house to the bus or the car to the store, not the chill in the air on a fall morning, but deep cold.

Serious cold.

Forty, fifty, even sixty below zero—actual temperature, not windchill—seems to change everything. Steel becomes brittle and breaks, shatters; breath taken straight into the throat will freeze the lining and burst blood vessels; eyes exposed too long will freeze; fingers and toes freeze, turn

10   black, and break off. These are all known, normal parts of intense cold.

But it changes beauty as well. Things are **steeped** in a new clarity, a clear focus. Sound seems to ring and the very air seems to be filled with diamonds when ice crystals form.

On a river in Alaska, while training, I once saw a place where a whirlpool had frozen into a cone, open at the

Illustration by Ronald Himler.

bottom, like a beautiful trap waiting to suck the whole team down. When I stopped to look at it, with the water roaring through at the bottom, the dogs became nervous
20 and stared down into the center as if mystified and were very glad when we moved on.

After a time I stopped trapping. That change—as with many changes—occurred because of the dogs. As mentioned, I had hunted when I was young, trapping and killing many animals. I never thought it wrong until the dogs came. And then it was a simple thing, almost a silly thing, that caused the change.

Columbia had a sense of humor and I saw it.

In the summer the dogs live in the kennel area, each
30 dog with his own house, on a chain that allows him to move in a circle. They can run only with the wheeled carts on cool nights, and sometimes they get bored being tied up. To **alleviate** the boredom, we give the dogs large beef bones to chew and play with. They get a new bone every other day or so. These bones are the center of much **contention**—we call them Bone Wars. Sometimes dogs clear across the kennel

The word *whole,* in line 17, means "entire." Its **homophone** is *hole,* meaning "hollowed-out place" or "cavity."

Re-read lines 22–28. What happened to cause the narrator to stop trapping? Underline the cause.

_____

_____

_____

_____

_____

_____

_____

_____

_____

_____

_____

_____

alleviate (ə·lē′vē·āt′) *v.:* relieve; reduce.

contention (kən·ten′shən) *n.:* conflict; struggle. Paulsen is playing on the phrase *bone of contention,* meaning "subject about which there is disagreement."

_____

_____

_____

_____

_____

_____

_____

_____

_____

_____

_____

will hold their bones up in the air, look at each other, raise their hair, and start growling at each other, posturing and bragging about their bones.

40   But not Columbia.

    Usually Columbia just chewed on his bone until the meat was gone. Then he buried it and waited for the next bone. I never saw him fight or get involved in Bone Wars and I always thought him a simple—perhaps a better word would be primitive—dog, basic and very wolflike, until one day when I was sitting in the kennel.

    I had a notebook and I was sitting on the side of Cookie's roof, writing—the dogs are good company for working—when I happened to notice Columbia doing

50 something strange.

    He was sitting quietly on the outside edge of his circle, at the maximum length of his chain. With one paw he was pushing his bone—which still had a small bit of meat on it—out and away from him, toward the next circle.

    Next to Columbia was a dog named Olaf. While Columbia was relatively passive, Olaf was very aggressive. Olaf always wanted to fight and he spent much time arguing over bones, females, the weather—anything and everything that caught his fancy. He was much scarred from fighting,

60 with notched ears and lines on his muzzle, but he was a very good dog—strong and honest—and we liked him.

    Being next to Columbia, Olaf had tried many times to get him to argue or bluster, but Columbia always ignored him.

    Until this morning.

    Carefully, slowly, Columbia pushed the bone toward Olaf's circle.

    And of all the things that Olaf was—tough, strong, honest—he wasn't smart. As they say, some are smarter

70 than others, and some are still not so smart, and then there was Olaf. It wouldn't be fair to call Olaf dumb—dogs don't measure those things like people—but even in the dog world he would not be known as a whip. Kind of a big bully who was also a bit of a doofus.

When he saw Columbia pushing the bone toward him, he began to reach for it. Straining against his chain, turning and trying to get farther and farther, he reached as far as he could with the middle toe on his right front foot, the claw going out as far as possible.

80 But not quite far enough. Columbia had measured it to the millimeter. He slowly pushed the bone until it was so close that Olaf's claw—with Olaf straining so hard his eyes bulged—just barely touched it.

Columbia sat back and watched Olaf straining and pushing and fighting, and when this had gone on for a long time—many minutes—and Olaf was still straining for all he was worth, Columbia leaned back and laughed.

"Heh, heh, heh . . ."

Then Columbia walked away.

90 And I could not kill or trap any longer.

It happened almost that fast. I had seen dogs with compassion for each other and their young and with anger and joy and hate and love, but this humor went into me more than the other things.

It was so complicated.

To make the joke up in his mind, the joke with the bone and the bully, and then set out to do it, carefully and quietly, to do it, then laugh and walk away—all of it was so complicated, so complex, that it triggered a chain reaction

100 in my mind.

If Columbia could do that, I thought, if a dog could do that, then a wolf could do that. If a wolf could do that, then

INFER

Re-read lines 80–89. Why is Columbia keeping the bone out of Olaf's reach?

_____

_____

_____

_____

_____

_____

_____

RETELL

Pause at line 89. Retell what happens between Columbia and Olaf.

_____

_____

_____

_____

_____

_____

_____

_____

a deer could do that. If a deer could do that, then a beaver, and a squirrel, and a bird, and, and, and . . .

And I quit trapping then.

It was wrong for me to kill.

But I had this problem. I had gone over some kind of line with the dogs, gone back into some primitive state of **exaltation** that I wanted to study. I wanted to run them

110 and learn from them. But it seemed to be wasteful (the word *immature* also comes to mind) to just run them. I thought I had to have a trap line to justify running the dogs, so I kept the line.

But I did not trap. I ran the country and camped and learned from the dogs and studied where I would have trapped if I were going to trap. I took many imaginary beaver and muskrat but I did no more sets and killed no more animals. I will not kill anymore.

Yet the line existed. Somehow in my mind—and until

120 writing this I have never told another person about this— the line still existed and when I had "trapped" in one area, I would extend the line to "trap" in another, as is proper when you actually trap. Somehow the phony trapping gave me a purpose for running the dogs and would until I began to train them for the Iditarod, a dog-sled race across Alaska, which I had read about in *Alaska* magazine.

But it was on one of these "trapping" runs that I got my third lesson,[1] or awakening.

There was a point where an old logging trail went

130 through a small, sharp-sided gully—a tiny canyon. The trail came down one wall of the gully—a drop of fifty or so feet—then scooted across a frozen stream and up the other side. It might have been a game trail that was slightly widened or an old foot trail that had not caved in. Whatever

---

1. **my third lesson:** The first two lessons are described in the two previous chapters of *Woodsong.*

it was, I came onto it in the middle of January. The dogs were very excited. New trails always get them tuned up and they were fairly smoking as we came to the edge of the gully.

I did not know it was there and had been letting them run, not riding the sled brake to slow them, and we virtually shot off the edge.

The dogs stayed on the trail, but I immediately lost all control and went flying out into space with the sled. As I did, I kicked sideways, caught my knee on a sharp snag, and felt the wood enter under the kneecap and tear it loose.

I may have screamed then.

The dogs ran out on the ice of the stream but I fell onto it. As these things often seem to happen, the disaster snowballed.

The trail crossed the stream directly at the top of a small frozen waterfall with about a twenty-foot drop. Later I saw the beauty of it, the falling lobes[2] of blue ice that had grown as the water froze and refroze, layering on itself. . . .

But at the time I saw nothing. I hit the ice of the streambed like dropped meat, bounced once, then slithered over the edge of the waterfall and dropped another twenty feet onto the frozen pond below, landing on the torn and separated kneecap.

I have been injured several times running dogs— cracked rib, a broken left leg, a broken left wrist, various parts frozen or cut or bitten while trying to stop fights— but nothing ever felt like landing on that knee.

I don't think I passed out so much as my brain simply exploded.

Again, I'm relatively certain I must have screamed or grunted, and then I wasn't aware of much for two, perhaps three minutes as I squirmed around trying to regain some part of my mind.

---

2. **lobes** *n.:* rounded pieces that jut out.

WORD STUDY

Brake (line 139) and *break* are **homophones.** What does each word mean?

_____

_____

Tear (line 144) is pronounced (ter) and means "rip." *Tear* (tir) is its **homograph,** and refers to what falls from our eyes when we are sad.

INFER

Why do you think the narrator saw nothing at the time of his accident (line 153)?

_____

_____

_____

PREDICT

Pause at line 163. What do you predict will happen to the narrator? On what do you base your prediction?

_____

_____

_____

_____

_____

_____

_____

IDENTIFY

Pause at line 178. Underline the detail that tells you what dog teams usually do when the person driving the sled falls off.

VOCABULARY

chagrin (shə·grin′) n.: embarrassment and annoyance caused by disappointment or failure.

PREDICT

Pause at line 184. What do you think will happen now?

_____

_____

_____

_____

_____

_____

_____

_____

_____

_____

_____

_____

IDENTIFY

Circle the details in lines 190–213 that tell you that Obeah is the lead dog of the sled team.

When things settled down to something I could control, I opened my eyes and saw that my snow pants and the jeans beneath were ripped in a jagged line for about a foot. Blood was welling out of the tear, soaking the cloth and the ice underneath the wound.

Shock and pain came in waves and I had to close my eyes several times. All of this was in minutes that seemed like hours, and I realized that I was in serious trouble. Contrary to popular belief, dog teams generally do not stop and wait for a musher[3] who falls off. They keep going, often for many miles.

Lying there on the ice, I knew I could not walk. I didn't think I could stand without some kind of crutch, but I knew I couldn't walk. I was a good twenty miles from home, at least eight or nine miles from any kind of farm or dwelling.

It may as well have been ten thousand miles.

There was some self-pity creeping in, and not a little **chagrin** at being stupid enough to just let them run when I didn't know the country. I was trying to skootch myself up to the bank of the gully to get into a more comfortable position when I heard a sound over my head.

I looked up, and there was Obeah looking over the top of the waterfall, down at me.

I couldn't at first believe it.

He whined a couple of times, moved back and forth as if he might be going to drag the team over the edge, then disappeared from view. I heard some more whining and growling, then a scrabbling sound, and was amazed to see that he had taken the team back up the side of the gully and dragged them past the waterfall to get on the gully wall just over me.

---

3. **musher** (mush′ər) n.: person who travels over snow by dog sled.

200　　　They were in a horrible tangle, but he dragged them along the top until he was well below the waterfall, where he scrambled down the bank with the team almost literally falling on him. They dragged the sled up the frozen streambed to where I was lying.

　　　On the scramble down the bank Obeah had taken them through a thick stand of cockleburs. Great clumps of burs wadded between their ears and down their backs.

　　　He pulled them up to me, concern in his eyes and making a soft whine, and I reached into his ruff and pulled
210　his head down and hugged him and was never so happy to see anybody probably in my life. Then I felt something and looked down to see one of the other dogs—named Duberry—licking the wound in my leg.

　　　She was licking not with the excitement that prey blood would cause but with the gentle licking that she would use when cleaning a pup, a wound lick.

　　　I brushed her head away, fearing infection, but she persisted. After a moment I lay back and let her clean it, still holding on to Obeah's ruff, holding on to a friend.

220　　　And later I dragged myself around and untangled them and unloaded part of the sled and crawled in and tied my leg down. We made it home that way, with me sitting in the sled; and later, when my leg was sewed up and healing and I was sitting in my cabin with the leg propped up on pillows by the woodstove; later, when all the pain was gone and I had all the time I needed to think of it . . . later I thought of the dogs.

　　　How they came back to help me, perhaps to save me. I knew that somewhere in the dogs, in their humor and the
230　way they thought, they had great, old knowledge; they had something we had lost.

　　　And the dogs could teach me.

FLUENCY

As you read the boxed passage aloud, imagine that you are the narrator, Gary Paulsen. Try to show with your tone of voice how your feelings change from the beginning to the end of the passage.

INTERPRET

Pause at line 213. List three adjectives that you would use to describe the actions of Obeah and Duberry. Explain why you listed, or did not list, *intelligent* as one of your adjectives.

_____

_____

_____

_____

_____

INFER

How have the narrator's experiences with dogs changed his perspective on them (lines 228–232)? What does the narrator believe he can learn from dogs?

_____

_____

_____

_____

_____

In Trouble

SKILLS FOCUS

Literary Skills
Analyze setting.

"Follow the Setting" Chart   Many stories have more than one setting. You have to follow the story wherever it takes you. Remember that when the story takes you to different settings, the whole mood of the story can change. In this selection, Gary Paulsen takes you to four different settings, ranging from steel-breaking cold parts of Alaska to a toasty-warm cabin.

Use this chart to follow the setting. The first column is filled in for you. Fill in the rest of the chart, and you'll have a path to the story's settings.

Where the story events occur	When the story occurs	Setting words from the story	Mood the setting creates
a river in Alaska	probably winter	"whirlpool had frozen into a cone," "water roaring through at the bottom"	beautiful, but scary
the kennel area			
a "trapping" run			
Paulsen's cabin			

Skills Review

In Trouble

VOCABULARY AND COMPREHENSION

A. Sound-Alikes and Look-Alikes   Fill in the blanks with the correct words from the Word Bank. Then, circle the two word pairs that are **homophones,** words that are spelled differently but sound the same. Then, underline the words that are **homographs,** words that are spelled the same but that have different meanings.

Word Bank

steeped

alleviate

contention

exaltation

chagrin

In my class, there was a lot of (1) _____ about whether country or rock music is best. To (2) _____ the tension that had built up, we decided to go to an outdoor concert featuring both types of bands. When we got there, the weather was perfect, and the night was (3) _____ with music as we settled on the grass to listen. When the country band played its latest hit, the crowd was filled with wild joy and (4) _____. The same thing happened when the rock group played. Both bands had a lot of class. To our (5) _____, we realized that the only thing that matters is music, not what type it is.

B. Reading Comprehension   Answer each question below.

1. How does Columbia show a sense of humor? _____

_____

2. What causes the narrator to stop trapping animals? _____

_____

3. How is the narrator injured? _____

_____

4. How is the narrator rescued after he gets hurt? _____

_____

SKILLS FOCUS

Vocabulary Skills
Understand homophones and homographs.

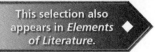

This selection also appears in *Elements of Literature.* ◆

There Will Come Soft Rains

by Ray Bradbury

LITERARY FOCUS: SETTING AS CHARACTER

Usually **setting** is in the background of a story, while characters—people and animals—take care of the action. But what if the setting demands a bigger role? Or even a starring part? In some stories the setting moves out of the background and becomes a character. For example, in a story about a woman lost in the desert, the main **conflict** could be between the person and the setting. The desert may seem to act against the woman like a character—by pounding her with hot sun, threatening her with rattlesnakes, and hiding water from her.

Read on to find out where and when "There Will Come Soft Rains" is set. It's a setting you probably won't forget soon.

READING SKILLS: TEXT STRUCTURES (CHRONOLOGY)

Most stories are told in **chronological order**—the events are presented in the order in which they occur. In other words, you learn what happens first, then you learn what happens next, and so on.

In "There Will Come Soft Rains," the story that follows, the events are told in chronological order. In fact, we learn what happens from one hour to the next.

SKILLS FOCUS

Literary Skills
Understand the role of setting.

Reading Skills
Understand chronological order.

Vocabulary Skills
Use context clues.

VOCABULARY DEVELOPMENT

PREVIEW SELECTION VOCABULARY

Become familiar with these words before you read "There Will Come Soft Rains."

paranoia (par′ə·noi′ə) *n.:* mental disorder that causes people to feel unreasonable distrust and suspicion.

The house was so concerned with self-protection that it almost seemed to suffer from paranoia.

cavorting (kə·vôrt′iŋ) *v.* used as *adj.:* leaping about; frolicking.

Images of panthers could be seen cavorting on the walls of the nursery.

tremulous (trem′yo͞o·ləs) *adj.:* trembling.

The tremulous branches swayed in the night breezes.

oblivious (ə·bliv′ē·əs) *adj.:* unaware.

The mechanical house was oblivious of events in the world outside.

sublime (sə·blīm′) *adj.:* majestic; grand.

The sublime poetry was recited until the very end.

CLARIFYING WORD MEANINGS: WORDS IN CONTEXT

Context refers to the sentence or paragraph in which a word appears. Context clues can help you figure out a word's meaning. There are different kinds of **context clues,** including definitions, restatements, examples, and contrasts. Here are some examples:

DEFINITION: Something that is **automatic** *works by itself.*

RESTATEMENT: His reflexes were **automatic.** *He didn't think before acting.*

EXAMPLE: **Automatic** machines have changed the way we live. *Think, for example, of the impact that furnaces, heart-lung machines, and even answering machines have had on our lives.*

CONTRAST: *Unlike regular vacuum cleaners,* **automatic** vacuum cleaners do not need to be pushed or pulled.

When you come across unfamiliar words in "There Will Come Soft Rains," look for context clues to help you figure out what those words mean.

There Will Come Soft Rains

Ray Bradbury

Tom Leonard.

INFER

Pause at line 6. Why do you think the house is empty?

_____

_____

_____

_____

IDENTIFY

Circle the details in lines 1–16 that identify the **setting**—the time and place of the story.

7:00 In the living room the voice-clock sang, *Ticktock, seven o'clock, time to get up, time to get up, seven o'clock!* as if it were afraid that nobody would. The morning house lay empty. The clock ticked on, repeating and repeating its sounds into the emptiness. *Seven-nine, breakfast time, seven-nine!*

In the kitchen the breakfast stove gave a hissing sigh and ejected from its warm interior eight pieces of perfectly browned toast, eight eggs sunny side up, sixteen slices of

10 bacon, and two coffees.

"Today is August 4, 2026," said a second voice from the kitchen ceiling, "in the city of Allendale, California." It repeated the date three times for memory's sake. "Today is Mr. Featherstone's birthday. Today is the anniversary of Tilita's marriage. Insurance is payable, as are the water, gas, and light bills."

Somewhere in the walls, relays clicked, memory tapes glided under electric eyes.

8:01 *Eight-one, tick-tock, eight-one o'clock, off to school,*
20 *off to work, run, run, eight-one!* But no doors slammed, no carpets took the soft tread of rubber heels. It was raining outside. The weather box on the front door sang quietly: "Rain, rain, go away; rubbers, raincoats for today . . ." And the rain tapped on the empty house, echoing.

Outside, the garage chimed and lifted its door to reveal the waiting car. After a long wait the door swung down again.

At eight-thirty the eggs were shriveled and the toast was like stone. An aluminum wedge scraped them into the sink, where hot water whirled them down a metal throat
30 which digested and flushed them away to the distant sea. The dirty dishes were dropped into a hot washer and emerged twinkling dry.

Nine-fifteen, sang the clock, *time to clean.*

Out of warrens[1] in the wall, tiny robot mice darted. The rooms were acrawl with the small cleaning animals, all rubber and metal. They thudded against chairs, whirling their moustached runners, kneading the rug nap, sucking gently at hidden dust. Then, like mysterious invaders, they popped into their burrows. Their pink electric eyes faded.
40 The house was clean.

10:00 *Ten o'clock.* The sun came out from behind the rain. The house stood alone in a city of rubble

---

1. **warrens** *n.:* small, crowded spaces. The little holes in the ground in which rabbits live are called warrens.

INFER

What happens—or doesn't happen—between 8:01 A.M. and 9:15 A.M. that suggests that all is not well with the humans who own this house (lines 19–32)?

INFER

Underline the details in lines 41–45 that tell you how this house is different from the other houses in the neighborhood. What seems to have happened to the city?

Write a number, from 1 to 5, over the details describing each of the five silhouettes on the wall of the house. What has caused the five silhouettes to be "burned on wood" (lines 46–60)?

_____

_____

_____

_____

_____

Personification is a figure of speech in which an object or animal is spoken of as if it has human qualities. Circle the words and phrases in lines 63–71 that portray the house's human qualities.

paranoia (par'ə·noi'ə) *n.:* mental disorder that causes people to feel unreasonable distrust and suspicion.

Who are the gods who have gone away (lines 73–75)?

_____

_____

_____

_____

and ashes. This was the one house left standing. At night the ruined city gave off a radioactive glow which could be seen for miles.

Ten-fifteen. The garden sprinklers whirled up in golden founts, filling the soft morning air with scatterings of brightness. The water pelted windowpanes, running down the charred west side where the house had been burned
50 evenly free of its white paint. The entire west face of the house was black, save for five places. Here the silhouette in paint of a man mowing a lawn. Here, as in a photograph, a woman bent to pick flowers. Still farther over, their images burned on wood in one titanic instant, a small boy, hands flung into the air; higher up, the image of a thrown ball, and opposite him a girl, hands raised to catch a ball which never came down.

The five spots of paint—the man, the woman, the children, the ball—remained. The rest was a thin charcoaled
60 layer.

The gentle sprinkler rain filled the garden with falling light.

Until this day, how well the house had kept its peace. How carefully it had inquired, "Who goes there? What's the password?" and, getting no answer from lonely foxes and whining cats, it had shut up its windows and drawn shades in an old-maidenly preoccupation with self-protection which bordered on a mechanical **paranoia.**

It quivered at each sound, the house did. If a sparrow
70 brushed a window, the shade snapped up. The bird, startled, flew off! No, not even a bird must touch the house!

The house was an altar with ten thousand attendants, big, small, servicing, attending, in choirs. But the gods had gone away, and the ritual of the religion continued senselessly, uselessly.

12:00 *Twelve noon.*

A dog whined, shivering, on the front porch.

The front door recognized the dog voice and opened. The dog, once huge and fleshy, but now gone to bone and
80   covered with sores, moved in and through the house, tracking mud. Behind it whirred angry mice, angry at having to pick up mud, angry at inconvenience.

For not a leaf fragment blew under the door but what the wall panels flipped open and the copper scrap rats flashed swiftly out. The offending dust, hair, or paper, seized in miniature steel jaws, was raced back to the burrows. There, down tubes which fed into the cellar, it was dropped into the sighing vent of an incinerator which sat like evil Baal[2] in a dark corner.

90   The dog ran upstairs, hysterically yelping to each door, at last realizing, as the house realized, that only silence was here.

It sniffed the air and scratched the kitchen door. Behind the door, the stove was making pancakes which filled the house with a rich baked odor and the scent of maple syrup.

The dog frothed at the mouth, lying at the door, sniffing, its eyes turned to fire. It ran wildly in circles, biting at its tail, spun in a frenzy, and died. It lay in the parlor for an hour.

100   **2:00** *Two o'clock,* sang a voice.

Delicately sensing decay at last, the regiments of mice hummed out as softly as blown gray leaves in an electrical wind.

Two-fifteen.

The dog was gone.

In the cellar, the incinerator glowed suddenly and a whirl of sparks leaped up the chimney.

---

2. **Baal** (bāʹəl): in the Bible, the god of Canaan, whom the Israelites came to regard as a false god.

Re-read lines 77–99. This section is filled with **images,** details that appeal to your senses. Circle three images that appeal to three different senses.

PREDICT

Pause at line 107. Will the house continue to go on doing its work forever? Tell what you think might happen next.

IDENTIFY

The children's nursery is vividly described. Underline the details in lines 118–132 that bring that **setting** to life.

VOCABULARY

cavorting (kə·vôrt′iŋ) v. used as *adj.:* leaping about; frolicking.

INFER

Flip back through the story, noting the times of day that are called out. Why does Bradbury include the exact times of specific events? How does knowing the exact time increase the **suspense**?

_____

_____

_____

_____

_____

_____

_____

_____

_____

_____

_____

_____

_____

Two thirty-five.

110　Bridge tables sprouted from patio walls. Playing cards fluttered onto pads in a shower of pips.[3] Martinis manifested on an oaken bench with egg-salad sandwiches. Music played.

But the tables were silent and the cards untouched.

At four o'clock the tables folded like great butterflies back through the paneled walls.

Four-thirty.

The nursery walls glowed.

Animals took shape: yellow giraffes, blue lions, pink antelopes, lilac panthers **cavorting** in crystal substance. The

120　walls were glass. They looked out upon color and fantasy. Hidden films clocked through well-oiled sprockets,[4] and the walls lived. The nursery floor was woven to resemble a crisp cereal[5] meadow. Over this ran aluminum roaches and iron crickets, and in the hot, still air butterflies of delicate red tissue wavered among the sharp aromas of animal spoors![6] There was the sound like a great matted yellow hive of bees within a dark bellows, the lazy bumble of a purring lion. And there was the patter of okapi[7] feet and the murmur of a fresh jungle rain, like other hoofs, falling upon the summer-

130　starched grass. Now the walls dissolved into distances of parched weed, mile on mile, and warm endless sky. The animals drew away into thorn brakes[8] and water holes.

It was the children's hour.

 Five o'clock. The bath filled with clear hot water.

---

3. **pips** *n.:* figures on cards.
4. **sprockets** *n.:* wheels with points designed to fit into the holes along the edges of a filmstrip.
5. **cereal** *n.* used as *adj.:* of grasses that produce grain.
6. **spoors** *n.:* animal tracks or droppings.
7. **okapi** (ō·kä′pē) *n.:* African animal related to the giraffe but with a much shorter neck.
8. **thorn brakes:** clumps of thorns; thickets.

Six, seven, eight o'clock. The dinner dishes manipulated like magic tricks, and in the study a *click.* In the metal stand opposite the hearth where a fire now blazed up warmly, a cigar popped out, half an inch of soft gray ash on it, smoking, waiting.

140 *Nine o'clock.* The beds warmed their hidden circuits, for nights were cool here.

Nine-five. A voice spoke from the study ceiling:

"Mrs. McClellan, which poem would you like this evening?"

The house was silent.

The voice said at last, "Since you express no preference, I shall select a poem at random." Quiet music rose to back the voice. "Sara Teasdale. As I recall, your favorite. . . .

> *There will come soft rains and the smell of the ground,*
> 150 *And swallows circling with their shimmering sound;*
>
> *And frogs in the pools singing at night,*
> *And wild plum trees in **tremulous** white;*
>
> *Robins will wear their feathery fire,*
> *Whistling their whims on a low fence-wire;*
>
> *And not one will know of the war, not one*
> *Will care at last when it is done.*
>
> *Not one would mind, neither bird nor tree,*
> *If mankind perished utterly;*
>
> *And Spring herself, when she woke at dawn*
> 160 *Would scarcely know that we were gone."*

RETELL

Retell in two or three sentences what is happening in the poem (lines 149–160).

_____
_____
_____
_____
_____
_____
_____
_____

COMPARE & CONTRAST

How is nature in the poem like nature in this story?

_____
_____
_____
_____
_____
_____
_____
_____
_____

VOCABULARY

tremulous (trem′yoo·ləs) *adj.:* trembling. *Tremulous* also means "fearful" or "timid."

PREDICT

Pause at line 165, and tell how you think the house might "die."

_____

_____

_____

_____

_____

_____

_____

_____

INTERPRET

A **conflict** has arisen in the story. On one side of the conflict is the house and all the scientific progress and advanced machinery it stands for. Whom or what is the house battling?

_____

_____

_____

_____

_____

_____

_____

_____

The fire burned on the stone hearth, and the cigar fell away into a mound of quiet ash on its tray. The empty chairs faced each other between the silent walls, and the music played.

10:00 At ten o'clock the house began to die.

The wind blew. A falling tree bough crashed through the kitchen window. Cleaning solvent,[9] bottled, shattered over the stove. The room was ablaze in an instant!

"Fire!" screamed a voice. The house lights flashed,

170 water pumps shot water from the ceilings. But the solvent spread on the linoleum, licking, eating, under the kitchen door, while the voices took it up in chorus: "Fire, fire, fire!"

The house tried to save itself. Doors sprang tightly shut, but the windows were broken by the heat and the wind blew and sucked upon the fire.

The house gave ground as the fire in ten billion angry sparks moved with flaming ease from room to room and then up the stairs. While scurrying water rats squeaked

---

9. solvent _n.:_ something that can dissolve something else (here, something that dissolves dirt). _Solvent, dissolve,_ and _solution_ have the same Latin root, _solvere,_ which means "to loosen."

from the walls, pistoled their water, and ran for more. And
180   the wall sprays let down showers of mechanical rain.

But too late. Somewhere, sighing, a pump shrugged to
a stop. The quenching rain ceased. The reserve water supply
which had filled baths and washed dishes for many quiet
days was gone.

The fire crackled up the stairs. It fed upon Picassos and
Matisses[10] in the upper halls, like delicacies, baking off the
oily flesh, tenderly crisping the canvases into black shavings.

Now the fire lay in beds, stood in windows, changed
the colors of drapes!

190   And then, reinforcements.

From attic trapdoors, blind robot faces peered down
with faucet mouths gushing green chemical.

The fire backed off, as even an elephant must at the
sight of a dead snake. Now there were twenty snakes whip-
ping over the floor, killing the fire with a clear cold venom
of green froth.

But the fire was clever. It had sent flame outside the
house, up through the attic to the pumps there. An explo-
sion! The attic brain which directed the pumps was shattered
200   into bronze shrapnel on the beams.

The fire rushed back into every closet and felt of the
clothes hung there.

The house shuddered, oak bone on bone, its bared
skeleton cringing from the heat, its wire, its nerves revealed
as if a surgeon had torn the skin off to let the red veins and
capillaries quiver in the scalded air. Help, help! Fire! Run,
run! Heat snapped mirrors like the first brittle winter ice.
And the voices wailed, Fire, fire, run, run, like a tragic nursery rhyme, a dozen voices, high, low, like children dying in

---

10. **Picassos and Matisses:** paintings by Pablo Picasso (1881–1973), a
famous Spanish painter and sculptor who worked in France, and by
Henri Matisse (än·rē′ má·tēs′) (1869–1954), a famous French painter.

IDENTIFY

Underline at least three
details in lines 185–202 that
personify the fire—that
make the fire seem human.

FLUENCY

Read the boxed passage
aloud at least twice. Read for
basic meaning the first time
you read. Before you read the
passage aloud a second time,
mark the lines to show which
ones you will read loudly,
softly, quickly, or slowly.

210 a forest, alone, alone. And the voices fading as the wires popped their sheathings[11] like hot chestnuts. One, two, three, four, five voices died.

In the nursery the jungle burned. Blue lions roared, purple giraffes bounded off. The panthers ran in circles, changing color, and ten million animals, running before the fire, vanished off toward a distant steaming river. . . .

Ten more voices died. In the last instant under the fire avalanche, other choruses, **oblivious,** could be heard announcing the time, playing music, cutting the lawn by 220 remote-control mower, or setting an umbrella frantically out and in, the slamming and opening front door, a thousand things happening, like a clock shop when each clock strikes the hour insanely before or after the other, a scene of maniac confusion, yet unity; singing, screaming, a few last cleaning mice darting bravely out to carry the horrid ashes away! And one voice, with **sublime** disregard for the situation, read poetry aloud in the fiery study, until all the film spools burned, until all the wires withered and the circuits cracked.

The fire burst the house and let it slam flat down, puff-230 ing out skirts of spark and smoke.

In the kitchen, an instant before the rain of fire and timber, the stove could be seen making breakfasts at a psychopathic[12] rate, ten dozen eggs, six loaves of toast, twenty dozen bacon strips, which, eaten by fire, started the stove working again, hysterically hissing!

The crash. The attic smashing into kitchen and parlor. The parlor into cellar, cellar into subcellar. Deep freeze, armchair, film tapes, circuits, beds, and all like skeletons thrown in a cluttered mound deep under.

240 Smoke and silence. A great quantity of smoke.

---

11. **sheathings** *n.:* protective coverings.
12. **psychopathic** (sī′kō·path′ik) *adj.:* insane.

Dawn showed faintly in the east. Among the ruins, one wall stood alone. Within the wall, a last voice said, over and over again and again, even as the sun rose to shine upon the heaped rubble and steam:

"Today is August 5, 2026, today is August 5, 2026, today is . . ."

Tom Leonard.

EVALUATE

What idea about scientific advances is Bradbury warning us about? Tell whether or not you agree with his message. Give reasons for your opinion.

There Will Come Soft Rains

SKILLS FOCUS

Reading Skills
Analyze chronological order.

"What's *Really* Going On?" Chart   In this story, Ray Bradbury describes some hideous events. But as the reader, you have to keep asking yourself the question "What's *really* going on here?" It is not always clear what is actually happening. For help following the story, use this time chart. Each tinted row contains a time and a main story event that the writer tells us happened at that time. Fill in each untinted box with what you think is *really* happening at that time. The first one is done for you.

Summary of Main Events   **What's *Really* Going On?**

7:00 A clock announces the time. A stove fixes breakfast automatically.	
It seems as if the house has been abandoned by people, but it's still operating as if it's alive.	
8:01 Garage door opens, but no one comes out. House is cleaned by robot mice.	
10:00 House is the only one in the city. Rest of city is in ashes and glows as if from radiation. Images of people are on the wall of the house.	
12:00 A starving dog walks into the house and searches for people. Dog dies in house.	
2:00 Bridge tables pop out from the walls. Nursery walls seem to come alive.	
5:00 Bath fills with water, and dinner dishes are washed. The house prepares for bedtime.	
10:00 House catches fire. Robots try to put out fire. The house burns down.	

Skills Review

There Will Come Soft Rains

VOCABULARY AND COMPREHENSION

A. Clarifying Meanings: Words in Context   Fill in the blanks with the correct Word Bank words. Then, underline the context clues.

1. The _____ music filled our hearts with its greatness.

2. People suffering from _____ tend to look at people

   with suspicion and distrust.

3. We could see the children jumping around the playground,

   _____ with their friends.

4. _____, the scared little dog hid behind a chair.

5. The smiling, calm mother seemed _____ to the

   chaos around her.

B. Reading Comprehension   Answer each question below.

1. When and where does this story take place? _____

   _____

2. What details tell you the city has been destroyed? _____

   _____

3. What happens to the dog? _____

   _____

4. At the end of the story, what happens to the house? _____

   _____

SKILLS FOCUS

Vocabulary Skills
Use context clues.

The Secret by Arthur C. Clarke

LITERARY FOCUS: SETTING AND PLOT

Setting, the time and place of a story, is an important part of many stories. A story's setting may even affect **plot** events. Think, for example, about a struggle between two friends that takes place in 2005 on a California beach in the height of summer. Then, imagine that struggle taking place two hundred years ago on a farm in New England in December. The actions, speech, and clothing of the people in the struggle would be very different, wouldn't they?

Setting is key in the story that follows. As you read, put yourself in the world of the characters—on a colony on the moon!

READING SKILLS: RE-READING TO CLARIFY

Successful readers often re-read difficult text in order to understand it better. When you encounter a story passage that you find hard, try the following tips:

- Re-read a sentence or passage whose meaning escapes you. To re-read, go back over the text slowly and carefully, paying close attention to details.
- Re-read a sentence or passage aloud to help you clarify its meaning.
- Re-read and reword the passage in simpler language, breaking it up into shorter units.

SKILLS FOCUS

Literary Skills
Understand setting.

Reading Skills
Re-read to clarify text.

Vocabulary Skills
Use context clues.

VOCABULARY DEVELOPMENT

PREVIEW SELECTION VOCABULARY

Before you read "The Secret," get to know these words from the story.

lunar (lōō′nər) *adj.:* of or on the moon.

Astronauts used a lunar rover to explore the moon's surface.

novelty (näv′əl·tē) *n.:* newness; freshness.

For many scientists at the spaceport, the novelty of space travel was gone.

receding (ri·sēd′iŋ) *v.:* moving back.

The achievements of early space explorers were receding in importance, becoming more and more distant events.

infernal (in·fur′nəl) *adj.:* inhuman; hellish.

The ash and pumice of the moon's surface created an infernal landscape.

hull (hul) *n.:* the frame of a vehicle.

An air-lock device was clamped against the outer hull of the tractor.

radial (rā′dē·əl) *adj.:* branching out from a center, like rays.

Radial corridors, like the spokes of a wheel, led toward the center of the dome.

trifling (trī′fliŋ) *adj.:* of little importance.

That hamsters normally have a short life span was a commonly known and trifling fact.

implications (im′pli·kā′shənz) *n.:* something implied or suggested; possible effects.

The scientist was more interested in his discovery than in the implications it would have for the people on Earth.

CLARIFYING WORD MEANINGS: RESTATEMENT

If a word is unfamiliar, **context clues** can sometimes help you figure out its meaning. You'll often find context clues among the words and phrases that surround the word you want to define. One type of context clue is **restatement.** This type of clue provides you with a paraphrase of what was previously said. In the sentence below, the italicized word provides a clue to the meaning of *novelty.*

Playing the video game was once a **novelty,** but now that the *newness* had worn off, she found the game boring.

As you read "The Secret," be on the lookout for context clues.

THE SECRET

Arthur C. Clarke

The moon.

IDENTIFY

Pause at line 10. Circle the name of the character introduced in this paragraph. Where does he work? What is his job?

_____

_____

_____

_____

_____

_____

VOCABULARY

lunar (lo͞o′nər) *adj.:* of or on the moon.

novelty (näv′əl·tē) *n.:* newness; freshness.

Henry Cooper had been on the moon for almost two weeks before he discovered that something was wrong. At first it was only an ill-defined suspicion, the sort of hunch that a hardheaded science reporter would not take too seriously. He had come here, after all, at the United Nations Space Administration's own request. UNSA had always been hot on public relations—especially just before budget time, when an overcrowded world was screaming for more roads and schools and sea farms, and complaining about the bil-

10 lions being poured into space.

So here he was, doing the **lunar** circuit for the second time, and beaming back two thousand words of copy a day. Although the **novelty** had worn off, there still remained the wonder and mystery of a world as big as Africa, thoroughly mapped, yet almost completely unexplored. A stone's throw away from the pressure domes, the labs, the spaceports, was a yawning emptiness that would challenge men for centuries to come.

Some parts of the moon were almost too familiar, of course. Who had not seen that dusty scar in the Mare Imbrium,[1] with its gleaming metal pylon and the plaque that announced in the three official languages of Earth:

ON THIS SPOT

AT 2001 UT

13 SEPTEMBER 1959

THE FIRST MAN-MADE OBJECT

REACHED ANOTHER WORLD

Cooper had visited the grave of Lunik II—and the more famous tomb of the men who had come after it. But these things belonged to the past; already, like Columbus and the Wright brothers, they were **receding** into history. What concerned him now was the future.

When he had landed at Archimedes[2] Spaceport, the Chief Administrator had been obviously glad to see him, and had shown a personal interest in his tour. Transportation, accommodation, and official guide were all arranged. He could go anywhere he liked, ask any questions he pleased. UNSA trusted him, for his stories had always been accurate, his attitude friendly. Yet the tour had gone sour; he did not know why, but he was going to find out.

He reached for the phone and said: "Operator? Please get me the Police Department. I want to speak to the Inspector General."

---

1. **Mare Imbrium** (mä′rā′ im′brē·əm): Latin for "Sea of Showers." The Mare Imbrium is a "sea"—a huge dark, flat area—on the moon.
2. **Archimedes** (är′kə·mē′dēz): Greek mathematician and inventor (287?–212 B.C.).

INFER

Pause at line 49. Who is
Chandra Coomaraswamy?

_____

_____

_____

_____

_____

_____

_____

_____

INFER

Re-read lines 50–70. How
would you describe Cooper's
friend Chandra?

_____

_____

_____

_____

_____

_____

_____

_____

_____

Presumably Chandra Coomaraswamy possessed a uniform, but Cooper had never seen him wearing it. They met, as arranged, at the entrance to the little park that was Plato City's chief pride and joy. At this time in the morning of the artificial twenty-four-hour "day" it was almost deserted, and they could talk without interruption.

50   As they walked along the narrow gravel paths, they chatted about old times, the friends they had known at college together, the latest developments in interplanetary politics. They had reached the middle of the park, under the exact center of the great blue-painted dome, when Cooper came to the point.

"You know everything that's happening on the moon, Chandra," he said. "And you know that I'm here to do a series for UNSA—hope to make a book out of it when I get back to Earth. So why should people be trying to hide

60   things from me?"

It was impossible to hurry Chandra. He always took his time to answer questions, and his few words escaped with difficulty around the stem of his hand-carved Bavarian pipe.

"What people?" he asked at length.

"You've really no idea?"

The Inspector General shook his head.

"Not the faintest," he answered; and Cooper knew that he was telling the truth. Chandra might be silent, but he

70   would not lie.

"I was afraid you'd say that. Well, if you don't know any more than I do, here's the only clue I have—and it frightens me. Medical research is trying to keep me at arm's length."

"Hmm," replied Chandra, taking his pipe from his mouth and looking at it thoughtfully.

"Is that all you have to say?"

"You haven't given me much to work on. Remember, I'm only a cop: I lack your vivid journalistic imagination."

"All I can tell you is that the higher I get in Medical Research, the colder the atmosphere becomes. Last time I was here, everyone was very friendly, and gave me some fine stories. But now, I can't even meet the Director. He's always too busy, or on the other side of the moon. Anyway, what sort of man is he?"

"Dr. Hastings? Prickly little character. Very competent, but not easy to work with."

"What could he be trying to hide?"

"Knowing you, I'm sure you have some interesting theories."

"Oh, I thought of narcotics, and fraud, and political conspiracies—but they don't make sense, in these days. So what's left scares the heck out of me."

Chandra's eyebrows signaled a silent question mark.

"Interplanetary plague," said Cooper bluntly.

"I thought that was impossible."

"Yes—I've written articles myself proving that the life forms on other planets have such alien chemistries that they can't react with us, and that all our microbes and bugs took millions of years to adapt to our bodies. But I've always wondered if it was true. Suppose a ship has come back from Mars, say, with something *really* vicious—and the doctors can't cope with it?"

There was a long silence. Then Chandra said: "I'll start investigating. I don't like it either, for here's an item you probably don't know. There were three nervous breakdowns in the Medical Division last month—and that's very, very unusual."

PREDICT

Pause at line 78. Do you think Chandra will help Cooper? Explain.

_____

_____

_____

_____

_____

_____

IDENTIFY

Re-read lines 94–102. Underline the things Cooper is afraid might be happening. If this story were taking place on Earth, would Cooper's worries be the same? Explain.

_____

_____

_____

_____

_____

IDENTIFY

Re-read lines 103–107. Circle the interesting but frightening fact that Chandra tells Cooper about.

He glanced at his watch, then at the false sky, which seemed so distant, yet which was only two hundred feet
110 above their heads.

"We'd better get moving," he said. "The morning shower's due in five minutes."

The call came two weeks later, in the middle of the night— the real lunar night. By Plato City time, it was Sunday morning.

"Henry? Chandra here. Can you meet me in half an hour at air lock five? Good—I'll see you."

This was it, Cooper knew. Air lock at five meant they were going outside the dome. Chandra had found something.

120 The presence of the police driver restricted conversa- tion as the tractor moved away from the city along the road

---

INFER

Pause at line 119. Why might Chandra want to meet with Cooper outside the air lock?

roughly bulldozed across the ash and pumice. Low in the south, Earth was almost full, casting a brilliant blue-green light over the **infernal** landscape. However hard one tried, Cooper told himself, it was difficult to make the moon appear glamorous. But nature guards her greatest secrets well; to such places men must come to find them.

The multiple domes of the city dropped below the sharply curved horizon. Presently, the tractor turned aside
130 from the main road to follow a scarcely visible trail. Ten minutes later, Cooper saw a single glittering hemisphere ahead of them, standing on an isolated ridge of rock. Another vehicle, bearing a red cross, was parked beside the entrance. It seemed that they were not the only visitors.

Nor were they unexpected. As they drew up to the dome, the flexible tube of the air-lock coupling[3] groped out toward them and snapped into place against their tractor's outer **hull**. There was a brief hissing as pressure equalized. Then Cooper followed Chandra into the building.

140 The air-lock operator led them along curving corridors and **radial** passageways toward the center of the dome. Sometimes they caught glimpses of laboratories, scientific instruments, computers—all perfectly ordinary, and all deserted on this Sunday morning. They must have reached the heart of the building, Cooper told himself when their guide ushered them into a large circular chamber and shut the door softly behind them.

It was a small zoo. All around them were cages, tanks, jars containing a wide selection of the fauna and flora[4] of
150 Earth. Waiting at its center was a short, grey-haired man, looking very worried, and very unhappy.

<mark>VISUALIZE</mark>

Re-read lines 120–134. Underline the details that help you picture the lunar **setting**.

<mark>VOCABULARY</mark>

infernal (in·fur′nəl) *adj.:* inhuman; hellish.

hull (hul) *n.:* the frame of a vehicle.

radial (rā′dē·əl) *adj.:* branching out from a center, like rays.

<mark>PREDICT</mark>

Pause at line 151. Why do you think Chandra has led Cooper to a zoo?

_____
_____
_____
_____
_____
_____
_____
_____
_____
_____
_____
_____

---

3. **coupling** (kup′lin) *n.:* mechanical device for joining together two parts or pieces of something.
4. **fauna and flora** (fô′nə *and* flôr′ə): Latin for "animals and plants."

IDENTIFY

Re-read lines 172–178. What is the secret?

_____

_____

_____

_____

_____

_____

_____

_____

_____

_____

VOCABULARY

trifling (trī′fliŋ) *adj.:* of little importance.

implications (im·pli·kā′shənz) *n.:* something implied or suggested; possible effects.

FLUENCY

Read aloud the boxed passage containing dialogue between Hastings and Cooper several times. Each time you read, work at making your voice sound natural and distinct when you read each character's lines.

"Dr. Hastings," said Coomaraswamy, "meet Mr. Cooper." The Inspector General turned to his companion and added, "I've convinced the Doctor that there's only one way to keep you quiet—and that's to tell you everything."

"Frankly," said Hastings, "I'm not sure if I care at all any more." His voice was unsteady, barely under control, and Cooper thought, Hello! There's another breakdown on the way.

160 The scientist wasted no time on such formalities as shaking hands. He walked to one of the cages, took out a small bundle of fur, and held it toward Cooper.

"Do you know what this is?" he asked abruptly.

"Of course. A hamster—the commonest lab animal."

"Yes," said Hastings. "A perfectly ordinary golden hamster. Except that this one is five years old—like all the others in this cage."

"Well? What's odd about that?"

"Oh, nothing, nothing at all . . . except for the **trifling**
170 fact that hamsters live for only two years. And we have some here that are getting on for ten."

For a moment no one spoke; but the room was not silent. It was full of rustlings and slitherings and scratchings, of faint whimpers and tiny animal cries. Then Cooper whispered: "My God—you've found a way of prolonging life!"

"No," retorted Hastings. "We've not found it. The moon has given it to us . . . as we might have expected, if we'd looked in front of our noses."

He seemed to have gained control over his emotions—
180 as if he was once more the pure scientist, fascinated by a discovery for its own sake and heedless of its **implications.**

"On Earth," he said, "we spend our whole lives fighting gravity. It wears down our muscles, pulls our stomachs out of shape. In seventy years, how many tons of blood does the heart lift through how many miles? And all that work, all that strain is reduced to a sixth here on the moon, where a one-hundred-and-eighty-pound human weighs only thirty pounds."

"I see," said Cooper slowly. "Ten years for a hamster—and how long for a man?"

"It's not a simple law," answered Hastings. "It varies with the size and the species. Even a month ago, we weren't certain. But now we're quite sure of this: on the moon, the span of human life will be at least two hundred years."

"And you've been trying to keep it secret!"

"You fool! Don't you understand?"

"Take it easy, Doctor—take it easy," said Chandra softly.

With an obvious effort of will, Hastings got control of himself again. He began to speak with such icy calm that his words sank like freezing raindrops into Cooper's mind.

"Think of them up there," he said, pointing to the roof, to the invisible Earth whose looming presence no one on the moon could ever forget. "Six billion of them, packing all the continents to the edges—and now crowding over into the sea beds. And here—" he pointed to the ground—"only a hundred thousand of *us,* on an almost empty world. But a world where we need miracles of technology and engineering merely to exist, where a man with an IQ of only a hundred and fifty can't even get a job.

"And now we find that we can live for two hundred years. Imagine how they're going to react to *that* news! This is your problem now, Mister Journalist; you've asked for it, and you've got it. Tell me this please—I'd really be interested to know—*just how are you going to break it to them?*"

He waited, and waited. Cooper opened his mouth, then closed it again, unable to think of anything to say.

In the far corner of the room, a baby monkey started to cry.

PREDICT

Pause at line 214. What might the people on Earth do if they learn the secret?

_____
_____
_____
_____
_____
_____
_____
_____
_____

EXTEND

Pause at line 218. From what you've learned about Henry Cooper, do you think he will reveal the secret? Explain.

_____
_____
_____
_____
_____
_____
_____
_____
_____

The Secret

Setting Chart   Fill in the following chart with details from the story that help create its **setting.** Remember, even details about people's jobs and the weather may help to develop a story's setting.

Literary Skills
Analyze setting.

Setting	
Details Revealing Time	**Details Revealing Place**

Skills Review

The Secret

VOCABULARY AND COMPREHENSION

A. Clarifying Word Meanings: Context Clues Match the Word Bank words to each restatement clue, given at right.

_____ **1.** lunar   **a.** branching out

_____ **2.** novelty   **b.** hellish

_____ **3.** receding   **c.** new thing; fad

_____ **4.** infernal   **d.** of the moon

_____ **5.** hull   **e.** ebbing; moving back

_____ **6.** radial   **f.** unimportant

_____ **7.** trifling   **g.** possible effects

_____ **8.** implications   **h.** framework

> **Word Bank**
>
> lunar
> novelty
> receding
> infernal
> hull
> radial
> trifling
> implications

B. Reading Comprehension Answer each question below.

1. Why does Henry Cooper become suspicious when he's visiting the moon? _____

_____

_____

2. What has Dr. Hastings's research revealed? _____

_____

_____

3. Why has Dr. Hastings been unwilling to make his discovery known?

_____

_____

_____

SKILLS FOCUS

Vocabulary Skill
Use context clues.

Collection

4

The Human Spirit

Academic Vocabulary for Collection 4

These are the terms you should know
as you read and analyze the selections in this collection.

———

Subject The topic of a work of literature. The subject is not the
same as the theme. The subject can generally be stated in a
single word or phrase, such as *loyalty, good losers, memories,
nature,* and so on.

Theme An idea or a truth about life that a work of literature reveals.
A theme can be expressed in one or more sentences. A theme
on the subject of loyalty might be "True friends don't desert
each other."

Universal Themes Themes that can be found in literature from different times, places, and cultures. For example, a love story written
in ancient Persia may explore the same theme as a poem written
in seventeenth-century England.

Recurring Themes Themes that reappear with great frequency in
literature. One such theme is "Love heals all wounds."

Before You Read

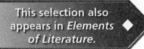This selection also appears in *Elements of Literature*. ◆

The Diary of Anne Frank, Act One, Scenes 1 and 2

by Frances Goodrich and Albert Hackett

LITERARY FOCUS: THEME

Stories, poems, and plays all explore a **theme**—an idea or a truth about human life or human behavior. It's what the writer is saying about life. Sometimes a theme is powerful enough to make us look at the world in a new way or to understand something we never understood before.

The Diary of Anne Frank is a complex work that explores more than one theme. As you read the following excerpt from that play, look for ideas about life that are expressed by the characters and their actions.

READING SKILLS: MAKING GENERALIZATIONS

A **generalization** is a broad statement that can be applied to many individuals, experiences, and situations. It is a type of conclusion you draw after considering as many facts as possible. A **valid** generalization is one that is logical and true. It must be based on evidence or facts and apply to many specific individuals or instances. Making a generalization about a story, poem, or play can help you to identify the theme. Here's an example:

SKILLS FOCUS

Literary Skills
Identify and analyze themes.

Reading Skills
Make generalizations.

Vocabulary Skills
Clarify word meanings through synonyms and antonyms.

Facts	Generalization
Joe and Isa play on the same ball team. Both Joe and Isa want to pitch. Isa is chosen to pitch. Joe wishes him luck. Joe is called in to finish the game when Isa is injured.	It takes more than one player to win a game.

Theme
Working together is the key to success.

PLAY

VOCABULARY DEVELOPMENT

PREVIEW SELECTION VOCABULARY

Before you read the excerpt from the play, get to know these words.

conspicuous (kən·spik′yoo·əs) *adj.:* obvious; noticeable.

The Nazis required all Jews to wear a conspicuous yellow Star of David on their clothing.

unabashed (un′ə·basht′) *adj.:* unembarrassed; unashamed.

Anne's unabashed comments sometimes embarrassed her mother.

loathe (lōth) *v.:* hate.

Anne loathed having her mother treat her like a baby.

CLARIFYING WORD MEANINGS: SYNONYMS AND ANTONYMS

A **synonym** is a word or phrase that shares the same meaning with another word. An **antonym** is a word that means the opposite of another word. Synonyms and antonyms are sometimes used as **context clues** to give readers extra help figuring out the meaning of an unfamiliar or difficult word. Here are some examples:

	Synonym	Antonym
conspicuous	Her cousin's expensive earrings were conspicuous—very *noticeable*—when she wore her hair up for the party.	Unlike her cousin, who liked to be conspicuous, Mary Lou preferred to stay *hidden* at large gatherings.
unabashed	He was unabashed, absolutely *unembarrassed,* by the accusation of cheating.	Although he was unabashed at the accusation, I felt *ashamed*.
loathe	The couple loathe the play. They really *hate* it.	A lot of people loathe the play, but I *like* it.

The Diary of Anne Frank

ACT ONE, SCENES 1 AND 2

Frances Goodrich and Albert Hackett

© Anne Frank Fonds-Basel/Anne Frank House-Amsterdam/ Getty Images.

BACKGROUND: Literature and Real Life

Anne Frank was a Jewish girl who was born in Frankfurt, Germany, in 1929. When she was four, her family moved to Amsterdam, the Netherlands, to escape anti-Jewish measures being introduced in Germany. In 1940, however, the Netherlands surrendered to the invading German army. Anne and her family went into hiding to avoid capture. Anne Frank started writing her diary in 1942 when she was thirteen years old. The diary begins with stories of boyfriends, parties, and school life. It closes two years later, just days before Anne is captured and put in a Nazi concentration camp. Anne Frank's diary recounts how she and her family lived in hiding until they were discovered and imprisoned in 1944. She died of typhus in a German prison camp when she was fifteen. But her story lives on through dozens of translations and the stage adaptation you are about to read.

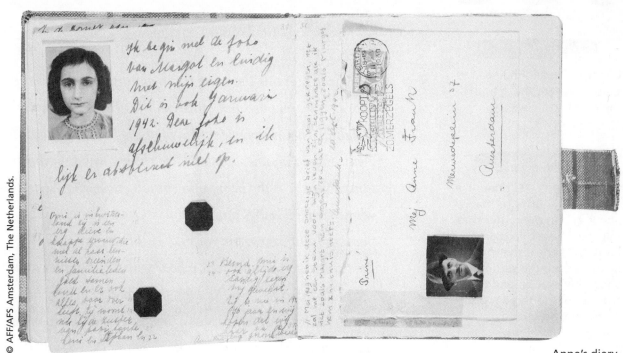

Anne's diary.

Characters

Occupants of the Secret Annex:

Anne Frank

Margot Frank, her older sister

Mr. Frank, their father

Mrs. Frank, their mother

Peter Van Daan

Mr. Van Daan, his father

Mrs. Van Daan, his mother

Mr. Dussel, a dentist

Workers in Mr. Frank's Business:

Miep Gies,[1] a young Dutchwoman

Mr. Kraler,[2] a Dutchman

Setting: Amsterdam, the Netherlands, July 1942 to August 1944; November 1945.

---

1. **Miep Gies** (mēp khēs).
2. **Kraler** (krä′lər).

Act One

SCENE 1

*The scene remains the same throughout the play. It is the top
floor of a warehouse and office building in Amsterdam,
Holland. The sharply peaked roof of the building is outlined
against a sea of other rooftops stretching away into the distance. Nearby is the belfry of a church tower, the Westertoren,
whose carillon[3] rings out the hours. Occasionally faint sounds
float up from below: the voices of children playing in the street,
the tramp of marching feet, a boat whistle from the canal.[4]*

10 *The three rooms of the top floor and a small attic space
above are exposed to our view. The largest of the rooms is in
the center, with two small rooms, slightly raised, on either
side. On the right is a bathroom, out of sight. A narrow, steep
flight of stairs at the back leads up to the attic. The rooms are
sparsely furnished, with a few chairs, cots, a table or two. The
windows are painted over or covered with makeshift blackout
curtains. In the main room there is a sink, a gas ring for cooking, and a wood-burning stove for warmth.*

*The room on the left is hardly more than a closet. There
is a skylight in the sloping ceiling. Directly under this room is*
20 *a small, steep stairwell, with steps leading down to a door.
This is the only entrance from the building below. When the
door is opened, we see that it has been concealed on the outer
side by a bookcase attached to it.*

*The curtain rises on an empty stage. It is late afternoon,
November 1945.*

*The rooms are dusty, the curtains in rags. Chairs and
tables are overturned.*

---

3. **carillon** (kar′ə·län′) *n.:* set of bells, each of which produces a
   single tone.
4. **canal** *n.:* artificial waterway. Amsterdam, which was built on soggy
   ground, has more than one hundred canals, built to help drain the
   land. The canals are used like streets.

IDENTIFY

Underline details in lines 1–8
that tell where the action of
the play takes place.

VISUALIZE

Re-read lines 9–23. Underline
words and phrases such as
above and *in the center* that
tell you where things are
located. Then, in the space
below, sketch the **setting**.
Show the location and rela-
tive size of the three rooms,
bathroom, attic, steps, and
door.

Setting Sketch

The door at the foot of the small stairwell swings open.
MR. FRANK *comes up the steps into view. He is a gentle, cul-*
30 *tured European in his middle years. There is still a trace of
a German accent in his speech.*

    *He stands looking slowly around, making a supreme effort
at self-control. He is weak, ill. His clothes are threadbare.*

    *After a second he drops his rucksack on the couch and
moves slowly about. He opens the door to one of the smaller
rooms and then abruptly closes it again, turning away. He goes
to the window at the back, looking off at the Westertoren as
its carillon strikes the hour of six; then he moves restlessly on.*

    From the street below we hear the sound of a barrel
40 *organ and children's voices at play. There is a many-colored
scarf hanging from a nail.* MR. FRANK *takes it, putting it
around his neck. As he starts back for his rucksack, his eye is
caught by something lying on the floor. It is a woman's white
glove. He holds it in his hand and suddenly all of his self-
control is gone. He breaks down crying.*

    We hear footsteps on the stairs. MIEP GIES *comes up, looking
for* MR. FRANK. MIEP *is a Dutchwoman of about twenty-two. She
wears a coat and hat, ready to go home. She is pregnant. Her
attitude toward* MR. FRANK *is protective, compassionate.*

50   **Miep.** Are you all right, Mr. Frank?

    Mr. Frank (*quickly controlling himself*). Yes, Miep, yes.

    Miep. Everyone in the office has gone home. . . . It's
after six. (*Then, pleading*) Don't stay up here, Mr. Frank.
What's the use of torturing yourself like this?

    Mr. Frank. I've come to say goodbye . . . . I'm leaving
here, Miep.

    Miep. What do you mean? Where are you going? Where?

    Mr. Frank. I don't know yet. I haven't decided.

IDENTIFY

Underline three details in lines 28–45 that show that Mr. Frank tries to control his feelings before he breaks down crying.

INFER

Pause at line 45. Why might the sight of the glove cause Mr. Frank to cry?

_____
_____
_____
_____
_____
_____
_____
_____
_____
_____
_____
_____
_____
_____
_____
_____
_____
_____

INFER

Circle the phrase that Mr. Frank uses to describe himself in line 67. Why does he want to leave Amsterdam?

_____

_____

_____

_____

_____

_____

_____

_____

INFER

What inference can you make about why Mr. Frank might want the papers burned (line 81)?

_____

_____

_____

_____

_____

_____

_____

_____

Miep. Mr. Frank, you can't leave here! This is your

60 home! Amsterdam is your home. Your business is here, waiting for you. . . . You're needed here. . . . Now that the war is over, there are things that . . .

Mr. Frank. I can't stay in Amsterdam, Miep. It has too many memories for me. Everywhere, there's something . . . the house we lived in . . . the school . . . that street organ playing out there . . . I'm not the person you used to know, Miep. I'm a bitter old man. (*Breaking off*) Forgive me. I shouldn't speak to you like this . . . after all that you did for us . . . the suffering . . .

70 **Miep.** No. No. It wasn't suffering. You can't say we suffered. (*As she speaks, she straightens a chair which is overturned.*)

Mr. Frank. I know what you went through, you and Mr. Kraler. I'll remember it as long as I live. (*He gives one last look around.*) Come, Miep. (*He starts for the steps, then remembers his rucksack, going back to get it.*)

Miep (*hurrying up to a cupboard*). Mr. Frank, did you see? There are some of your papers here. (*She brings a bundle of papers to him.*) We found them in a heap of rubbish

80 on the floor after . . . after you left.

Mr. Frank. Burn them. (*He opens his rucksack to put the glove in it.*)

Miep. But, Mr. Frank, there are letters, notes . . .

Mr. Frank. Burn them. All of them.

Miep. Burn this? (*She hands him a paperbound notebook.*)

Mr. Frank (*quietly*). Anne's diary. (*He opens the diary and begins to read.*) "Monday, the sixth of July, nineteen forty-two." (*To* MIEP) Nineteen forty-two. Is it possible,

90 Miep? . . . Only three years ago. (*As he continues his reading, he sits down on the couch.*) "Dear Diary, since you and

I are going to be great friends, I will start by telling you about myself. My name is Anne Frank. I am thirteen years old. I was born in Germany the twelfth of June, nineteen twenty-nine. As my family is Jewish, we emigrated to Holland when Hitler came to power."

[*As* MR. FRANK *reads on, another voice joins his, as if coming from the air. It is* ANNE's *voice.*]

Mr. Frank and Anne's Voice. "My father started a business, importing spice and herbs. Things went well for us until nineteen forty. Then the war came, and the Dutch capitulation, followed by the arrival of the Germans. Then things got very bad for the Jews."

[MR. FRANK's *voice dies out.* ANNE's *voice continues alone. The lights dim slowly to darkness. The curtain falls on the scene.*]

Anne's Voice. You could not do this and you could not do that. They forced Father out of his business. We had to wear yellow stars.[5] I had to turn in my bike. I couldn't go to a Dutch school anymore. I couldn't go to the movies or ride in an automobile or even on a streetcar, and a million other things. But somehow we children still managed to have fun. Yesterday Father told me we were going into hiding. Where, he wouldn't say. At five o'clock this morning Mother woke me and told me to hurry and get dressed. I was to put on as many clothes as I could. It would look too suspicious if we walked along carrying suitcases. It wasn't until we were on our way that I learned where we were going. Our hiding place was to be upstairs in the building where Father used to

Movie Still Archives.

5. **yellow stars:** The Nazis ordered all Jews to sew a large Star of David (a six-pointed star) on their outer clothing so that they could be easily recognized as Jews.

The Diary of Anne Frank, Act One, Scenes 1 and 2   **131**

ANALYZE

Most of this play is in the form of a **flashback**, an interruption in the present action of the plot to show events that happened at an earlier time. The play starts in 1945, after the end of World War II. Then, as Mr. Frank looks at Anne's diary, the scene flashes back to 1942, when Anne was writing in her diary. Circle the paragraph where the voices of Mr. Frank and Anne blur together. Why do you think the writers have father and daughter speaking together at this point?

_____

_____

_____

_____

IDENTIFY

Underline three details in lines 107–114 that tell you how life changed for Anne after the Dutch surrendered and the Germans arrived in the Netherlands.

INFER

Why does the Frank family go into hiding (line 116)?

_____

_____

_____

Compare the description of
the rooms here, in 1942
(lines 128–129), with their
description in 1945 at the
beginning of the play (lines
1–27). How has the appearance of the rooms changed?

_____

_____

_____

_____

_____

_____

_____

_____

_____

_____

_____

_____

Stage directions often reveal
characters' thoughts and
actions. Read lines 130–144.
Circle the text that describes
Mr. and Mrs. Van Daan's
emotional state.

have his business. Three other people were coming in with us . . . the Van Daans and their son Peter . . . Father knew the Van Daans but we had never met them. . . .

[*During the last lines the curtain rises on the scene. The lights dim on.* ANNE's *voice fades out.*]

SCENE 2

It is early morning, July 1942. The rooms are bare, as before, but they are now clean and orderly.

130   MR. VAN DAAN, *a tall, portly man in his late forties, is in the main room, pacing up and down, nervously smoking a cigarette. His clothes and overcoat are expensive and well cut.*

MRS. VAN DAAN *sits on the couch, clutching her possessions: a hatbox, bags, etc. She is a pretty woman in her early forties. She wears a fur coat over her other clothes.*

PETER VAN DAAN *is standing at the window of the room on the right, looking down at the street below. He is a shy, awkward boy of sixteen. He wears a cap, a raincoat, and long Dutch trousers, like plus fours.[6] At his feet is a black case, a*

140   *carrier for his cat.*

The yellow Star of David is **conspicuous** *on all of their clothes.*

Mrs. Van Daan (*rising, nervous, excited*). Something's happened to them! I know it!

Mr. Van Daan. Now, Kerli!

Mrs. Van Daan. Mr. Frank said they'd be here at seven o'clock. He said . . .

Mr. Van Daan. They have two miles to walk. You can't expect . . .

150   **Mrs. Van Daan.** They've been picked up. That's what's happened. They've been taken . . .

---

6. **plus fours** *n.:* baggy trousers that end in cuffs just below the knees.

[MR. VAN DAAN *indicates that he hears someone coming.*]

Mr. Van Daan. You see?

[PETER *takes up his carrier and his school bag, etc., and goes into the main room as* MR. FRANK *comes up the stairwell from below.* MR. FRANK *looks much younger now. His movements are brisk, his manner confident. He wears an overcoat and carries his hat and a small cardboard box. He crosses to the* VAN DAANS, *shaking hands with each of them.*]

160   **Mr. Frank.** Mrs. Van Daan, Mr. Van Daan, Peter. (*Then, in explanation of their lateness*) There were too many of the Green Police[7] on the streets . . . we had to take the long way around.

[*Up the steps come* MARGOT FRANK, MRS. FRANK, MIEP (*not pregnant now*), *and* MR. KRALER. *All of them carry bags, packages, and so forth. The Star of David is conspicuous on all of the* FRANKS' *clothing.* MARGOT *is eighteen, beautiful, quiet, shy.* MRS. FRANK *is a young mother, gently bred, reserved. She, like* MR. FRANK, *has a slight German accent.*

170 MR. KRALER *is a Dutchman, dependable, kindly.*

     As MR. KRALER *and* MIEP *go upstage to put down their parcels,* MRS. FRANK *turns back to call* ANNE.]

     Mrs. Frank. Anne?

[ANNE *comes running up the stairs. She is thirteen, quick in her movements, interested in everything, mercurial[8] in her emotions. She wears a cape and long wool socks and carries a school bag.*]

     Mr. Frank (*introducing them*). My wife, Edith. Mr. and Mrs. Van Daan (MRS. FRANK *hurries over, shaking hands with*
180 *them.*) . . . their son, Peter . . . my daughters, Margot and Anne.

---

7. **Green Police:** Nazi police, who wore green uniforms.
8. **mercurial** (mər·kyoor'ē·əl) *adj.:* changeable.

COMPARE & CONTRAST

Compare this description of Mr. Frank, in 1942 (lines 156–159), with the description of him at the beginning of the play, in 1945. How have those three years changed him?

_____

_____

_____

_____

_____

_____

INFER

Re-read lines 174–177. Notice how the description of Anne helps to reveal her **character**. List three adjectives that describe your first impression of her.

_____

_____

_____

_____

_____

_____

_____

_____

_____

Factory with the Secret Annex. To see a floor plan of this building, turn to page 164.

CLARIFY

Miep and Mr. Kraler are helping the Franks settle in. How do Miep and Mr. Kraler know the Franks? (Look at the list of characters on page 127 for help.)

[ANNE *gives a polite little curtsy as she shakes* MR. VAN DAAN'S *hand. Then she immediately starts off on a tour of investigation of her new home, going upstairs to the attic room.*

MIEP *and* MR. KRALER *are putting the various things they have brought on the shelves.*]

Mr. Kraler. I'm sorry there is still so much confusion.

Mr. Frank. Please. Don't think of it. After all, we'll have plenty of leisure to arrange everything ourselves.

190   **Miep** (*to* MRS. FRANK). We put the stores of food you sent in here. Your drugs are here . . . soap, linen here.

Mrs. Frank. Thank you, Miep.

Miep. I made up the beds . . . the way Mr. Frank and Mr. Kraler said. (*She starts out.*) Forgive me. I have to hurry. I've got to go to the other side of town to get some ration books[9] for you.

Mrs. Van Daan. Ration books? If they see our names on ration books, they'll know we're here.

Mr. Kraler. There isn't anything . . .

---

9. **ration books:** books of stamps or coupons issued by the government during wartime. People could purchase scarce items, such as food, clothing, and gasoline, only with these coupons.

Miep. Don't worry. Your names won't be on them. (*As she hurries out*) I'll be up later.

Mr. Frank. Thank you, Miep.

Mrs. Frank (*to* MR. KRALER). It's illegal, then, the ration books? We've never done anything illegal.

Mr. Frank. We won't be living here exactly according to regulations.

[*As* MR. KRALER *reassures* MRS. FRANK, *he takes various small things, such as matches and soap, from his pockets, handing them to her.*]

Mr. Kraler. This isn't the black market,[10] Mrs. Frank. This is what we call the white market . . . helping all of the hundreds and hundreds who are hiding out in Amsterdam.

[*The carillon is heard playing the quarter-hour before eight.* MR. KRALER *looks at his watch.* ANNE *stops at the window as she comes down the stairs.*]

Anne. It's the Westertoren!

Mr. Kraler. I must go. I must be out of here and downstairs in the office before the workmen get here. (*He starts for the stairs leading out.*) Miep or I, or both of us, will be up each day to bring you food and news and find out what your needs are. Tomorrow I'll get you a better bolt for the door at the foot of the stairs. It needs a bolt that you can throw yourself and open only at our signal. (*To* MR. FRANK) Oh . . . You'll tell them about the noise?

Mr. Frank. I'll tell them.

Mr. Kraler. Goodbye, then, for the moment. I'll come up again, after the workmen leave.

Mr. Frank. Goodbye, Mr. Kraler.

Mrs. Frank (*shaking his hand*). How can we thank you?

[*The others murmur their goodbyes.*]

---

10. **black market:** place or system for buying and selling goods illegally, without ration stamps.

INFER

Re-read lines 207–212. How does Mr. Kraler feel about the German occupation of the Netherlands? What might happen to him and to Miep if the Germans find out they're hiding two Jewish families?

PREDICT

Pause at line 228. How do you think the Franks and the Van Daans will get along in the cramped space where they must live? Make a prediction based on what you know about the characters so far.

Mr. Kraler. I never thought I'd live to see the day when a man like Mr. Frank would have to go into hiding. When you think—

[*He breaks off, going out.* MR. FRANK *follows him down the steps, bolting the door after him. In the interval before he returns,* PETER *goes over to* MARGOT, *shaking hands with her. As* MR. FRANK *comes back up the steps,* MRS. FRANK *questions him anxiously.*]

Mrs. Frank. What did he mean, about the noise?

240 **Mr. Frank.** First let us take off some of these clothes.

[*They all start to take off garment after garment. On each of their coats, sweaters, blouses, suits, dresses is another yellow Star of David.* MR. *and* MRS. FRANK *are underdressed quite simply. The others wear several things: sweaters, extra dresses, bathrobes, aprons, nightgowns, etc.*]

Mr. Van Daan. It's a wonder we weren't arrested, walking along the streets . . . Petronella with a fur coat in July . . . and that cat of Peter's crying all the way.

Anne (*as she is removing a pair of panties*). A cat?

250 **Mrs. Frank** (*shocked*). Anne, please!

Anne. It's all right. I've got on three more.

[*She pulls off two more. Finally, as they have all removed their surplus clothes, they look to* MR. FRANK, *waiting for him to speak.*]

Mr. Frank. Now. About the noise. While the men are in the building below, we must have complete quiet. Every sound can be heard down there, not only in the workrooms but in the offices too. The men come at about eight-thirty and leave at about five-thirty. So, to be perfectly safe, from
260 eight in the morning until six in the evening we must move only when it is necessary, and then in stockinged feet. We must not speak above a whisper. We must not run any

INFER

Why are the characters wearing so many layers of clothing (lines 240–248)?

WORD STUDY

Surplus, in line 253, is made of the affix *sur–,* meaning "over" and the word *plus,* meaning "more." A **synonym** for surplus is "extra."

water. We cannot use the sink or even, forgive me, the w.c.[11] The pipes go down through the workrooms. It would be heard. No trash . . . (MR. FRANK *stops abruptly as he hears the sound of marching feet from the street below. Everyone is motionless, paralyzed with fear.* MR. FRANK *goes quietly into the room on the right to look down out of the window.* ANNE *runs after him, peering out with him. The tramping feet pass without stopping. The tension is relieved.* MR. FRANK, *followed by* ANNE, *returns to the main room and resumes his instructions to the group.*) . . . No trash must ever be thrown out which might reveal that someone is living up here . . . not even a potato paring. We must burn everything in the stove at night. This is the way we must live until it is over, if we are to survive.

[*There is silence for a second.*]

Mrs. Frank. Until it is over.

Mr. Frank (*reassuringly*). After six we can move about . . . we can talk and laugh and have our supper and read and play games . . . just as we would at home. (*He looks at his watch.*) And now I think it would be wise if we all went to our rooms, and were settled before eight o'clock. Mrs. Van Daan, you and your husband will be upstairs. I regret that there's no place up there for Peter. But he will be here, near us. This will be our common room, where we'll meet to talk and eat and read, like one family.

Mr. Van Daan. And where do you and Mrs. Frank sleep?

Mr. Frank. This room is also our bedroom.

Mrs. Van Daan. That isn't right. We'll sleep here and you take the room upstairs.

Mr. Van Daan. It's your place.

Mr. Frank. Please. I've thought this out for weeks. It's the best arrangement. The only arrangement.

INTERPRET

Why is the group silent after Mr. Frank's speech (line 277)?

INTERPRET

Pause at line 294. Which person in the group has the leadership role? How do you know?

---

11. **w.c.:** short for "water closet," or toilet.

IDENTIFY

Circle the details in lines 298–301 that tell why the Franks are sharing their hiding place with the Van Daans.

INTERPRET

Re-read lines 311–312. Do you think Anne slept well because she's too young to understand the danger she's in? What do you learn about her **character** from this statement?

Mrs. Van Daan (*to* MR. FRANK). Never, never can we thank you. (*Then, to* MRS. FRANK) I don't know what would have happened to us, if it hadn't been for Mr. Frank.

Mr. Frank. You don't know how your husband helped me when I came to this country . . . knowing no one . . .

300   not able to speak the language. I can never repay him for that. (*Going to* MR. VAN DAAN) May I help you with your things?

Mr. Van Daan. No. No. (*To* MRS. VAN DAAN) Come along, liefje.[12]

Mrs. Van Daan. You'll be all right, Peter? You're not afraid?

Peter (*embarrassed*). Please, Mother.

[*They start up the stairs to the attic room above.* MR. FRANK *turns to* MRS. FRANK.]

Mr. Frank. You too must have some rest, Edith. You

310   didn't close your eyes last night. Nor you, Margot.

Anne. I slept, Father. Wasn't that funny? I knew it was the last night in my own bed, and yet I slept soundly.

Mr. Frank. I'm glad, Anne. Now you'll be able to help me straighten things in here. (*To* MRS. FRANK *and* MARGOT) Come with me. . . . You and Margot rest in this room for the time being. (*He picks up their clothes, starting for the room on the right.*)

Mrs. Frank. You're sure . . . ? I could help . . . And Anne hasn't had her milk . . .

320   **Mr. Frank.** I'll give it to her. (*To* ANNE *and* PETER) Anne, Peter . . . it's best that you take off your shoes now, before you forget. (*He leads the way to the room, followed by* MARGOT.)

Mrs. Frank. You're sure you're not tired, Anne?

Anne. I feel fine. I'm going to help Father.

Mrs. Frank. Peter, I'm glad you are to be with us.

---

12. **liefje** (lēf′hyə): Dutch for "little dear one."

Peter. Yes, Mrs. Frank.

[MRS. FRANK *goes to join* MR. FRANK *and* MARGOT.

During the following scene MR. FRANK *helps* MARGOT *and*

330   MRS. FRANK *to hang up their clothes. Then he persuades them*

both to lie down and rest. The VAN DAANS, *in their room*

above, settle themselves. In the main room ANNE *and* PETER

remove their shoes. PETER *takes his cat out of the carrier.*]

Anne. What's your cat's name?

Peter. Mouschi.[13]

Anne. Mouschi! Mouschi! Mouschi! (*She picks up*

the cat, walking away with it. To PETER) I love cats. I have

one . . . a darling little cat. But they made me leave her

behind. I left some food and a note for the neighbors to

340   take care of her. . . . I'm going to miss her terribly. What

is yours? A him or a her?

Peter. He's a tom. He doesn't like strangers. (*He takes*

the cat from her, putting it back in its carrier.)

Anne (*unabashed*). Then I'll have to stop being a

stranger, won't I? Is he fixed?

Peter (*startled*). Huh?

Anne. Did you have him fixed?

Peter. No.

Anne. Oh, you ought to have him fixed—to keep him

350   from—you know, fighting. Where did you go to school?

Peter. Jewish Secondary.

Anne. But that's where Margot and I go! I never saw

you around.

Peter. I used to see you . . . sometimes . . .

Anne. You did?

Peter. . . . in the schoolyard. You were always in the

middle of a bunch of kids. (*He takes a penknife from his*

pocket.)

Anne. Why didn't you ever come over?

---

13. **Mouschi** (mōō'shē).

MAKE A GENERALIZATION

Re-read Anne and Peter's conversation in lines 334–361. What does this **dialogue** tell you about how teenagers interact?

VOCABULARY

unabashed (un'ə·basht') *adj.:* unembarrassed; unashamed.

Peter. I'm sort of a lone wolf. (*He starts to rip off his Star of David.*)

Anne. What are you doing?

Peter. Taking it off.

Anne. But you can't do that. They'll arrest you if you go out without your star.

[*He tosses his knife on the table.*]

Peter. Who's going out?

Anne. Why, of course! You're right! Of course we don't need them anymore. (*She picks up his knife and starts to take her star off.*) I wonder what our friends will think when we don't show up today?

Peter. I didn't have any dates with anyone.

Anne. Oh, I did. I had a date with Jopie to go and play ping-pong at her house. Do you know Jopie de Waal?[14]

Peter. No.

Anne. Jopie's my best friend. I wonder what she'll think when she telephones and there's no answer? . . . Probably she'll go over to the house. . . . I wonder what she'll think . . . we left everything as if we'd suddenly been called away . . . breakfast dishes in the sink . . . beds not made . . . (*As she pulls off her star, the cloth underneath shows clearly the color and form of the star.*) Look! It's still there! (PETER *goes over to the stove with his star.*) What're you going to do with yours?

Peter. Burn it.

Anne. (*She starts to throw hers in, and cannot.*) It's funny, I can't throw mine away. I don't know why.

Peter. You can't throw . . . ? Something they branded you with . . . ? That they made you wear so they could spit on you?

---

14. **Jopie de Waal** (yō′pē də väl′).

COMPARE & CONTRAST

Pause at line 365. Describe ways in which Peter's personality is different from Anne's.

_____

_____

_____

_____

_____

_____

_____

_____

_____

_____

_____

_____

_____

_____

_____

_____

_____

FLUENCY

With a partner, read the boxed passage aloud. Notice the punctuation marks. Be sure to read questions differently from exclamations. Wherever you see ellipses, like these . . . , pause briefly.

Anne. I know. I know. But after all, it is the Star of David, isn't it?

[*In the bedroom, right,* MARGOT *and* MRS. FRANK *are lying down.* MR. FRANK *starts quietly out.*]

Peter. Maybe it's different for a girl.

[MR. FRANK *comes into the main room.*]

Mr. Frank. Forgive me, Peter. Now let me see. We must find a bed for your cat. (*He goes to a cupboard.*) I'm glad you brought your cat. Anne was feeling so badly about
400   hers. (*Getting a used small washtub*) Here we are. Will it be comfortable in that?

Peter (*gathering up his things*). Thanks.

Mr. Frank (*opening the door of the room on the left*). And here is your room. But I warn you, Peter, you can't grow anymore. Not an inch, or you'll have to sleep with your feet out of the skylight. Are you hungry?

Peter. No.

Mr. Frank. We have some bread and butter.

Peter. No, thank you.

410   **Mr. Frank.** You can have it for luncheon then. And tonight we will have a real supper . . . our first supper together.

Peter. Thanks. Thanks. (*He goes into his room. During the following scene he arranges his possessions in his new room.*)

Mr. Frank. That's a nice boy, Peter.

Anne. He's awfully shy, isn't he?

Mr. Frank. You'll like him, I know.

Anne. I certainly hope so, since he's the only boy I'm likely to see for months and months.

420   [MR. FRANK *sits down, taking off his shoes.*]

Mr. Frank. Annele,[15] there's a box there. Will you open it?

INFER

Pause at line 392. Why did the Nazis force Jews to wear the Star of David? What does the Star of David mean to Anne?

_____

_____

_____

_____

_____

_____

_____

_____

PREDICT

Pause at line 419. What do you think Anne and Peter's relationship will be like?

_____

_____

_____

_____

_____

_____

_____

_____

_____

---

15. **Annele** (än′ə·lə): Yiddish for "little Anne" (like "Annie").

PREDICT

Do you think Anne's experiences in the Secret Annex will be like a "summer boardinghouse" (line 428)? Why or why not?

_____

_____

_____

_____

_____

_____

_____

_____

IDENTIFY

Pause at line 453. What does Anne realize about "going into hiding" that she had not realized before?

_____

_____

_____

_____

_____

_____

_____

_____

_____

[_He indicates a carton on the couch._ ANNE _brings it to the center table. In the street below, there is the sound of children playing._]

Anne (_as she opens the carton_). You know the way I'm going to think of it here? I'm going to think of it as a boardinghouse. A very peculiar summer boardinghouse, like the one that we— (_She breaks off as she pulls out some photo-_
430 _graphs._) Father! My movie stars! I was wondering where they were! I was looking for them this morning . . . and Queen Wilhelmina![16] How wonderful!

Mr. Frank. There's something more. Go on. Look further. (_He goes over to the sink, pouring a glass of milk from a thermos bottle._)

Anne (_pulling out a pasteboard-bound book_). A diary! (_She throws her arms around her father._) I've never had a diary. And I've always longed for one. (_She looks around the room._) Pencil, pencil, pencil, pencil. (_She starts down the stairs._) I'm going down to the office to get a pencil.
440

Mr. Frank. Anne! No! (_He goes after her, catching her by the arm and pulling her back._)

Anne (_startled_). But there's no one in the building now.

Mr. Frank. It doesn't matter. I don't want you ever to go beyond that door.

Anne (_sobered_). Never . . . ? Not even at nighttime, when everyone is gone? Or on Sundays? Can't I go down to listen to the radio?

Mr. Frank. Never. I am sorry, Anneke.[17] It isn't safe.
450 No, you must never go beyond that door.

[_For the first time_ ANNE _realizes what "going into hiding" means._]

Anne. I see.

---

16. **Queen Wilhelmina** (vĭl′hĕl·mē′nä) (1880–1962): queen of the Netherlands from 1890 to 1948.
17. **Anneke** (än′ə·kə): another affectionate nickname for Anne.

Mr. Frank. It'll be hard, I know. But always remember this, Anneke. There are no walls, there are no bolts, no locks that anyone can put on your mind. Miep will bring us books. We will read history, poetry, mythology. (*He gives her the glass of milk.*) Here's your milk. (*With his arm about her, they go over to the couch, sitting down side by side.*) As a matter of fact, between us, Anne, being here has certain advantages for you. For instance, you remember the battle you had with your mother the other day on the subject of overshoes? You said you'd rather die than wear overshoes? But in the end you had to wear them? Well now, you see, for as long as we are here, you will never have to wear overshoes! Isn't that good? And the coat that you inherited from Margot, you won't have to wear that anymore. And the piano! You won't have to practice on the piano. I tell you, this is going to be a fine life for you!

[ANNE's *panic is gone.* PETER *appears in the doorway of his room, with a saucer in his hand. He is carrying his cat.*]

Peter. I . . . I . . . I thought I'd better get some water for Mouschi before . . .

Mr. Frank. Of course.

[*As he starts toward the sink, the carillon begins to chime the hour of eight. He tiptoes to the window at the back and looks down at the street below. He turns to* PETER, *indicating in pantomime that it is too late.* PETER *starts back for his room. He steps on a creaking board. The three of them are frozen for a minute in fear. As* PETER *starts away again,* ANNE *tiptoes over to him and pours some of the milk from her glass into the saucer for the cat.* PETER *squats on the floor, putting the milk before the cat.* MR. FRANK *gives* ANNE *his fountain pen and then goes into the room at the right. For a second* ANNE *watches the cat; then she goes over to the center table and opens her diary.*]

INTERPRET

What does Mr. Frank mean in lines 455–456 when he says, "There are no walls, there are no bolts, no locks that anyone can put on your mind"?

_____

_____

_____

_____

_____

_____

_____

IDENTIFY

Why is it "too late" for Peter to give water to Mouschi (lines 477–478)?

_____

_____

_____

_____

_____

_____

_____

_____

_____

_____

_____

_____

_____

_____

_____

_____

_____

_____

_____

_____

_____

_____

_____

_____

_____

_____

_____

_____

loathe (lōth) v.: hate.

In the room at the right, MRS. FRANK *has sat up quickly at the sound of the carillon.* MR. FRANK *comes in and sits down beside her on the settee,*[18] *his arm comfortingly around her.*

490 *Upstairs, in the attic room,* MR. *and* MRS. VAN DAAN *have hung their clothes in the closet and are now seated on the iron bed.* MRS. VAN DAAN *leans back, exhausted.* MR. VAN DAAN *fans her with a newspaper.*

ANNE *starts to write in her diary. The lights dim out; the curtain falls.*

In the darkness ANNE'*s voice comes to us again, faintly at first and then with growing strength.*]

Anne's Voice. I expect I should be describing what it feels like to go into hiding. But I really don't know yet myself. I only know it's funny never to be able to go out-
500 doors . . . never to breathe fresh air . . . never to run and shout and jump. It's the silence in the nights that frightens me most. Every time I hear a creak in the house or a step on the street outside, I'm sure they're coming for us. The days aren't so bad. At least we know that Miep and Mr. Kraler are down there below us in the office. Our protectors, we call them. I asked Father what would happen to them if the Nazis found out they were hiding us. Pim[19] said that they would suffer the same fate that we would. . . . Imagine!
510 They know this, and yet when they come up here, they're always cheerful and gay, as if there were nothing in the world to bother them. . . . Friday, the twenty-first of August, nineteen forty-two. Today I'm going to tell you our general news. Mother is unbearable. She insists on treating me like a baby, which I **loathe**. Otherwise things are going better. The weather is . . .

[*As* ANNE'*s voice is fading out, the curtain rises on the scene.*]

---

18. **settee** (se·tē′) *n.:* small couch.
19. **Pim:** family nickname for Mr. Frank.

The Diary of Anne Frank, Act One, Scenes 1 and 2

Generalization Chart   A **generalization** is a broad statement about a topic. You can make a generalization by drawing a conclusion based on details or evidence. Often, making a generalization about people or events in a story can lead you to identify the work's theme.

SKILLS FOCUS

Literary Skills
Analyze theme.

In the chart below, list details from the excerpt of *The Diary of Anne Frank*. Then, review those details and see if you can make a generalization about what you've read.

Detail
Detail
Detail
Detail
Generalization

Skills Review

The Diary of Anne Frank, Act One, Scenes 1 and 2

VOCABULARY AND COMPREHENSION

Word Bank

conspicuous

unabashed

loathe

A. Clarifying Meanings: Synonyms and Antonyms   Write the word from the Word Bank that goes with each synonym and antonym pair.

1. _____ (hated; liked)

2. _____ (unembarrassed; ashamed)

3. _____ (noticeable; hidden)

B. Reading Comprehension   Answer each question below.

1. Why did Anne and her family move to Holland? _____

_____

_____

2. Write three rules that members of the Secret Annex had to follow.

_____

_____

3. Why did Peter tear off the Star of David that was sewn onto his

clothing? _____

_____

_____

4. What did Mr. Frank give to Anne to make her feel better while they

were in hiding? _____

_____

_____

SKILLS FOCUS

Vocabulary Skills
Use synonyms and antonyms to clarify word meanings.

Camp Harmony by Monica Sone
In Response to Executive Order 9066 by Dwight Okita

These selections also appear in *Elements of Literature.*

LITERARY FOCUS: RECURRING THEMES

A **theme** is a truth about life that is revealed through literature. Some themes appear time and again in literature all over the world. For example, a theme such as "Parents deserve respect" might be explored in ancient myths as well as in modern novels, in movies, and in TV shows. Such themes are called **recurring themes.** (*Recur* means "occur again.")

As you read the selections that follow, identify the themes they explore. Then, see if you can identify other works that share those themes.

READING SKILLS: MAKING GENERALIZATIONS

A **generalization** is a broad statement based on several particular situations. In making a generalization, you combine evidence of different kinds to draw a conclusion that is **valid,** or both logical and true. Here is a generalization drawn from specific historical facts.

FACTS:

- The Fugitive Slave Act of 1793 required that captured runaways be returned to the states from which they had escaped.
- The 1793 act did not provide a way for the act to be enforced.
- The Fugitive Slave Act of 1850 required that fugitives who had escaped to free states be captured and returned to the South.
- The 1850 act set penalties for interfering with the capture of fugitives.

GENERALIZATION:

The Fugitive Slave Act of 1850 was harsher than the 1793 act.

As you read the next two selections, think about a generalization you might draw from the writers' experiences.

SKILLS FOCUS

Literary Skills
Understand recurring themes.

Reading Skills
Make generalizations.

Vocabulary Skills
Clarify word meanings through restatement.

VOCABULARY DEVELOPMENT

PREVIEW SELECTION VOCABULARY

Before you read "Camp Harmony," take time to get to know these words:

tersely (tụrs′lē) *adv.:* briefly and clearly; without unnecessary words.

The child tersely stated, "Pigs—dirty."

laconically (lə·kän′ik·lē) *adv.:* with few words.

He announced laconically, "Soup."

breach (brēch) *n.:* opening.

The narrator squeezed into a breach in the wall of people.

riveted (riv′it·id) *v.:* fastened or held firmly, as if by rivets (metal bolts or pins).

The family watched, riveted with fear, as the stove turned red hot.

vigil (vij′əl) *n.:* watch.

Armed guards kept an around-the-clock vigil in the camp.

CLARIFYING WORD MEANINGS: RESTATEMENT

Writers sometimes provide **restatements** of difficult words right in the surrounding text. A restatement is a paraphrase; it says the same thing using different words. In the examples that follow, the restatement of each vocabulary word is italicized.

- The note was **tersely** worded. The writer *wasted no words.*
- The teacher spoke **laconically,** *answering* questions *with one- or two-word replies.*
- There was a **breach,** *or crack,* in the wall.
- We *stared*—**riveted**—at the fireworks display.
- When my cat was sick I kept **vigil,** *guarding him all night,* until dawn came and he felt better.

Camp Harmony

Monica Sone

BACKGROUND: Literature and Social Studies

In 1942, many thousands of Japanese Americans living on the West Coast were sent to internment camps. They had committed no crime, but the United States had gone to war with Japan. Executive Order 9066 made their confinement legal. Ironically, many of the evacuated families had sons or brothers serving with the U.S. Army in the war overseas. Most of the 120,000 Japanese Americans detained spent three years behind barbed wire. Released in 1945, at the end of World War II, they returned home to find their property stolen and their livelihoods gone. They had to wait more than forty years for an apology and compensation from the U.S. government.

When our bus turned a corner and we no longer had to smile and wave, we settled back gravely in our seats. Everyone was quiet except for a chattering group of university students, who soon started singing college songs. A few people turned and glared at them, which only served to increase the volume of their singing. Then suddenly a baby's sharp cry rose indignantly above the hubbub. The singing stopped immediately, followed by a guilty silence. Three seats behind us, a young mother held a wailing red-faced infant in her arms, bouncing it up and down. Its angry little face emerged from multiple layers of kimonos, sweaters, and blankets, and it, too, wore the white pasteboard tag[1] pinned to its blanket. A young man stammered

---

IDENTIFY

An **autobiography** is an account of a person's life, written by himself or herself. Circle the pronouns in the first sentence that tell you that the narrator takes part in this story.

_____

_____

_____

WORD STUDY

Indignantly (in·dig'nənt·lē), in line 7, is an adverb that means "with anger caused by something felt to be unjust."

---

1. **white pasteboard tag:** All Japanese American families registering for evacuation were given numbered tags to wear and to attach to their luggage. Monica's family became family number 10710.

Excerpt (retitled "Camp Harmony") from *Nisei Daughter* by Monica Sone. Copyright © 1953 and renewed © 1981 by Monica Sone. Reproduced by permission of **Little, Brown and Company**.

Wrath (rath) means "rage"
or "fury." Knowing that,
what does *wrathful* (line 14)
mean?

_____

_____

_____

_____

_____

_____

_____

_____

In lines 17–30, the narrator
admires the scenery, but is
she really enjoying the ride?
How does she feel about this
trip? Underline the details
that support your ideas.

_____

_____

_____

_____

_____

_____

_____

_____

out an apology as the mother gave him a wrathful look. She
hunted frantically for a bottle of milk in a shopping bag,
and we all relaxed when she had found it.

We sped out of the city southward along beautiful
stretches of farmland, with dark, newly turned soil. In the
beginning we devoured every bit of scenery which flashed

20   past our window and admired the massive-muscled work-
horses plodding along the edge of the highway, the rich
burnished copper color of a browsing herd of cattle, the
vivid spring green of the pastures, but eventually the same-
ness of the country landscape palled[2] on us. We tried to
sleep to escape from the restless anxiety which kept bob-
bing up to the surface of our minds. I awoke with a start
when the bus filled with excited buzzing. A small group of
straw-hatted Japanese farmers stood by the highway, waving at us. I felt a sudden warmth toward them, then a

30   twinge of pity. They would be joining us soon.

About noon we crept into a small town. Someone said,
"Looks like Puyallup, all right." Parents of small children
babbled excitedly, "Stand up quickly and look over there.
See all the chick-chicks and fat little piggies?" One little

Topaz, August 1943 (1943) by Suiko Mikami. Watercolor.

---

2. **palled** (pôld) *v.*: became boring or tiresome.

city boy stared hard at the hogs and said **tersely,** "They're bachi—dirty!"

Our bus idled a moment at the traffic signal, and we noticed at the left of us an entire block filled with neat rows of low shacks, resembling chicken houses. Someone com-

40 mented on it with awe, "Just look at those chicken houses. They sure go in for poultry in a big way here." Slowly the bus made a left turn, drove through a wire-fence gate, and to our dismay, we were inside the oversized chicken farm. The bus driver opened the door, the guard stepped out and stationed himself at the door again. Jim, the young man who had shepherded us into the buses, popped his head inside and sang out, "OK, folks, all off at Yokohama, Puyallup."

We stumbled out, stunned, dragging our bundles after us. It must have rained hard the night before in Puyallup,

50 for we sank ankle deep into gray, glutinous[3] mud. The receptionist, a white man, instructed us courteously, "Now, folks, please stay together as family units and line up. You'll be assigned your apartment."

We were standing in Area A, the mammoth parking lot of the state fairgrounds. There were three other separate areas, B, C, and D, all built on the fairgrounds proper, near the baseball field and the racetracks. This camp of army barracks was hopefully called Camp Harmony.

We were assigned to apartment 2–I–A, right across from

60 the bachelor quarters. The apartments resembled elongated,[4] low stables about two blocks long. Our home was one room, about eighteen by twenty feet, the size of a living room. There was one small window in the wall opposite the one door. It was bare except for a small, tinny wood-burning stove crouching in the center. The flooring consisted of two-by-fours laid directly on the earth, and dandelions were

---

3. **glutinous** (glo͞ot″n·əs) *adj.*: sticky; gluey.
4. **elongated** (ē·lôŋ′gāt′id) *v.* used as *adj.*: lengthened.

INTERPRET

Yokohama is a seaport city south of Tokyo, Japan. Puyallup is a city in Washington State, near Tacoma. Why do you think Jim identifies their destination as Yokohama, Puyallup (line 47)?

_____

_____

_____

_____

_____

_____

VOCABULARY

tersely (tʉrs′lē) *adv.*: briefly and clearly; without unnecessary words.

VISUALIZE

Underline the details in lines 59–69 that help you picture the room. Sketch the room in the space below.

Pause at line 77. What do the mother's comments about the dandelions reveal about her **character**?

_____

_____

_____

_____

_____

_____

_____

_____

VOCABULARY

laconically (lə·kän′ik·lē) *adv.:* with few words. *Laconically* and *tersely* are synonyms.

INTERPRET

How does the author's poem, created quickly and meant as a joke, relate to her family's situation (lines 82–86)?

_____

_____

_____

_____

_____

_____

_____

_____

_____

already pushing their way up through the cracks. Mother was delighted when she saw their shaggy yellow heads. "Don't anyone pick them. I'm going to cultivate them."

70 Father snorted, "Cultivate them! If we don't watch out, those things will be growing out of our hair."

Just then Henry stomped inside, bringing the rest of our baggage. "What's all the excitement about?"

Sumi replied **laconically,** "Dandelions."

Henry tore off a fistful. Mother scolded, "Arra! Arra! Stop that. They're the only beautiful things around here. We could have a garden right in here."

"Are you joking, Mama?"

I chided Henry, "Of course she's not. After all, she has

80 to have some inspiration to write poems, you know, with all the 'nari keri's.'[5] I can think of a poem myself right now:

Oh, Dandelion, Dandelion,

Despised and uprooted by all,

Dance and bob your golden heads

For you've finally found your home

With your yellow fellows, nari keri, amen!"

Henry said, thrusting the dandelions in Mother's black hair, "I think you can do ten times better than that, Mama."

Sumi reclined on her sea bag[6] and fretted, "Where do

90 we sleep? Not on the floor, I hope."

"Stop worrying," Henry replied disgustedly.

Mother and Father wandered out to see what the other folks were doing and they found people wandering in the mud, wondering what other folks were doing. Mother

---

5. **Nari keri** (nä·*rē* ke·*rē*): a phrase used to end many Japanese poems. It is meant to convey wonder and awe.
6. **sea bag** *n.:* large canvas bag like the ones sailors use to carry their personal belongings. Each person was allowed to bring only one sea bag of bedding and two suitcases of clothing to the internment camps.

returned shortly, her face lit up in an ecstatic smile, "We're in luck. The latrine is right nearby. We won't have to walk blocks."

We laughed, marveling at Mother who could be so poetic and yet so practical. Father came back, bent double
100 like a woodcutter in a fairy tale, with stacks of scrap lumber over his shoulder. His coat and trouser pockets bulged with nails. Father dumped his loot in a corner and explained, "There was a pile of wood left by the carpenters and hundreds of nails scattered loose. Everybody was picking them up, and I hustled right in with them. Now maybe we can live in style, with tables and chairs."

The block leader knocked at our door and announced lunchtime. He instructed us to take our meal at the nearest mess hall. As I untied my sea bag to get out my pie plate,
110 tin cup, spoon, and fork, I realized I was hungry. At the mess hall we found a long line of people. Children darted in and out of the line, skiing in the slithery mud. The young stood impatiently on one foot, then the other, and scowled, "The food had better be good after all this wait." But the issei[7] stood quietly, arms folded, saying very little.

Department of Special Collections, Charles E. Young Research Library, UCLA.

Progress After One Year, the Mess Hall Line (1943)
by Kango Takamura. Watercolor.

---

7. **issei** (ē'sā') *n.:* Japanese who immigrated to North America. Issei were forbidden by law to become U.S. citizens.

Notes _____

_____
_____
_____
_____
_____
_____

COMPARE & CONTRAST

Re-read lines 92–106. In what way are the mother and father alike? Explain, using details from the story.

DRAW CONCLUSIONS

Pause at line 133. Based on what you've read so far, what conclusion can you draw about conditions in Japanese internment camps?

_____

_____

_____

_____

_____

VOCABULARY

breach (brēch) *n.:* opening; *Breach* usually refers to a breakthrough in a wall or in a line of defense.

VISUALIZE

In the space below, redraw the room you sketched earlier. This time, show the door, window, and stove, as well as the arrangement of the cots. On each cot, write the name of the person assigned to it.

A light drizzle began to fall, coating bare black heads with tiny sparkling raindrops. The chow line inched forward.

120 Lunch consisted of two canned sausages, one lob of boiled potato, and a slab of bread. Our family had to split up, for the hall was too crowded for us to sit together. I wandered up and down the aisles, back and forth along the crowded tables and benches, looking for a few inches to squeeze into. A small issei woman finished her meal, stood up, and hoisted her legs modestly over the bench, leaving a space for one. Even as I thrust myself into the **breach,** the space had shrunk to two inches, but I worked myself into it. My dinner companion, hooked just inside my right elbow, was a baldheaded, gruff-looking issei man who seemed to resent nestling at mealtime. Under my left elbow 130 was a tiny, mud-spattered girl. With busy, runny nose, she was belaboring her sausages, tearing them into shreds and mixing them into the potato gruel which she had made with water. I choked my food down.

We cheered loudly when trucks rolled by, distributing canvas army cots for the young and hardy, and steel cots for the older folks. Henry directed the arrangement of the cots. Father and Mother were to occupy the corner nearest the wood stove. In the other corner, Henry arranged two cots in an L shape and announced that this was the combina- 140 tion living room–bedroom area, to be occupied by Sumi and myself. He fixed a male den for himself in the corner nearest the door. If I had had my way, I would have arranged everyone's cots in one neat row, as in Father's hotel dormitory.

We felt fortunate to be assigned to a room at the end of the barracks, because we had just one neighbor to worry about. The partition wall separating the rooms was only seven feet high, with an opening of four feet at the top, so at night, Mrs. Funai next door could tell when Sumi was

150 still sitting up in bed in the dark, putting her hair up. "Mah, Sumi-chan," Mrs. Funai would say through the plank wall, "are you curling your hair tonight, again? Do you put it up every night?" Sumi would put her hands on her hips and glare defiantly at the wall.

The block monitor, an impressive nisei[8] who looked like a star tackle, with his crouching walk, came around the first night to tell us that we must all be inside our room by nine o'clock every night. At ten o'clock, he rapped at the door again, yelling, "Lights out!" and Mother rushed to

160 turn the light off not a second later.

Throughout the barracks, there was a medley[9] of creaking cots, whimpering infants, and explosive night coughs. Our attention was **riveted** on the intense little wood stove, which glowed so violently I feared it would melt right down to the floor. We soon learned that this condition lasted for only a short time, after which it suddenly turned into a deep freeze. Henry and Father took turns at the stove to produce the harrowing[10] blast which all but singed our army blankets but did not penetrate through them. As it grew quieter in

170 the barracks, I could hear the light patter of rain. Soon I felt the splat! splat! of raindrops digging holes into my face. The dampness on my pillow spread like a mortal bleeding, and I finally had to get out and haul my cot toward the center of the room. In a short while, Henry was up. "I've got multiple leaks, too. Have to complain to the landlord first thing in the morning."

IDENTIFY

Imagery is description that appeals to the senses. Circle the images in lines 161–176. Then, draw an arrow from each image and label it with the sense it appeals to: sight, hearing, and touch.

VOCABULARY

riveted (riv′it·id) v.: fastened or held firmly, as if by rivets (metal bolts or pins).

INFER

Underline two images in lines 161–176 that reveal the author's anger at the conditions in the barracks. Why do you think Henry tells his sister (the author) he's going to complain to the landlord? Who is the landlord?

---

8. **nisei** (nē′sā′) n.: native U.S. or Canadian citizen born of Japanese immigrant parents.
9. **medley** (med′lē) n.: jumble; mixture.
10. **harrowing** (har′ō·iŋ) adj.: extremely distressing.

FLUENCY

Read the boxed passage aloud. Imagine you are the author. Try to capture the despair and anger she feels about the way she and her family have been treated.

VOCABULARY

vigil (vij′əl) *n.*: watch; act of staying awake to keep watch.

INTERPRET

Think back over the events in this true story. What idea about life, or **theme,** is the author sharing with you?

_____

_____

_____

_____

_____

_____

_____

_____

_____

_____

_____

_____

_____

_____

_____

_____

180

190

All through the night I heard people getting up, dragging cots around. I stared at our little window, unable to sleep. I was glad Mother had put up a makeshift curtain on the window, for I noticed a powerful beam of light sweeping across it every few seconds. The lights came from high towers placed around the camp, where guards with tommy guns kept a twenty-four-hour **vigil.** I remembered the wire fence encircling us, and a knot of anger tightened in my breast. What was I doing behind a fence, like a criminal? If there were accusations to be made, why hadn't I been given a fair trial? Maybe I wasn't considered an American anymore. My citizenship wasn't real, after all. Then what was I? I was certainly not a citizen of Japan, as my parents were. On second thought, even Father and Mother were more alien residents of the United States than Japanese nationals, for they had little tie with their mother country. In their twenty-five years in America, they had worked and paid their taxes to their adopted government as any other citizen.

200

Of one thing I was sure. The wire fence was real. I no longer had the right to walk out of it. It was because I had Japanese ancestors. It was also because some people had little faith in the ideas and ideals of democracy. They said that after all these were but words and could not possibly ensure loyalty. New laws and camps were surer devices. I finally buried my face in my pillow to wipe out burning thoughts and snatch what sleep I could.

In Response to Executive Order 9066

All Americans of Japanese Descent Must Report to Relocation Centers

Dwight Okita

Dear Sirs:
Of course I'll come. I've packed my galoshes
and three packets of tomato seeds. Denise calls them
"love apples." My father says where we're going
they won't grow.

I am a fourteen-year-old girl with bad spelling
and a messy room. If it helps any, I will tell you
I have always felt funny using chopsticks
and my favorite food is hot dogs.

10 My best friend is a white girl named Denise—
we look at boys together. She sat in front of me
all through grade school because of our names:
O'Connor, Ozawa. I know the back of Denise's head
    very well.
I tell her she's going bald. She tells me I copy on tests.
15 We're best friends.

I saw Denise today in Geography class.
She was sitting on the other side of the room.

"In Response to Executive Order 9066" from *Crossing with the Light* by Dwight Okita. Copyright © 1992 by **Dwight Okita.** Published by Tia Chucha Press, Chicago. Reproduced by permission of the author.

INTERPRET

How would you describe the speaker's **tone** in lines 1–5? What is the "invitation" she has received?

_____

_____

_____

_____

_____

_____

_____

_____

_____

_____

IDENTIFY

Underline words and phrases the speaker uses to describe herself in lines 6–9.

INFER

Pause at line 19. Why do you think Denise speaks so cruelly to her former friend?

_____
_____
_____
_____
_____
_____
_____
_____
_____

"You're trying to start a war," she said, "giving secrets away
to the Enemy. Why can't you keep your big mouth shut?"

20 I didn't know what to say.
I gave her a packet of tomato seeds
and asked her to plant them for me, told her
when the first tomato ripened
she'd miss me.

Japanese American internees line up for a meal at the internment camp in Puyallup, Washington.

© Seattle Post-Intelligencer Collection; Museum of History & Industry/CORBIS.

INTERPRET

Re-read lines 20–24. What point is the speaker making about her friend's unfair attitude?

_____
_____
_____
_____
_____
_____
_____
_____

Camp Harmony / In Response to Executive Order 9066

Comparison Chart   The details in a literary selection work together to reflect a **theme,** or truth about life. Different writers may explore the same theme but use different topics and details to convey that theme. Themes that are explored time and time again are called **recurring themes.** Fill in the following chart with important details from "Camp Harmony" and "In Response to Executive Order 9066." Then, identify a theme that applies to both works.

SKILLS FOCUS

Literary Skills
Analyze recurring themes.

Important Details from "Camp Harmony"	Important Details from "In Response to Executive Order 9066"
Recurring Theme	

Skills Review

Camp Harmony/In Response to Executive Order 9066

VOCABULARY AND COMPREHENSION

A. Clarifying Meanings: Verify by Restating Write a sentence for each word in the Word Bank. Then, follow the directions below each answer line.

1. _____

   Substitute the word *curtly* or *concisely* for **tersely**.

2. _____

   Replace **laconically** with *briefly* or *abruptly*.

3. _____

   Use *crack* in place of **breach**.

4. _____

   Substitute *fixed firmly* for **riveted**.

5. _____

   Use *watch* for **vigil**.

B. Reading Comprehension Answer each question below.

1. In "Camp Harmony," where is the Sone family sent? Why are they

   sent there? _____

   _____

2. How is the camp like a prison? Use details from the selection. _____

   _____

3. Who is the speaker of "In Response to Executive Order 9066"? _____

   _____

4. Why does the speaker give Denise tomato seeds? _____

   _____

A Family in Hiding

by Miep Gies with Alison Leslie Gold

LITERARY FOCUS: THEME

A **theme** is the general idea or insight about life that a work of literature reveals. In some literary works the theme is expressed directly in a sentence or in a passage ("There's no place like home"). In most selections, however, the theme is implied through characters' actions, events that take place, and so on. You need to think about all the elements of a work before you state its theme. Use the tips described below to help you identify the theme of "A Family in Hiding."

READING SKILLS: FINDING THEME

The theme of a literary work emerges from all its elements. To put your finger on the theme of a selection, use the following tips:

- **The title.** Sometimes the title hints at the theme of a work.
- **The characters.** What do the characters discover that could have meaning for other people's lives? How do they reveal the theme in their thoughts, words, and feelings?
- **Key passages.** Look for passages of description, dialogue, or narration that reveal insights about the characters' experiences or about life.
- **The resolution.** How does the selection end? What has the main character learned about life?

SKILLS FOCUS

Literary Skills
Understand theme.

Reading Skills
Find theme.

Vocabulary Skills
Use context clues.

VOCABULARY DEVELOPMENT

PREVIEW SELECTION VOCABULARY

Get to know these words before you read "A Family in Hiding."

enthusiasm (en·thōō′zē·az′əm) *n.:* energetic interest.

> *Anne always showed enthusiasm when visitors arrived.*

allotted (ə·lät′id) *v.:* handed out; given.

> *Miep and Henk were allotted the room normally shared by Anne and Margot.*

insatiable (in·sā′shə·bəl) *adj.:* unable to be satisfied.

> *The occupants of the Annex were insatiable for the company of others.*

reverberated (ri·vur′bə·rāt′əd) *v.:* echoed.

> *The ringing of the clock reverberated through the rooms of the Annex.*

CLARIFYING WORD MEANINGS: CONTEXT CLUES

What do you do when you don't know the meaning of a word? One strategy is to use **context clues** that you find in the words and sentences surrounding the word. These clues can help you guess the meaning. Here are four types of context clues you should get familiar with. The italicized words or phrases provide context clues for each boldface word.

DEFINITION: Look for words that define or provide a synonym for the unfamiliar word.

  Her eyes were **imploring** me, *begging* for an invitation to the party.

RESTATEMENT: Find words that restate the unfamiliar word's meaning.

  He **bristled** at the remark. I'm not sure why he *got so angry.*

EXAMPLE: Look for examples that reveal the meaning of the unfamiliar word.

  Her nerves were **taut,** *like a rope tightly drawn.*

CONTRAST: Find words that contrast the unfamiliar word with a word or phrase you already know.

  Although she tried to be **congenial,** *no one wanted to be her friend.*

A Family in Hiding

Miep Gies with Alison Leslie Gold

BACKGROUND: Literature and Real Life

The Diary of Anne Frank would never have been published if it weren't for
Miep Gies (mēp khēs). Miep saved Anne's diaries and the family photographs
that she found in the attic after the family had been taken by the Nazi police.
The next selection is from Miep Gies's book *Anne Frank Remembered,*
which she published in 1987. In it, she describes a night in the Secret Annex.

Before reading the selection, here is what you should know:

- Henk is Miep's husband.
- Jo Koophuis is managing the factory that once belonged to Otto Frank.

Anne and the others had been after us to come and sleep
upstairs in the hiding place. There was something always
imploring about the way they asked, so one day I took
some things from home with me to work, some night-
clothes for Henk and myself.

When I announced to Anne and Mrs. Frank that we
would finally come to spend the night, the **enthusiasm** was
extraordinary. You'd have thought that Queen Wilhelmina
herself was about to make a visit. Rubbing her hands
10 together, Anne was filled with excitement. "Miep and Henk
will be sleeping over tonight," she ran to tell the others
upstairs.

> **INFER**
>
> *Imploring* (line 3) means
> "begging." It comes from a
> Latin word meaning "cry out;
> weep." What does this word
> suggest about the Frank
> family?
>
> _____
>
> _____
>
> _____
>
> _____
>
> **VOCABULARY**
>
> **enthusiasm**
> (en·thōō′zē·az′əm) *n.:*
> energetic interest.

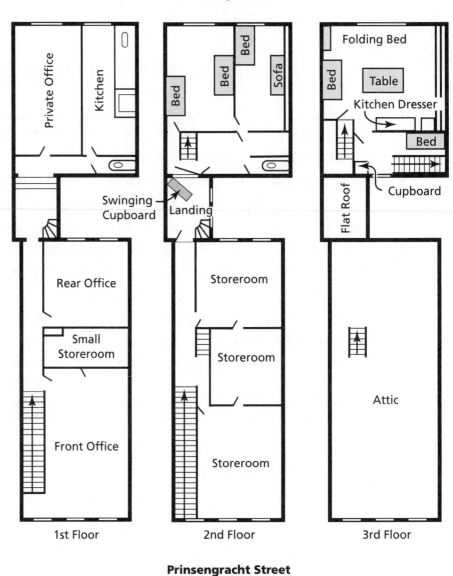

Backyards

Private Office

Kitchen

Bed

Bed

Bed

Sofa

Folding Bed

Bed

Table

Kitchen Dresser

Bed

Swinging Cupboard

Landing

Flat Roof

Cupboard

Rear Office

Storeroom

Small Storeroom

Storeroom

Attic

Front Office

Storeroom

1st Floor

2nd Floor

3rd Floor

PP/FA, Inc.

Prinsengracht Street

Hoping to moderate her mood, I told Mrs. Frank, "We don't want any fuss."

Mrs. Frank smiled, put her hand on my shoulder, and squeezed. On my way out, I repeated my request to Mr. Frank, who was climbing downstairs: "Now, no fuss, please."

With a smile on his face, he shook his head. "No, no, of
20 course not."

During the day I told Jo Koophuis of our plan. After work Henk came, and when the last worker had gone home at five-thirty, the end of the workday, Mr. Koophuis bade us good night. He locked the door of the building behind him. The office was quite silent with everyone gone. We made sure that the lights had been turned off; then we went up the stairway, pulled open the bookcase, and went in. I closed it behind us.

Each of our friends greeted us happily as we made our way upstairs. "The last worker has gone," I informed them. Right away, there were voices, footsteps, the toilet flushing, a cabinet shutting. Already, it was noisy upstairs; the place had come alive.

Anne directed us toward the bedroom she shared with Margot. At Anne's insistence, Henk and I had been **allotted** their room. Anne and Margot were going into the room with their parents for the night. Anne pulled me to her bed, neatly made up, and told me she wanted me to put my things there. Amused, I told her that I'd be honored, and put my night things on her bed, and Henk's on Margot's bed.

Shortly, it was time for the radio broadcasts, and the entire group trooped down to Mr. Frank's office below to pull up chairs and gather around the Phillips radio on the table. The whole room bristled with excitement when the near-and-yet-so-far voice of Radio Orange came through the radio. "Here is Radio Orange. All things went well today. The English . . ." and on it went, filling us with hope and with information, our only real connection to the still-free outside world.

When it was time to sit down to eat, Henk and I were given seats of honor, as we had been at our anniversary dinner. All nine of us squeezed in around the table.

COMPARE & CONTRAST

Pause at line 33. How was the Annex at night different from the Annex by day?

_____

_____

_____

_____

_____

_____

_____

_____

VOCABULARY

allotted (ə·lät′id) v.: handed out; given.

INFER

Re-read the paragraph beginning on line 42. Which side, the Allies or the Nazis, was Radio Orange most likely on?

_____

_____

_____

_____

_____

_____

VOCABULARY

insatiable (in·sā′shə·bəl) adj.: unable to be satisfied. In other words, they couldn't get enough of the pleasure of company.

IDENTIFY

Pause at line 67. What important realization does Miep come to here?

_____

_____

_____

_____

_____

_____

_____

_____

_____

_____

_____

_____

_____

_____

VOCABULARY

reverberated (ri·vʉr′bə·rāt′əd) v.: echoed.

This time, Mrs. Frank and Margot had supervised the cooking. The food was tasty and filling.

With the blackout frames up and the electric light on, along with the heat from the cooking, the room became toasty-warm, cozy. We sat long over coffee and dessert, talking, our friends devouring the novelty of our presence.

60 They seemed to be **insatiable** for our company.

As I sat, I became aware of what it meant to be imprisoned in these small rooms. As this feeling registered, I felt a taste of the helpless fear that these people were filled with, day and night. Yes, for all of us it was wartime, but Henk and I had the freedom to come and go as we pleased, to stay in or go out. These people were in a prison, a prison with locks inside the doors.

Reluctantly, we said good-nights, remembering that Mr. and Mrs. Van Daan could not go to bed until we'd

70 gone. Henk and I and the Frank family trooped down the stairway to the floor below. Here we said a second round of good-nights, and Henk and I got ready for bed in our little room, surrounded by Anne's movie-star faces on the wall.

I climbed into Anne's hard little bed, which was very toasty with blanket upon blanket, so many blankets that I couldn't imagine how Anne could ever be taken with a chill. The room was cool otherwise, and as I settled in as cozily as I could, I could hear every sound being made in the other rooms: Mr. Van Daan coughing, the squeak of

80 springs, the sound of a slipper dropping beside a bed, the toilet flushing, Mouschi [the cat] landing on his padded feet somewhere above me.

The Westertoren clock struck at fifteen-minute intervals. I'd never heard it so loud; it echoed and **reverberated** through the rooms. The church was right across the back gardens from the Annex. In the office, the building blocked the sound. During the day, by the time I heard the ringing in my front office, the sound had been muted and cushioned by the entire building. It was

90 soothing and distant.

All through the night I heard each ringing of the Westertoren clock. I never slept; I couldn't close my eyes. I heard the sound of a rainstorm begin, the wind come up. The quietness of the place was overwhelming. The fright of these people who were locked up here was so thick I could feel it pressing down on me. It was like a thread of terror pulled taut. It was so terrible it never let me close my eyes.

For the first time I knew what it was like to be a Jew in hiding.

© Bob Krist/CORBIS.

The Westertoren clock tower.

WORD STUDY

Underline the context clue that helps you guess that *muted* (line 89) means "muffled" or "softened."

What do we mean when we say that someone is mute?

_____

_____

_____

_____

WORD STUDY

Re-read lines 96–97. What **figure of speech,** or imaginative comparison, does Miep use to help us feel her terror? Underline it.

INTERPRET

Read through the story again, and identify the most important passage. What idea about life, or **theme,** does that passage convey?

_____

_____

_____

_____

_____

_____

_____

_____

A Family in Hiding

Literary Skills
Analyze theme.

Theme Chart   A **theme** is a truth or an insight about life. Nearly every literary work explores a theme. Fill in the chart below with details from "A Family in Hiding." Then, review the details and identify the theme of the story.

	Details from "A Family in Hiding"
Title of Work:	
Characters' Thoughts/Actions:	
Key Passages:	
Resolution:	
Theme	

Skills Review

A Family in Hiding

VOCABULARY AND COMPREHENSION

A. Clarifying Word Meanings: Context Clues   Fill in the blanks with words from the Word Bank. Use context clues to help you.

> Word Bank
>
> enthusiasm
> allotted
> insatiable
> reverberated

As I hid in the basement, without a prayer for survival, my hope never once subsided, and my craving for life remained (1) _____. This small space, which I had been (2) _____, apparently by fate, so unexpectedly brought forth wonderful feelings. My imagination raced. My heart and mind burst with (3) _____ for all that I had ever loved, both people and things. My inner voice was so loud that its sound (4) _____ inside my mind all during my confinement.

B. Reading Comprehension   Answer each question below.

1. Who is telling the story? _____

2. When is it safe for Miep and Henk to visit the Annex? _____

_____

_____

3. How do the people in the Annex receive news of the outside world?

_____

_____

4. At the end of the story, why does Miep find herself unable to sleep?

_____

_____

SKILLS FOCUS

Vocabulary Skills
Use context clues.

A Matter of Style

Modern Head by Roy Lichtenstein.
© Lee Snider/CORBIS.

Academic Vocabulary for Collection 5

These are the terms you should know
as you read and analyze the selections in this collection.

———

Style The way a writer uses language. Style results from **diction,** or word choice, as well as from sentence structure and tone.

Figures of Speech Imaginative comparisons between seemingly unlike things. Figures of speech are not meant to be understood as literally true. These are two common figures of speech:

- **Simile** A comparison between two unlike things, using a word such as *like, as, than,* or *resembles:* "My heart is like a singing bird."
- **Metaphor** A comparison in which two unlike things are said to be identical: "The road was a ribbon of moonlight."

Symbol A person, a place, a thing, or an event that has meaning in itself and that also stands for something beyond itself. A packet of flower seeds, for example, may symbolize hope for a better future.

Irony A contrast between expectation and reality. There are three common types of irony:

- **Verbal irony** Saying one thing but meaning the opposite. Calling a meek little kitten a "tiger," for example, is use of verbal irony.
- **Situational irony** What happens is the opposite of what we were led to expect.
- **Dramatic irony** When the audience or readers know something that a character does not know.

Imagery Language that appeals to the senses. Most images are visual, but images can appeal to the senses of hearing, touch, taste, and smell, or even to several senses at once.

Dialect A way of speaking that is characteristic of a geographical area or a certain group of people. Writers often use regional dialects to bring a character to life and to give a story a particular flavor.

Before You Read

This selection also appears in *Elements of Literature*.

The Tell-Tale Heart by Edgar Allan Poe

LITERARY FOCUS: NARRATOR

A **narrator** is a person who tells a story. A story's narrator may be a character in the story. Another type of narrator is outside the story and observes and reports on the action that takes place. We rely on a story's narrator to let us know what is going on. But what if the narrator can't be trusted? As you read "The Tell-Tale Heart," decide whether or not its narrator is truthful—or even sane.

IRONY: THE UNEXPECTED

Irony is a contrast between expectation and reality. Much of the horror in "The Tell-Tale Heart" comes from Poe's use of irony. Look for these three basic kinds of irony as you read the story:

- **Verbal irony**   What is said is the opposite of what is meant.
- **Situational irony**   What happens is different from or even opposite of what we expected.
- **Dramatic irony**   We know something a character doesn't know.

READING SKILLS: PREVIEWING

When you **preview** a selection, you look it over to see what lies ahead. You might scan the title and skim a paragraph or two to get an idea of the writer's subject and style. Preview Poe's story. What predictions can you make?

My Predictions

SKILLS FOCUS

Literary Skills
Understand narrator; understand irony.

Reading Skills
Preview the story.

Vocabulary Skills
Identify synonyms.

VOCABULARY DEVELOPMENT

PREVIEW SELECTION VOCABULARY

Become familiar with these words before you read "The Tell-Tale Heart."

acute (ə·kyo͞ot′) *adj.*: sharp.

> *His nervousness increased his acute sense of hearing.*

vexed (vekst) *v.*: disturbed.

> *He was vexed by the old man's eye.*

sagacity (sə·gas′ə·tē) *n.*: intelligence and good judgment.

> *He was proud of his powers and of his sagacity.*

refrained (ri·frānd′) *v.*: held back.

> *Though furious, he refrained from action.*

wary (wer′ē) *adj.*: cautious.

> *He was too wary to make a careless mistake.*

suavity (swäv′ə·tē) *n.*: smooth manner; smoothness.

> *The police showed perfect suavity.*

audacity (ô·das′ə·tē) *n.*: boldness.

> *He was impressed with his own audacity.*

vehemently (vē′ə·mənt·lē) *adv.*: forcefully.

> *He talked more vehemently, but he couldn't drown out the sound.*

gesticulations (jes·tik′yo͞o·lā′shənz) *n.*: energetic gestures.

> *His violent gesticulations did not disturb the police officers.*

derision (di·rizh′ən) *n.*: ridicule.

> *He hated the smiling derision of the police.*

CLARIFYING WORD MEANINGS: SYNONYMS

A **synonym** is a word that has the same or nearly the same meaning as another word. When you learn a new word, take note of its synonyms. Knowing its synonyms will help you remember the new word's meaning.

In the sentences below, a synonym is provided in parentheses for each boldface vocabulary word.

- "Above all was the sense of hearing **acute** (sharp)."
- "It was not the old man who **vexed** (annoyed) me, but his Evil Eye."
- "I had been too **wary** (cautious) for that."
- "I talked more quickly—more **vehemently** (forcefully); but the noise steadily increased."
- "Anything was more tolerable than this **derision** (ridicule)!"

THE TELL-TALE HEART

Edgar Allan Poe

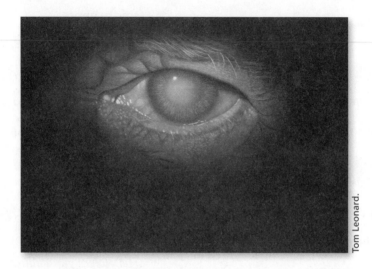

Tom Leonard.

True!—nervous—very, very dreadfully nervous I had been and am; but why *will* you say that I am mad? The disease had sharpened my senses—not destroyed—not dulled them. Above all was the sense of hearing **acute.** I heard all things in the heaven and in the earth. I heard many things in hell. How, then, am I mad? Hearken! and observe how healthily—how calmly I can tell you the whole story.

It is impossible to say how first the idea entered my brain; but once conceived, it haunted me day and night. 10 Object[1] there was none. Passion there was none. I loved the old man. He had never wronged me. He had never given me insult. For his gold I had no desire. I think it was his eye! Yes, it was this! One of his eyes resembled that of a

---

1. **object** (äb′jikt) *n.:* purpose or goal.

vulture—a pale blue eye, with a film over it. Whenever it fell upon me, my blood ran cold; and so by degrees—very gradually—I made up my mind to take the life of the old man and thus rid myself of the eye forever.

Now this is the point. You fancy me mad. Madmen know nothing. But you should have seen me. You should have seen how wisely I proceeded—with what caution—with what foresight—with what dissimulation² I went to work! I was never kinder to the old man than during the whole week before I killed him. And every night, about midnight, I turned the latch of his door and opened it—oh, so gently! And then, when I had made an opening sufficient for my head, I put in a dark lantern, all closed, closed, so that no light shone out, and then I thrust in my head. Oh, you would have laughed to see how cunningly I thrust it in! I moved it slowly—very, very slowly, so that I might not disturb the old man's sleep. It took me an hour to place my whole head within the opening so far that I could see him as he lay upon his bed. Ha! Would a madman have been so wise as this? And then, when my head was well in the room, I undid the lantern cautiously—oh, so cautiously—cautiously (for the hinges creaked)—I undid it just so much that a single thin ray fell upon the vulture eye. And this I did for seven long nights—every night just at midnight—but I found the eye always closed; and so it was impossible to do the work; for it was not the old man who **vexed** me, but his Evil Eye. And every morning, when the day broke, I went boldly into the chamber and spoke courageously to him, calling him by name in a hearty tone and inquiring how he had passed the night. So you see he would have been a very profound³ old man, indeed, to

---

2. **dissimulation** (di·sim′yoo·lā′shən) *n.:* disguising of intentions or feelings. (Look for a similar word at the end of the story.)
3. **profound** (prō·found′) *adj.:* deeply intellectual.

EVALUATE

In lines 18–33 the narrator claims to have several qualities that insane people *don't* have. Circle the qualities that he mentions. In your opinion, does having those qualities prove his sanity—or not?

_____

_____

_____

PREDICT

Pause at line 40. Do you think the narrator will kill the old man? Tell what you think will happen. Base your prediction on the details you already know.

_____

_____

_____

_____

_____

_____

_____

_____

_____

VOCABULARY

vexed (vekst) *v.:* disturbed; annoyed.

sagacity (sə·gas′ə·tē) *n.:* intelligence and good judgment.

Re-read lines 47–59. Why is it **ironic** that the old man feared robbers? (What should he have feared?)

_____

_____

_____

_____

_____

_____

_____

_____

Read the boxed passage at least twice to appreciate the author's unique **style**—the way he expresses himself. Notice the kinds of words and sentences he uses—long, short, simple, poetic, and so on. As you read aloud, change the pace of your reading to reflect the narrator's words. Decide which sentences you will read softly, perhaps even in a whisper. Pay special attention to Poe's use of *italic* type to show emphasis, and dashes to show abrupt changes in thought.

suspect that every night, just at twelve, I looked in upon him while he slept.

Upon the eighth night I was more than usually cautious in opening the door. A watch's minute hand moves more quickly than did mine. Never before that night had I *felt* the extent of my own powers—of my **sagacity.** I could scarcely contain my feelings of triumph. To think that there I was, opening the door, little by little, and he not even to dream of my secret deeds or thoughts. I fairly chuckled at the idea; and perhaps he heard me; for he moved on the bed suddenly, as if startled. Now you may think that I drew back—but no. His room was as black as pitch with the thick darkness (for the shutters were close fastened, through fear of robbers), and so I knew that he could not see the opening of the door, and I kept pushing it on steadily, steadily.

I had my head in, and was about to open the lantern, when my thumb slipped upon the tin fastening, and the old man sprang up in the bed, crying out—"Who's there?"

I kept quite still and said nothing. For a whole hour I did not move a muscle, and in the meantime I did not hear him lie down. He was still sitting up in the bed listening— just as I have done, night after night, hearkening to the deathwatches[4] in the wall.

Presently I heard a slight groan, and I knew it was the groan of mortal terror. It was not a groan of pain or of grief—oh, no!—it was the low, stifled sound that arises from the bottom of the soul when overcharged with awe. I knew the sound well. Many a night, just at midnight, when all the world slept, it has welled up from my own bosom, deepening, with its dreadful echo, the terrors that distracted me. I say I knew it well. I knew what the old man felt, and pitied him, although I chuckled at heart. I knew that he had

---

4. **deathwatches** *n.:* beetles that burrow into wood and make tapping sounds, which some people believe are a sign of approaching death.

been lying awake ever since the first slight noise, when he had turned in the bed. His fears had been ever since growing upon him. He had been trying to fancy them causeless but could not. He had been saying to himself—"It is nothing but the wind in the chimney—it is only a mouse crossing the floor," or "It is merely a cricket which has made a single chirp." Yes, he had been trying to comfort himself with these suppositions; but he had found all in vain. *All in vain;* because Death, in approaching him, had stalked with his black shadow before him and enveloped the victim. And it was the mournful influence of the unperceived shadow that caused him to feel—although he neither saw nor heard—to *feel* the presence of my head within the room.

When I had waited a long time, very patiently, without hearing him lie down, I resolved to open a little—a very, very little crevice in the lantern. So I opened it—you cannot imagine how stealthily, stealthily—until, at length, a single

Culver Pictures, Inc.

This illustration and the illustration on page 180 are from a short movie based on "The Tell-Tale Heart."

The Tell-Tale Heart **177**

_____

_____

_____

_____

_____

_____

INTERPRET

Pause at line 108. What do you think the narrator might be hearing when he thinks he hears the beating of the old man's heart?

_____

_____

_____

_____

_____

VOCABULARY

refrained (ri·frānd') *v.:* held back.

dim ray, like the thread of the spider, shot from out the crevice and full upon the vulture eye.

It was open—wide, wide open—and I grew furious as I gazed upon it. I saw it with perfect distinctness—all a dull blue, with a hideous veil over it that chilled the very marrow in my bones; but I could see nothing else of the old man's

100 face or person, for I had directed the ray, as if by instinct, precisely upon the damned spot.

And now have I not told you that what you mistake for madness is but overacuteness of the senses?—now, I say, there came to my ears a low, dull, quick sound, such as a watch makes when enveloped in cotton. I knew *that* sound well too. It was the beating of the old man's heart. It increased my fury, as the beating of a drum stimulates the soldier into courage.

But even yet I **refrained** and kept still. I scarcely

110 breathed. I held the lantern motionless. I tried how steadily I could maintain the ray upon the eye. Meantime the hellish tattoo[5] of the heart increased. It grew quicker and quicker and louder and louder every instant. The old man's *terror* must have been extreme! It grew louder, I say, louder every moment!—do you mark me well? I have told you that I am nervous: So I am. And now at the dead hour of the night, amid the dreadful silence of that old house, so strange a noise as this excited me to uncontrollable terror. Yet for some minutes longer I refrained and stood still. But the beating

120 grew louder, louder! I thought the heart must burst. And now a new anxiety seized me—the sound would be heard by a neighbor! The old man's hour had come! With a loud yell, I threw open the lantern and leaped into the room. He shrieked once—once only. In an instant I dragged him to the floor and pulled the heavy bed over him. I then smiled

---

5. **tattoo** *n.:* steady beat.

gaily to find the deed so far done. But, for many minutes, the heart beat on with a muffled sound. This, however, did not vex me; it would not be heard through the wall. At length it ceased. The old man was dead. I removed the bed
130 and examined the corpse. Yes, he was stone, stone dead. I placed my hand upon the heart and held it there many minutes. There was no pulsation. He was stone dead. His eye would trouble me no more.

If still you think me mad, you will think so no longer when I describe the wise precautions I took for the concealment of the body. The night waned,[6] and I worked hastily but in silence. First of all I dismembered the corpse. I cut off the head and the arms and the legs.

I then took up three planks from the flooring of the
140 chamber and deposited all between the scantlings.[7] I then replaced the boards so cleverly, so cunningly, that no human eye—not even *his*—could have detected anything wrong. There was nothing to wash out—no stain of any kind—no blood spot whatever. I had been too **wary** for that. A tub had caught all—ha! ha!

When I had made an end of these labors, it was four o'clock—still dark as midnight. As the bell sounded the hour, there came a knocking at the street door. I went down to open it with a light heart—for what had I *now* to fear?
150 There entered three men, who introduced themselves, with perfect **suavity,** as officers of the police. A shriek had been heard by a neighbor during the night; suspicion of foul play had been aroused; information had been lodged at the police office, and they (the officers) had been deputed[8] to search the premises.

___
6. **waned** (wānd) *v.:* gradually drew to a close.
7. **scantlings** *n.:* small beams of wood.
8. **deputed** (di·pyōōt′id) *v.:* appointed.

RETELL

Tell what happens on the eighth night (lines 47–133). Be sure to include the reason the narrator's behavior changes. Describe how he commits the murder.

_____

_____

_____

_____

_____

_____

_____

_____

INTERPRET

Pause at line 145. What's one example of something that the **narrator** has said—or done—or felt—that is evidence that he *is* mad?

_____

_____

_____

_____

VOCABULARY

wary (wer′ē) *adj.:* cautious.

suavity (swäv′ə·tē) *n.:* smoothness; politeness.

The Tell-Tale Heart **179**

Culver Pictures, Inc.

I smiled—for *what* had I to fear? I bade the gentlemen welcome. The shriek, I said, was my own in a dream. The old man, I mentioned, was absent in the country. I took my visitors all over the house. I bade them search—search *well*.
160   I led them, at length, to *his* chamber. I showed them his treasures, secure, undisturbed. In the enthusiasm of my confidence, I brought chairs into the room and desired them *here* to rest from their fatigues, while I myself, in the wild **audacity** of my perfect triumph, placed my own seat upon the very spot beneath which reposed the corpse of the victim.

The officers were satisfied. My *manner* had convinced them. I was singularly at ease. They sat, and while I answered cheerily, they chatted familiar things. But, ere long, I felt myself getting pale and wished them gone. My head ached,
170   and I fancied a ringing in my ears; but still they sat and still chatted. The ringing became more distinct—it continued and became more distinct: I talked more freely to get rid of

VOCABULARY

audacity (ô·das′ə·tē) *n.:* boldness.

the feeling: but it continued and gained definitiveness—until, at length, I found that the noise was *not* within my ears.

No doubt I now grew *very* pale—but I talked more fluently and with a heightened voice. Yet the sound increased—and what could I do? It was *a low, dull, quick sound—much such a sound as a watch makes when enveloped in cotton.* I gasped for breath—and yet the officers heard it not. I talked more quickly—more **vehemently;** but the noise steadily increased. I arose and argued about trifles, in a high key and with violent **gesticulations,** but the noise steadily increased. Why *would* they not be gone? I paced the floor to and fro with heavy strides, as if excited to fury by the observation of the men—but the noise steadily increased. Oh God! what *could* I do? I foamed—I raved—I swore! I swung the chair upon which I had been sitting and grated it upon the boards, but the noise arose over all and continually increased. It grew louder—louder—*louder!* And still the men chatted pleasantly, and smiled. Was it possible they heard not? Almighty God!—no, no! They heard!—they suspected!—they *knew!*—they were making a mockery of my horror!—this I thought, and this I think. But anything was better than this agony! Anything was more tolerable than this **derision!** I could bear those hypocritical smiles no longer! I felt that I must scream or die!—and now—again!—hark! louder! louder! louder! *louder!*—

"Villains!" I shrieked, "dissemble no more! I admit the deed!—tear up the planks!—here, here!—it is the beating of his hideous heart!"

INFER

What is happening to the narrator (lines 175–189)? What does he think he hears? What's your explanation for the sound he hears?

_____

_____

_____

_____

_____

INTERPRET

Poe once wrote that every word in a story should create a "single, overwhelming impression." In your opinion, what impression was he trying to create in this story?

_____

_____

_____

_____

VOCABULARY

vehemently (vē′ə·mənt·lē) *adv.:* forcefully; passionately.

gesticulations (jes·tik′yoo·lā′shənz) *n.:* energetic gestures.

derision (di·rizh′ən) *n.:* contempt; ridicule.

The Tell-Tale Heart

SKILLS FOCUS

Literary Skills
Analyze the narrator.

Narrator Evaluation Chart   The narrator of "The Tell-Tale Heart" claims that he is not mad. Do you agree? Fill out the graphic below by collecting evidence from the story. Focus on the narrator's thoughts, words, and actions. Then, write whether or not you think the narrator is a reliable source of information.

Narrator

Sane

Mad

I believe the narrator is _____

_____

_____

_____

_____

_____

Skills Review

The Tell-Tale Heart

VOCABULARY AND COMPREHENSION

A. Synonyms   Write the word from the Word Bank that best fits each group of synonyms.

Word Bank

acute
vexed
sagacity
refrained
wary
suavity
audacity
vehemently
gesticulations
derision

_____ 1. disturbed, annoyed, troubled

_____ 2. careful, cautious, leery

_____ 3. boldness, daring, brazenness

_____ 4. withheld, repressed, held back

_____ 5. forcefully, passionately, furiously

_____ 6. smoothness, politeness, fine manners

_____ 7. gestures, wild movements, spasms

_____ 8. scorn, ridicule, contempt

_____ 9. sharp, sensitive, severe

_____ 10. intelligence, smarts, good sense

B. Reading Comprehension   Answer each question below.

1. Why does the narrator decide to kill the old man? _____

_____

2. Why does the narrator think he is not mad? _____

_____

3. Who arrives at the narrator's door at night? Why have they come?

_____

_____

4. Why does the narrator finally confess to his crime? _____

_____

SKILLS FOCUS

Vocabulary Skills
Identify synonyms.

Before You Read

This selection also appears in *Elements of Literature*. ◆

Raymond's Run by Toni Cade Bambara

LITERARY FOCUS: ALLUSIONS

An **allusion** is a reference to a statement, a person, a place, or an event from literature, the arts, history, sports, TV, or the movies. When the narrator of "Raymond's Run" refers to herself as "Mercury," she expects you to know that in classical mythology, Mercury, the messenger of the gods, was known for being swift. Although allusions can enrich your reading experiences, they can become dated. Footnotes are provided with this selection to explain some of its allusions.

DIALECT

A **dialect** is a way of speaking that is characteristic of a certain geographical area or a certain group of people. Dialect can involve special pronunciation, vocabulary, and grammar. Everyone speaks a dialect of some kind. Writers use dialect to capture the voice of a particular person. When you read "Raymond's Run," you hear Squeaky's own true voice, in her regional dialect.

READING SKILLS: MAKING JUDGMENTS

You always make **judgments** as you read. You form opinions about the story's characters, plot, and style. You decide if the people and actions are believable. You may later revise your judgments when the story provides more information. Copy the headings below on a sheet of paper. As you read "Raymond's Run," make notes about the story's main characters. Note on the chart if and when your ideas about the characters change.

Characters	Judgments
Squeaky	
Raymond	
Gretchen	

SKILLS FOCUS

Literary Skills
Understand allusions and dialect.

Reading Skills
Make judgments.

Raymond's Run

Toni Cade Bambara

HRW Photo.

I don't have much work to do around the house like some
girls. My mother does that. And I don't have to earn my
pocket money by hustling; George runs errands for the big
boys and sells Christmas cards. And anything else that's got
to get done, my father does. All I have to do in life is mind
my brother Raymond, which is enough.

Sometimes I slip and say my little brother Raymond.
But as any fool can see he's much bigger and he's older too.
But a lot of people call him my little brother cause he needs
looking after cause he's not quite right. And a lot of smart
mouths got lots to say about that too, especially when George
was minding him. But now, if anybody has anything to say
to Raymond, anything to say about his big head, they have

10

IDENTIFY

Pause at line 6. What is the narrator's main responsibility in life? Underline the passage that tells you.

IDENTIFY

Read lines 7–20 carefully. Underline words and phrases that Squeaky uses that are **dialect.**

_____

_____

_____

_____

IDENTIFY

Who is telling you this story? Underline her name (lines 16–20).

_____

_____

_____

_____

_____

_____

_____

_____

IDENTIFY

Pause at line 38. Underline the reasons Squeaky thinks she's going to beat Gretchen this year.

_____

_____

_____

_____

_____

_____

_____

_____

_____

_____

to come by me. And I don't play the dozens[1] or believe in standing around with somebody in my face doing a lot of talking. I much rather just knock you down and take my chances even if I am a little girl with skinny arms and a squeaky voice, which is how I got the name Squeaky. And if things get too rough, I run. And as anybody can tell you,
20 I'm the fastest thing on two feet.

There is no track meet that I don't win the first-place medal. I used to win the twenty-yard dash when I was a little kid in kindergarten. Nowadays, it's the fifty-yard dash. And tomorrow I'm subject to run the quarter-meter relay all by myself and come in first, second, and third.

The big kids call me Mercury[2] cause I'm the swiftest thing in the neighborhood. Everybody knows that—except two people who know better, my father and me. He can beat me to Amsterdam Avenue with me having a two-fire-hydrant
30 headstart and him running with his hands in his pockets and whistling. But that's private information. Cause can you imagine some thirty-five-year-old man stuffing himself into PAL[3] shorts to race little kids? So as far as everyone's concerned, I'm the fastest and that goes for Gretchen, too, who has put out the tale that she is going to win the first-place medal this year. Ridiculous. In the second place, she's got short legs. In the third place, she's got freckles. In the first place, no one can beat me and that's all there is to it.

I'm standing on the corner admiring the weather and
40 about to take a stroll down Broadway so I can practice my breathing exercises, and I've got Raymond walking on the inside close to the buildings, cause he's subject to fits of fantasy and starts thinking he's a circus performer and that the curb is a tightrope strung high in the air. And some-

---

1. **play the dozens:** slang for "trade insults."
2. **Mercury:** in Roman mythology, messenger of the gods, known for his speediness.
3. **PAL:** Police Athletic League.

times after a rain he likes to step down off his tightrope right into the gutter and slosh around getting his shoes and cuffs wet. Then I get hit when I get home. Or sometimes if you don't watch him he'll dash across traffic to the island[4] in the middle of Broadway and give the pigeons a fit. Then I have to go behind him apologizing to all the old people sitting around trying to get some sun and getting all upset with the pigeons fluttering around them, scattering their newspapers and upsetting the waxpaper lunches in their laps. So I keep Raymond on the inside of me, and he plays like he's driving a stage coach which is OK by me so long as he doesn't run me over or interrupt my breathing exercises, which I have to do on account of I'm serious about my running, and I don't care who knows it.

Now some people like to act like things come easy to them, won't let on that they practice. Not me. I'll high-prance down 34th Street like a rodeo pony to keep my knees strong even if it does get my mother uptight so that she walks ahead like she's not with me, don't know me, is all by herself on a shopping trip, and I am somebody else's crazy child. Now you take Cynthia Procter for instance. She's just the opposite. If there's a test tomorrow, she'll say something like, "Oh, I guess I'll play handball this afternoon and watch television tonight," just to let you know she ain't thinking about the test. Or like last week when she won the spelling bee for the millionth time, "A good thing you got 'receive,' Squeaky, cause I would have got it wrong. I completely forgot about the spelling bee." And she'll clutch the lace on her blouse like it was a narrow escape. Oh, brother. But of course when I pass her house on my early morning trots around the block, she is practicing the scales on the piano over and over and over and over. Then in music class she always lets

Notes

FLUENCY

The boxed passage is written in **dialect**—in the "language" of a particular region. Read the passage aloud twice. See if you read more smoothly and naturally the second time you read.

---

4. **island** *n.*: traffic island, a car-free area in the middle of a street.

herself get bumped around so she falls accidentally on purpose onto the piano stool and is so surprised to find herself sitting there that she decides just for fun to try out the ole keys. And what do you know—Chopin's[5] waltzes just spring out of her fingertips and she's the most surprised thing in the world. A regular prodigy. I could kill people like that. I stay up all night studying the words for the spelling bee. And you can see me any time of day practicing running. I never walk if I can trot, and shame on Raymond if he can't keep up. But of course he does, cause if he hangs back someone's liable to walk up to him and get smart, or take his allowance from him, or ask him where he got that great big pumpkin head. People are so stupid sometimes.

So I'm strolling down Broadway breathing out and breathing in on counts of seven, which is my lucky number, and here comes Gretchen and her sidekicks: Mary Louise,

INFER

What **inference** can you make about Squeaky's character based on lines 59–89?

HRW Photo.

---

5. **Chopin's:** Frédéric François Chopin (shō′pan) (1810–1849), Polish composer and pianist.

who used to be a friend of mine when she first moved to Harlem from Baltimore and got beat up by everybody till I took up for her on account of her mother and my mother used to sing in the same choir when they were young girls, but people ain't grateful, so now she hangs out with the new girl Gretchen and talks about me like a dog; and Rosie, who is as fat as I am skinny and has a big mouth where Raymond is concerned and is too stupid to know that there is not a big deal of difference between herself and Raymond and that she can't afford to throw stones. So they are steady coming up Broadway and I see right away that it's going to be one of those Dodge City scenes[6] cause the street ain't that big and they're close to the buildings just as we are. First I think I'll step into the candy store and look over the new comics and let them pass. But that's chicken and I've got a reputation to consider. So then I think I'll just walk straight on through them or even over them if necessary. But as they get to me, they slow down. I'm ready to fight, cause like I said I don't feature a whole lot of chit-chat, I much prefer to just knock you down right from the jump and save everybody a lotta precious time.

"You signing up for the May Day races?" smiles Mary Louise, only it's not a smile at all. A dumb question like that doesn't deserve an answer. Besides, there's just me and Gretchen standing there really, so no use wasting my breath talking to shadows.

"I don't think you're going to win this time," says Rosie, trying to signify[7] with her hands on her hips all salty, completely forgetting that I have whupped her behind many times for less salt than that.

---

6. **Dodge City scenes:** showdowns like those in the television western *Gunsmoke,* which was set in Dodge City, Kansas. In a typical scene a marshal and an outlaw face off with pistols on an empty street.
7. **signify** *v.:* slang for "act boastful" or "insult someone."

MAKE A JUDGMENT
Underline Squeaky's ideas for settling her **conflict** with Gretchen and her friends (lines 106–113). Which of her ideas do you think is best?

_____

_____

_____

_____

_____

_____

_____

PREDICT
Pause at line 113. What do you think will happen when Squeaky and Raymond meet Gretchen and her friends?

_____

_____

_____

_____

_____

_____

_____

_____

_____

_____

_____

"I always win cause I'm the best," I say straight at Gretchen who is, as far as I'm concerned, the only one talking in this ventriloquist-dummy routine. Gretchen smiles, but it's not a smile, and I'm thinking that girls never really smile at each other because they don't know how and don't want to know how and there's probably no one to teach us how, cause grown-up girls don't know either. Then they all

130　look at Raymond who has just brought his mule team to a standstill. And they're about to see what trouble they can get into through him.

"What grade you in now, Raymond?"

"You got anything to say to my brother, you say it to me, Mary Louise Williams of Raggedy Town, Baltimore."

"What are you, his mother?" sasses Rosie.

"That's right, Fatso. And the next word out of anybody and I'll be *their* mother too." So they just stand there and Gretchen shifts from one leg to the other and so do they.

140　Then Gretchen puts her hands on her hips and is about to say something with her freckle-face self but doesn't. Then she walks around me looking me up and down but keeps walking up Broadway, and her sidekicks follow her. So me and Raymond smile at each other and he says, "Gidyap" to his team and I continue with my breathing exercises, strolling down Broadway toward the ice man on 145th with not a care in the world cause I am Miss Quicksilver[8] herself.

I take my time getting to the park on May Day because the track meet is the last thing on the program. The biggest

150　thing on the program is the May Pole dancing, which I can do without, thank you, even if my mother thinks it's a shame I don't take part and act like a girl for a change. You'd think my mother'd be grateful not to have to make me a white organdy dress with a big satin sash and buy me new white

INFER

Why doesn't Squeaky allow Raymond to answer Mary Louise's question (lines 134–135)?

---

8. **Quicksilver:** another name for mercury, a silver-colored liquid metal that flows rapidly.

baby-doll shoes that can't be taken out of the box till the big day. You'd think she'd be glad her daughter ain't out there prancing around a May Pole getting the new clothes all dirty and sweaty and trying to act like a fairy or a flower or whatever you're supposed to be when you should be try-
160   ing to be yourself, whatever that is, which is, as far as I am concerned, a poor black girl who really can't afford to buy shoes and a new dress you only wear once a lifetime cause it won't fit next year.

    I was once a strawberry in a Hansel and Gretel pageant when I was in nursery school and didn't have no better sense than to dance on tiptoe with my arms in a circle over my head doing umbrella steps and being a perfect fool just so my mother and father could come dressed up and clap. You'd think they'd know better than to encourage that kind of
170   nonsense. I am not a strawberry. I do not dance on my toes. I run. That is what I am all about. So I always come late to the May Day program, just in time to get my number pinned on and lay in the grass till they announce the fifty-yard dash.

    I put Raymond in the little swings, which is a tight squeeze this year and will be impossible next year. Then I look around for Mr. Pearson, who pins the numbers on. I'm really looking for Gretchen if you want to know the truth, but she's not around. The park is jam-packed. Parents in hats and corsages and breast-pocket handker-
180   chiefs peeking up. Kids in white dresses and light-blue suits. The parkees unfolding chairs and chasing the rowdy kids from Lenox[9] as if they had no right to be there. The big guys with their caps on backwards, leaning against the fence swirling the basketballs on the tips of their fingers, waiting for all these crazy people to clear out the park so they can play. Most of the kids in my class are carrying bass

---

9. **Lenox:** Lenox Avenue, a major street in Harlem (now called Malcolm X Boulevard).

INFER

What do Squeaky's feelings about May Pole dancing reveal about her (lines 148–163)?

INFER

Re-read Squeaky's description of the May Day crowd (lines 178–188). How do you think she feels about the people in the crowd?

In lines 192–193, Squeaky makes an **allusion** to "Jack and the Beanstalk." Underline the part of the text where you find out why she refers to Mr. Pearson by that name.

_____

_____

_____

_____

_____

_____

_____

MAKE A JUDGMENT

Why would Mr. Pearson suggest that Squeaky lose the race on purpose (lines 202–210)? Do you think his idea was a good one? Explain.

_____

_____

_____

_____

_____

_____

_____

_____

_____

drums and glockenspiels[10] and flutes. You'd think they'd put in a few bongos or something for real like that.

190 Then here comes Mr. Pearson with his clipboard and his cards and pencils and whistles and safety pins and fifty million other things he's always dropping all over the place with his clumsy self. He sticks out in a crowd because he's on stilts. We used to call him Jack and the Beanstalk to get him mad. But I'm the only one that can outrun him and get away, and I'm too grown for that silliness now.

"Well, Squeaky," he says, checking my name off the list and handing me number seven and two pins. And I'm thinking he's got no right to call me Squeaky, if I can't call him Beanstalk.

200 "Hazel Elizabeth Deborah Parker," I correct him and tell him to write it down on his board.

"Well, Hazel Elizabeth Deborah Parker, going to give someone else a break this year?" I squint at him real hard to see if he is seriously thinking I should lose the race on purpose just to give someone else a break. "Only six girls running this time," he continues, shaking his head sadly like it's my fault all of New York didn't turn out in sneakers. "That new girl should give you a run for your money." He looks around the park for Gretchen like a periscope in a submarine movie.

210 "Wouldn't it be a nice gesture if you were . . . to ahhh . . ."

I give him such a look he couldn't finish putting that idea into words. Grown-ups got a lot of nerve sometimes. I pin number seven to myself and stomp away, I'm so burnt. And I go straight for the track and stretch out on the grass while the band winds up with "Oh, the Monkey Wrapped His Tail Around the Flag Pole," which my teacher calls by some other name. The man on the loudspeaker is calling

---

10. **glockenspiels** (gläk'ən·spēlz') *n.:* musical instruments with flat metal bars that are struck with small hammers and produce bell-like sounds. Glockenspiels are often used in marching bands.

everyone over to the track and I'm on my back looking at the sky, trying to pretend I'm in the country, but I can't,

220 because even grass in the city feels hard as sidewalk, and there's just no pretending you are anywhere but in a "concrete jungle" as my grandfather says.

The twenty-yard dash takes all of two minutes cause most of the little kids don't know no better than to run off the track or run the wrong way or run smack into the fence and fall down and cry. One little kid, though, has got the good sense to run straight for the white ribbon up ahead so he wins. Then the second-graders line up for the thirty-yard dash and I don't even bother to turn my head to watch cause

230 Raphael Perez always wins. He wins before he even begins by psyching the runners, telling them they're going to trip on their shoelaces and fall on their faces or lose their shorts or something, which he doesn't really have to do since he is very fast, almost as fast as I am. After that is the forty-yard dash which I used to run when I was in first grade. Raymond is hollering from the swings cause he knows I'm about to do my thing cause the man on the loudspeaker has just announced the fifty-yard dash, although he might just as well be giving a recipe for angel food cake cause you can hardly

240 make out what he's sayin for the static. I get up and slip off my sweat pants and then I see Gretchen standing at the starting line, kicking her legs out like a pro. Then as I get into place I see that ole Raymond is on line on the other side of the fence, bending down with his fingers on the ground just like he knew what he was doing. I was going to yell at him but then I didn't. It burns up your energy to holler.

Every time, just before I take off in a race, I always feel like I'm in a dream, the kind of dream you have when you're sick with fever and feel all hot and weightless. I dream I'm

250 flying over a sandy beach in the early morning sun, kissing

INTERPRET

Underline Squeaky's observation of Gretchen as the race is about to begin (lines 240–242). Why is this detail significant?

_____

_____

_____

_____

_____

_____

_____

INFER

Why do you think Raymond is lining up along with the runners (lines 242–245)?

_____

_____

_____

_____

_____

_____

_____

_____

_____

HRW Photo.

PREDICT

Pause at line 270. Do you think Squeaky will win the race? Explain.

the leaves of the trees as I fly by. And there's always the smell of apples, just like in the country when I was little and used to think I was a choo-choo train, running through the fields of corn and chugging up the hill to the orchard. And all the time I'm dreaming this, I get lighter and lighter until I'm flying over the beach again, getting blown through the sky like a feather that weighs nothing at all. But once I spread my fingers in the dirt and crouch over the Get on Your Mark, the dream goes and I am solid again and am

260 telling myself, Squeaky you must win, you must win, you are the fastest thing in the world, you can even beat your father up Amsterdam if you really try. And then I feel my weight coming back just behind my knees then down to my feet then into the earth and the pistol shot explodes in my blood and I am off and weightless again, flying past the other runners, my arms pumping up and down and the whole world is quiet except for the crunch as I zoom over the gravel in the track. I glance to my left and there is no one. To the right, a blurred Gretchen, who's got her chin

270 jutting out as if it would win the race all by itself. And on the other side of the fence is Raymond with his arms down to his side and the palms tucked up behind him, running in his very own style, and it's the first time I ever saw that and

I almost stop to watch my brother Raymond on his first run. But the white ribbon is bouncing toward me and I tear past it, racing into the distance till my feet with a mind of their own start digging up footfuls of dirt and brake me short. Then all the kids standing on the side pile on me, banging me on the back and slapping my head with their May Day programs, for I have won again and everybody on 151st Street can walk tall for another year.

"In first place . . ." the man on the loudspeaker is clear as a bell now. But then he pauses and the loudspeaker starts to whine. Then static. And I lean down to catch my breath and here comes Gretchen walking back, for she's overshot the finish line too, huffing and puffing with her hands on her hips taking it slow, breathing in steady time like a real pro and I sort of like her a little for the first time. "In first place . . ." and then three or four voices get all mixed up on the loudspeaker and I dig my sneaker into the grass and stare at Gretchen who's staring back, we both wondering just who did win. I can hear old Beanstalk arguing with the man on the loudspeaker and then a few others running their mouths about what the stopwatches say. Then I hear Raymond yanking at the fence to call me and I wave to shush him, but he keeps rattling the fence like a gorilla in a cage like in them gorilla movies, but then like a dancer or something he starts climbing up nice and easy but very fast. And it occurs to me, watching how smoothly he climbs hand over hand and remembering how he looked running with his arms down to his side and with the wind pulling his mouth back and his teeth showing and all, it occurred to me that Raymond would make a very fine runner. Doesn't he always keep up with me on my trots? And he surely knows how to breathe in counts of seven cause he's always doing it at the dinner table, which drives my brother

280

290

300

INFER

Why has Squeaky decided she likes Gretchen "a little for the first time" (lines 287–288)?

IDENTIFY

What is Raymond doing when Squeaky realizes he could become a runner (lines 295–304)?

IDENTIFY

Pause at line 316. Underline two details from the previous paragraph that show Squeaky has changed.

COMPARE & CONTRAST

Pause at line 333. In what way are Squeaky's and Gretchen's smiles different from their earlier smiles (page 190, line 125)?

_____

_____

_____

_____

_____

_____

_____

INTERPRET

Why is this story titled "Raymond's Run" and *not* "Squeaky's Run"?

_____

_____

_____

_____

_____

_____

_____

George up the wall. And I'm smiling to beat the band cause if I've lost this race, or if me and Gretchen tied, or even if I've won, I can always retire as a runner and begin a whole new career as a coach with Raymond as my champion. After all, with a little more study I can beat Cynthia and her phony self at the spelling bee. And if I bugged my mother, I could get piano lessons and become a star. And I have a big rep[11] as the baddest thing around. And I've got a roomful of ribbons and medals and awards. But what has Raymond got to call his own?

So I stand there with my new plans, laughing out loud by this time as Raymond jumps down from the fence and runs over with his teeth showing and his arms down to the side, which no one before him has quite mastered as a running style. And by the time he comes over I'm jumping up and down so glad to see him—my brother Raymond, a great runner in the family tradition. But of course everyone thinks I'm jumping up and down because the men on the loudspeaker have finally gotten themselves together and compared notes and are announcing "In first place—Miss Hazel Elizabeth Deborah Parker." (Dig that.) "In second place—Miss Gretchen P. Lewis." And I look over at Gretchen wondering what the "P" stands for. And I smile. Cause she's good, no doubt about it. Maybe she'd like to help me coach Raymond; she obviously is serious about running, as any fool can see. And she nods to congratulate me and then she smiles. And I smile. We stand there with this big smile of respect between us. It's about as real a smile as girls can do for each other, considering we don't practice real smiling every day, you know, cause maybe we too busy being flowers or fairies or strawberries instead of something honest and worthy of respect . . . you know . . . like being people.

---

11. **rep** *n.:* slang for "reputation." People often create slang by clipping off parts of words.

Raymond's Run

Allusion Chart   An **allusion** is a reference to a person, a place, or a thing. Circle the allusion in each passage from "Raymond's Run." Then, explain what each allusion means.

SKILLS FOCUS

Literary Skills
Analyze allusions.

Allusion in "Raymond's Run"	What the Allusion Refers To
"The big kids call me Mercury cause I'm the swiftest thing in the neighborhood." (lines 26–27)	
"And what do you know—Chopin's waltzes just spring out of her fingertips. . . ." (lines 80–81)	
"I see right away that it's going to be one of those Dodge City scenes. . . ." (lines 103–104)	
"I was once a strawberry in a Hansel and Gretel pageant. . . ." (lines 164–165)	
"We used to call him Jack and the Beanstalk to get him mad." (lines 193–194)	

Skills Review

Raymond's Run

COMPREHENSION

Reading Comprehension   Answer each question below.

1. What qualities is Squeaky best known for? _____

_____

2. Why does Squeaky have to take care of her older brother? _____

_____

3. What does Squeaky do to prepare for the race? _____

_____

4. How is Squeaky different from Cynthia Procter? _____

_____

5. Why do the kids call Mr. Pearson "Jack and the Beanstalk"? _____

_____

6. How does Squeaky feel just before a race? _____

_____

7. What does Raymond do when Squeaky is about to run the race? _____

_____

8. What does Squeaky think of Gretchen following the race? _____

_____

9. Why does Squeaky want to be Raymond's track coach? _____

_____

10. Did your opinion of Squeaky change as you read the story? Tell why or why not.

_____

_____

A Dream Within a Dream by Edgar Allan Poe
Life by Naomi Long Madgett

LITERARY FOCUS: STYLE

The way a writer uses language is called **style.** Several elements create style: word choice, typical length of sentences, types of sentences, use or avoidance of figurative language and symbols, and so on. In the poems you're about to read, the writers' use of figurative language and symbols helps define their style.

Figurative language always suggests similarities between seemingly unrelated things, such as a person and a stick. The most common figures of speech are **similes** (which use the connecting words *like, as, than,* or *resembles*), **metaphors** (which use no connecting words), and **personification** (giving nonhuman things lifelike qualities).

> **Simile:** He was as tall and straight as a stick.
> **Metaphor:** He was a stick, unmoving and straight.
> **Personification:** The stick lay on the ground waiting to be picked up.

Symbols are people, places, or events that have meaning in themselves but that also stand for something beyond themselves. A robin, for example, has come to symbolize the arrival of spring.

READING SKILLS: READING POETRY FOR MEANING

When you read a story, do you pause at the end of each line? Of course not. The same is true of poetry. Instead of coming to a stop at the end of a line, see if the sense of the line carries over to the next line:

> And I hold within my hand
> Grains of the golden sand—

You would not come to a full stop after the word *hand* because the sense of the line is not a complete thought. Punctuation often lets you know where to make a brief or a full pause. If there is no punctuation in a poem, re-read the lines of poetry until its units of meaning become clear.

SKILLS FOCUS

Literary Skills
Understand a writer's style.

Reading Skills
Practice reading poetry.

A Dream Within a Dream

Edgar Allan Poe

IDENTIFY

What is the poem's **speaker** doing in lines 1 and 2?

_____

_____

_____

Take this kiss upon the brow!
And, in parting from you now,
Thus much let me avow—
You are not wrong, who deem
5   That my days have been a dream;
Yet if hope has flown away
In a night, or in a day,
In a vision, or in none,
Is it therefore the less *gone?*
10   *All* that we see or seem
Is but a dream within a dream.

INTERPRET

What might the **speaker** be referring to when he says "my days" (line 5)?

_____

_____

_____

I stand amid the roar
Of a surf-tormented shore,
And I hold within my hand
15   Grains of the golden sand—
How few! yet how they creep
Through my fingers to the deep,
While I weep—while I weep!
O God! can I not grasp
20   Them with a tighter clasp?
O God! can I not save
One from the pitiless wave?
Is *all* that we see or seem
But a dream within a dream?

INTERPRET

What might the grains of sand **symbolize** (line 15)?

_____

_____

_____

IDENTIFY

Re-read "A Dream Within a Dream." Circle words that rhyme, underline repetition, and put a star next to examples of **metaphor, personification,** and **symbol.**

Life

Naomi Long Madgett

© Royalty-Free/CORBIS.

Life is but a toy that swings on a bright gold chain

Ticking for a little while

To amuse a fascinated infant,

Until the keeper, a very old man,

5   Becomes tired of the game

And lets the watch run down.

IDENTIFY

To what is life compared in "Life"? Circle your answer.

INTERPRET

Who is the keeper? What might the "game" be (lines 4–5)?

_____

_____

_____

_____

_____

FLUENCY

Read aloud "A Dream Within a Dream." Then, read aloud "Life." In which poem is sound more important? Why?

_____

_____

_____

_____

_____

_____

ANALYZE

Re-read "Life," circling passages you find particularly effective. Then, underline the **figures of speech** and put a star next to any **symbols** the poet uses.

A Dream Within a Dream / Life

SKILLS FOCUS

Literary Skills
Analyze a
writer's style.

Style Chart   A writer's style, or certain way of using language, is often created by his or her use of figurative language and symbols. Find examples of **similes, metaphors, personification,** and **symbols** in "A Dream Within a Dream" and "Life," and write them in the chart below.

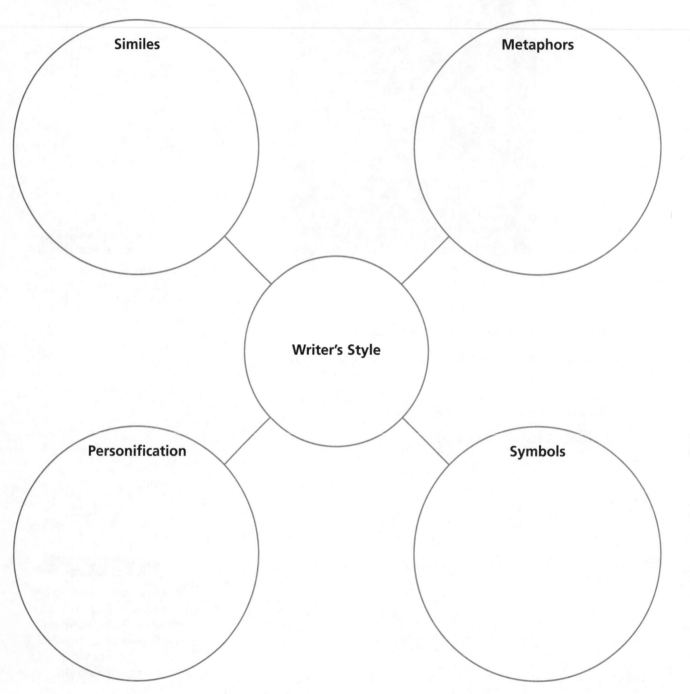

Similes

Metaphors

Writer's Style

Personification

Symbols

Skills Review

A Dream Within a Dream / Life

COMPREHENSION

Reading Comprehension Answer each question below. Circle the letter of the correct answer.

1. Which of the following statements best explains the situation in "A Dream Within a Dream"?

   a. A young child wakes from a dream.

   b. The speaker has just arrived by boat.

   c. The speaker is saying good-bye to a beloved person.

   d. The speaker regrets the end of a seaside vacation.

2. Which statement about "A Dream Within a Dream" is *not* accurate?

   f. Each stanza consists of eleven lines.

   g. Poe uses rhyme throughout the poem.

   h. Poe uses repetition in the last two lines of both stanzas.

   j. Words that rhyme with *dream* occur in lines 4, 10, and 23.

3. In "A Dream Within a Dream," what might the grains of sand symbolize?

   a. the ocean waves

   b. a vision of hope

   c. the passing days

   d. tiny crystals

4. Which of the following statements about "Life" is accurate?

   f. The poem is sad and dark.

   g. The poem compares life to a toy watch.

   h. The poem depends on repetition and rhyme.

   j. The poem contains dialogue.

Poetry:
Sound and Sense

Woman Playing a Mandolin by Pablo Picasso.
© Alexander Burkatowski/CORBIS.

Academic Vocabulary for Collection 6

These are the terms you should know
as you read and analyze the poems in this collection.

———————

ELEMENTS OF POETRY

Rhythm A musical quality produced by the repetition of stressed and unstressed syllables or by the repetition of other sound patterns.

Meter A regular pattern of stressed and unstressed syllables. The symbol ′ indicates a stressed syllable. The symbol ◡ indicates an unstressed syllable.

Rhyme The repetition of accented sounds in words that are close together in a poem. There are many kinds of rhymes:

- **End Rhyme** Rhymes appearing at the ends of lines. Example: "Listen, my children, and you shall *hear* / Of the midnight ride of Paul *Revere.*"
- **Internal Rhyme** Rhymes occurring within lines. Example: "Back into the chamber *turning,* all my soul within me *burning . . .*"

Rhyme Scheme The pattern of rhyme used in a poem. Rhyme schemes can be described using a series of letters. An eight-line poem in which the last words of the first two lines rhyme, the last words of the next two lines rhyme, and so on, would be labeled *aabbccdd.*

Alliteration The repetition of consonant sounds in words that are close together. Example: "The sun was shining on the sea."

Onomatopoeia The use of words whose sounds imitate or suggest their meaning. Examples include *screech* and *bang.*

TYPES OF POEMS

- **Ballad** A song or poem that tells a story, usually in short stanzas and simple language.
- **Narrative Poem** A poem that tells a story.
- **Lyric Poem** A poem that expresses the feelings or thoughts of a speaker.
- **Free Verse** Poetry without a regular meter or rhyme scheme.

This selection also appears in *Elements of Literature.*

Valentine for Ernest Mann

by Naomi Shihab Nye

LITERARY FOCUS: LYRIC POETRY

Poems that express thoughts and feelings are called **lyric poems.** Lyric poems are usually short and deal with a single, strong emotion. The word *lyric* comes from the word *lyre* (līr). A lyre is a stringed instrument, similar to a small harp. In ancient Greece, people used to recite poems while accompanying themselves on the lyre. As you read "Valentine for Ernest Mann," imagine the kind of instrument or music that might accompany it.

READING SKILLS: READING A POEM

To read poetry well, use these strategies:

- **Be aware of punctuation.** Don't stop reading at the end of a line of poetry unless you see punctuation there. Pause briefly for a comma, colon, semicolon, or dash, but don't make a full stop until you come to a period. If a poem doesn't contain any punctuation, read in thought units, pausing where the sense of the line indicates a stop.
- **Let the rhythm come through.** Avoid reading poems in a singsong way. Instead, read in a normal voice, as if you were speaking to a friend. The rhythm of the poem will emerge naturally.
- **Look for figures of speech.** Look for **metaphors** and **similes.** What comparisons do they reveal?
- **Find the subject and verb.** If a passage in a poem is not clear, look for the subject and verb. If word order has been inverted, rephrase the lines in natural word order. Decide how the other words are related to the subject and verb.
- **Read it again.** Almost no one "gets" a poem at the first reading. Re-read it until its meaning becomes clear.
- **Have fun.** Poets play with words, sounds, rhythm, and rhymes. As you interpret a poem, you are playing a game with the poet.
- **Listen to the poem.** Read the poem aloud. The speaker's voice adds meaning to a poem.

SKILLS FOCUS

Literary Skills
Understand the characteristics of lyric poetry.

Reading Skills
Use specific strategies to read a poem.

Valentine for Ernest Mann

Naomi Shihab Nye

You can't order a poem like you order a taco.
Walk up to the counter, say, "I'll take two"
and expect it to be handed back to you
on a shiny plate.

5   Still, I like your spirit.
Anyone who says, "Here's my address,
write me a poem," deserves something in reply.
So I'll tell a secret instead:
poems hide. In the bottoms of our shoes,
10   they are sleeping. They are the shadows
drifting across our ceilings the moment
before we wake up. What we have to do
is live in a way that lets us find them.

Once I knew a man who gave his wife
15   two skunks for a valentine.
He couldn't understand why she was crying.
"I thought they had such beautiful eyes."
And he was serious. He was a serious man
who lived in a serious way. Nothing was ugly
20   just because the world said so. He really
liked those skunks. So, he re-invented them
as valentines and they became beautiful.
At least, to him. And the poems that had been hiding
in the eyes of skunks for centuries
25   crawled out and curled up at his feet.

Maybe if we re-invent whatever our lives give us
we find poems. Check your garage, the odd sock
in your drawer, the person you almost like, but not quite.
And let me know.

INFER

Re-read lines 1–7. Who is the speaker talking to?

_____

_____

IDENTIFY

Lines 8–13 contain **personification;** they describe poems as if they were human. Underline what the speaker says poems do.

FLUENCY

Read lines 14-25 aloud, as if you were telling a story. Use your voice to express the meaning of the lines.

INFER

Lyric poetry captures a thought or an emotion. Re-read lines 26–29. What idea is the speaker trying to convey?

_____

_____

_____

INTERPRET

What does the "valentine" of the title refer to?

_____

"Valentine for Ernest Mann" from *Red Suitcase* by Naomi Shihab Nye. Copyright © 1994 by Naomi Shihab Nye. Reproduced by permission of **Bog Editions, Ltd.**

Valentine for Ernest Mann

SKILLS FOCUS

Literary Skills
Analyze a
lyric poem.

"Most Important Word" Chart   Lyric poems usually convey a single, strong emotion or thought. One way to identify that emotion or thought is to find the poem's most important word. Look for the most important word in "Valentine for Ernest Mann." Write the word in the space provided below. List the reasons you have chosen the word. At the bottom of the chart, describe the strong emotion or main thought that the poem conveys.

Most Important Word
Line(s) where the word appears:
Reasons for my choice:
Strong emotion or thought conveyed in the poem:

Skills Review

Valentine for Ernest Mann

COMPREHENSION

Reading Comprehension   Answer each question below.

1. Why is the speaker writing to Ernest Mann?

_____

_____

_____

2. What is the "secret" the speaker reveals?

_____

_____

_____

3. According to lines 9–12, what can poems do?

_____

_____

_____

4. Why did the man give his wife two skunks for a valentine?

_____

_____

_____

5. What does the poet mean by "re-inventing whatever our lives give us"?

_____

_____

_____

Before You Read

This selection also appears in *Elements of Literature*. ◆

Paul Revere's Ride

by Henry Wadsworth Longfellow

LITERARY FOCUS: NARRATIVE POEM

A **narrative poem** is a poem that tells a story. Like stories, narrative poems have characters, settings, conflict, and sometimes even dialogue. **Ballads** and **epics** are types of narrative poetry. The poem you're about to read tells a story about Paul Revere.

GALLOPING RHYTHM

Many poems, including narrative poems, contain special elements, such as rhythm, that create musical effects. **Rhythm** is the musical quality produced by the repetition of stressed and unstressed syllables. When the sounds occur in a regular pattern, we call it **meter.** The meter in "Paul Revere's Ride" sounds like a galloping horse: da da DUM da da DUM da da DUM da da DUM. Read on, and you'll see why so many people find this poem's rhythm memorable and exciting.

READING SKILLS: READING ALOUD

When you read a work aloud, you come to appreciate it more. Reading aloud is especially useful when you're reading a poem that has a specific rhythmic structure. The rhythm of your voice adds to the meaning of the words. As you read "Paul Revere's Ride," pause every so often to read it aloud and appreciate the writer's use of **galloping rhythm.**

Literary Skills
Understand the characteristics of narrative poetry; understand rhythm and meter.

Reading Skills
Use specific strategies to read a poem.

Paul Revere's Ride

Henry Wadsworth Longfellow

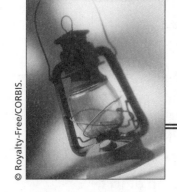

© Royalty-Free/CORBIS.

BACKGROUND: Literature and Social Studies

This poem is based loosely on historical events. On the night of April 18, 1775, Paul Revere, William Dawes, and Dr. Samuel Prescott set out from Boston to warn American colonists of a planned British raid on Concord, Massachusetts. The British wanted to arrest two Americans who were calling for armed resistance to England. The British also wanted to destroy a supply of arms in Concord. The next day armed volunteers known as minutemen confronted the British at Lexington and Concord. These were the first battles of the American Revolution.

Listen, my children, and you shall hear
Of the midnight ride of Paul Revere,
On the eighteenth of April, in Seventy-five;
Hardly a man is now alive
5   Who remembers that famous day and year.

He said to his friend, "If the British march
By land or sea from the town tonight,
Hang a lantern aloft in the belfry[1] arch
Of the North Church tower as a signal light—
10 One, if by land, and two, if by sea;
And I on the opposite shore will be,

CLARIFY

Read lines 6–14 carefully. Then, explain in your own words the system of signals that Revere arranges with his friend and the action he plans to take.

_____

_____

_____

_____

_____

_____

_____

_____

---

1. **belfry** (bel'frē) *n.* used as *adj.:* steeple of a church where bells are hung.

IDENTIFY

Circle details in lines 19–23 that describe the Somerset in a scary way.

INFER

Re-read lines 15–23. Explain why it takes bravery for Revere to row to Charlestown. What could happen to him?

Ready to ride and spread the alarm

Through every Middlesex village and farm,

For the country folk to be up and to arm."

15 Then he said, "Good night!" and with muffled oar

Silently rowed to the Charlestown shore,

Just as the moon rose over the bay,

Where swinging wide at her moorings² lay

The Somerset, British man-of-war;

20 A phantom ship, with each mast and spar³

Across the moon like a prison bar,

And a huge black hulk, that was magnified

By its own reflection in the tide.

Meanwhile, his friend, through alley and street,

25 Wanders and watches with eager ears,

Till in the silence around him he hears

The muster⁴ of men at the barrack door,

The sound of arms, and the tramp of feet,

And the measured tread of the grenadiers,⁵

30 Marching down to their boats on the shore.

Then he climbed the tower of the Old North Church,

By the wooden stairs, with stealthy tread,

To the belfry chamber overhead,

And startled the pigeons from their perch

35 On the somber rafters, that round him made

Masses and moving shapes of shade—

By the trembling ladder, steep and tall,

To the highest window in the wall,

IDENTIFY

Alliteration is the repetition of consonant sounds in words that are close together. Underline examples of alliteration in lines 31–41.

2. **moorings** *n.:* cables holding a ship in place so that it doesn't float away.
3. **mast and spar:** poles supporting a ship's sails.
4. **muster** *n.:* assembly; gathering.
5. **grenadiers** (gren'ə·dirz') *n.:* foot soldiers who carry and throw grenades.

Where he paused to listen and look down

40 A moment on the roofs of the town,

And the moonlight flowing over all.

Beneath, in the churchyard, lay the dead,

In their night encampment on the hill,

Wrapped in silence so deep and still

45 That he could hear, like a sentinel's[6] tread,

The watchful night wind, as it went

Creeping along from tent to tent,

And seeming to whisper, "All is well!"

A moment only he feels the spell

50 Of the place and the hour, and the secret dread

Of the lonely belfry and the dead;

For suddenly all his thoughts are bent

On a shadowy something far away,

Where the river widens to meet the bay—

55 A line of black that bends and floats

On the rising tide, like a bridge of boats.

Meanwhile, impatient to mount and ride,

Booted and spurred, with a heavy stride

On the opposite shore walked Paul Revere.

60 Now he patted his horse's side,

Now gazed at the landscape far and near,

Then, impetuous,[7] stamped the earth,

And turned and tightened his saddle girth;

But mostly he watched with eager search

65 The belfry tower of the Old North Church,

As it rose above the graves on the hill,

---

6. **sentinel's:** guard's.
7. **impetuous** (im·pech'o͞o·əs) *adj.:* impulsive; eager.

The speaker uses a **metaphor,** a comparison without using *like* or *as,* to compare the graveyard to a military camp (line 43). Another metaphor compares the gravestones to soldiers' tents (line 47). Circle the **simile,** the comparison that does use *like* or *as,* in lines 45–48. What is the wind compared to?

_____

_____

_____

_____

INFER

What is the "shadowy something" (line 53) that Revere's friend sees from his lookout?

_____

_____

_____

_____

PREDICT

Pause at line 56. What do you think Revere's friend will do next? (Remember the plan!)

_____

_____

_____

_____

IDENTIFY

What do the two lamps (line 72) in the church belfry signify? How will the British be coming?

_____

_____

_____

_____

_____

_____

_____

_____

Lonely and spectral[8] and somber and still.

And lo! as he looks, on the belfry's height

A glimmer, and then a gleam of light!

70   He springs to the saddle, the bridle he turns,

But lingers and gazes, till full on his sight

A second lamp in the belfry burns!

A hurry of hoofs in a village street,

A shape in the moonlight, a bulk in the dark,

75   And beneath, from the pebbles, in passing, a spark

Struck out by a steed flying fearless and fleet:

That was all! And yet, through the gloom and the light,

The fate of a nation was riding that night;

And the spark struck out by that steed, in his flight,

80   Kindled the land into flame with its heat.

He has left the village and mounted the steep,

And beneath him, tranquil and broad and deep,

Is the Mystic, meeting the ocean tides;

And under the alders[9] that skirt its edge,

85   Now soft on the sand, now loud on the ledge,

Is heard the tramp of his steed as he rides.

FLUENCY

Read the boxed passage aloud. Then, read it aloud a second time. Try to capture the **rhythm** of galloping hooves. Notice how the **alliteration,** with its repeated consonant sounds, suggests the sound of hooves striking the ground.

It was twelve by the village clock,

When he crossed the bridge into Medford town.

He heard the crowing of the cock,

90   And the barking of the farmer's dog,

And felt the damp of the river fog,

That rises after the sun goes down.

IDENTIFY

In lines 81–92, circle one **image** that appeals to each of the following senses: sight, hearing, and touch. Draw an arrow from each circled image, and write the sense the image appeals to.

---

8. spectral _adj._: ghostly.

9. alders (ôl′dərz) _n._: shrubs and trees of the birch family.

It was one by the village clock,

When he galloped into Lexington.

95 He saw the gilded weathercock[10]

Swim in the moonlight as he passed,

And the meetinghouse windows, blank and bare,

Gaze at him with a spectral glare,

As if they already stood aghast[11]

100 At the bloody work they would look upon.

It was two by the village clock,

When he came to the bridge in Concord town.

He heard the bleating of the flock,

And the twitter of birds among the trees,

105 And felt the breath of the morning breeze

Blowing over the meadows brown.

And one was safe and asleep in his bed

Who at the bridge would be first to fall,

Who that day would be lying dead,

110 Pierced by a British musket ball.

You know the rest. In the books you have read,

How the British Regulars fired and fled—

How the farmers gave them ball for ball,

From behind each fence and farmyard wall,

115 Chasing the redcoats down the lane,

Then crossing the fields to emerge again

Under the trees at the turn of the road,

And only pausing to fire and load.

---

10. **weathercock** *n.:* weathervane made to look like a rooster (cock).
   Weathervanes indicate the direction in which the wind is blowing.
11. **aghast** (ə·gast′) *adj.:* shocked; horrified.

INFER

What "bloody work" would the windows look upon (lines 97–100)?

_____

_____

_____

_____

_____

_____

_____

PARAPHRASE

In your own words, describe the events of the battle that the speaker tells of in lines 111–118.

_____

_____

_____

_____

_____

_____

_____

_____

_____

_____

_____

_____

_____

_____

Based on the details in this poem, do you agree that Paul Revere was a true hero? Tell why or why not.

_____

_____

_____

_____

_____

_____

_____

_____

_____

_____

_____

So through the night rode Paul Revere;

120 And so through the night went his cry of alarm

To every Middlesex village and farm—

A cry of defiance and not of fear,

A voice in the darkness, a knock at the door,

And a word that shall echo forevermore!

125 For, borne on the night wind of the Past,

Through all our history, to the last,

In the hour of darkness and peril and need,

The people will waken and listen to hear

The hurrying hoofbeats of that steed,

130 And the midnight message of Paul Revere.

Paul Revere's Ride

Story Map   Like other stories, narrative poems have a **plot,** a series of related events. A story map shows how one plot element leads to another. Fill in the story map for "Paul Revere's Ride" below. Add events to the map if you need to.

Literary Skills
Analyze a
narrative poem.

Characters	Setting (if important)	Problem or Conflict

Event 1

↓

Event 2

↓

Event 3

↓

Climax

↓

Resolution

Skills Review

Paul Revere's Ride

COMPREHENSION

Reading Comprehension   Answer the questions below.

1. Who was responsible for putting the lights in the belfry?

2. What did the two lights in the church belfry signify?

3. Where does Paul Revere ride after he sees the two lights in the belfry? What does he intend to do?

4. The poet says "the fate of the nation" was riding that night. Explain what he meant.

5. Who won the battle that night, the British or the citizens of Middlesex? Explain.

POEMS

Lincoln Monument: Washington
by Langston Hughes

Mr. Longfellow and His Boy
by Carl Sandburg

LITERARY FOCUS: LYRIC POETRY AND NARRATIVE POETRY

A **lyric poem** is usually short and conveys a single, strong emotion or idea. A **narrative poem** is usually longer than a lyric poem. It tells a story, a series of related events. Like a story, it has characters, setting, a plot, and sometimes dialogue.

"Lincoln Monument: Washington" is a lyric poem. As you read it, look for the single idea or emotion the poet is expressing. Then, read the narrative poem "Mr. Longfellow and His Boy" to learn of a series of events that span decades.

READING SKILLS: FINDING UNITS OF MEANING (STANZAS)

A **stanza** is a group of lines that forms a single unit of a poem. A stanza is like a paragraph in prose: It often expresses a unit of thought. Some stanzas have a fixed number of lines and a regular rhyme scheme. Other stanzas, such as those used in free verse, may vary in length.

As you read the poems that follow, pay close attention to stanza breaks. Ask yourself: "What thought or idea is conveyed in each stanza?"

SKILLS FOCUS

Literary Skills
Understand the characteristics of lyric poetry and narrative poetry.

Reading Skills
Use specific strategies to read a poem.

Lincoln Monument: Washington

Langston Hughes

> **BACKGROUND: Literature and Social Studies**
> Here is what you need to know before reading the poems:
> - Langston Hughes wrote "Lincoln Monument: Washington" in 1927. The Lincoln Monument was dedicated in 1927.
> - Carl Sandburg wrote "Mr. Longfellow and His Boy" in 1941, during World War II, when Franklin Delano Roosevelt was president of the United States and Winston Churchill was prime minister of England.
> - The poem that Sandburg quotes was written by Henry Wadsworth Longfellow in 1849. Abraham Lincoln became president of the United States in 1861.

IDENTIFY

Alliteration is the repetition of consonant sounds in words close together. Circle letters in lines 1–5 that create alliteration. What effect does the use of alliteration create?

_____

_____

INTERPRET

Abraham Lincoln died in 1865. How, then, would you explain lines 4–5?

_____

_____

_____

Let's go see old Abe
Sitting in the marble and the moonlight,
Sitting lonely in the marble and the moonlight,
Quiet for ten thousand centuries, old Abe.
5 Quiet for a million, million years.

Quiet—

And yet a voice forever
Against the
Timeless walls
10 Of time—
Old Abe.

Mr. Longfellow and His Boy

An old-fashioned recitation to be read aloud

Carl Sandburg

Mr. Longfellow, Henry Wadsworth Longfellow,
    the Harvard professor,
    the poet whose pieces you see in all the schoolbooks,
"Tell me not in mournful numbers
5   life is but an empty dream . . ."
Mr. Longfellow sits in his Boston library writing,
Mr. Longfellow looks across the room
    and sees his nineteen-year-old boy
propped up in a chair at a window,
10 home from the war,
a rifle ball through right and left shoulders.

In his diary the father writes about his boy:
    "He has a wound through him a foot long.
    He pretends it does not hurt him."
15 And the father if he had known
would have told the boy propped up in a chair
how one of the poems written in that room
    made President Lincoln cry.
And both the father and the boy
20 would have smiled to each other and felt good
about why the President had tears over that poem.

Noah Brooks, the California newspaperman,
could have told the Longfellows how one day
Brooks heard the President saying two lines:

DRAW CONCLUSIONS

Longfellow was born in 1807 and died in 1882. What war would his son (see lines 8–11) have been wounded in?

_____

_____

_____

INFER

Why would Longfellow and his son have "felt good" that Longfellow's poem "made President Lincoln cry" (lines 15–21)?

_____

_____

_____

_____

_____

_____

_____

WORD STUDY

Re-read lines 25–26. These lines of the poem that made Lincoln cry use the **metaphor** of a sailing ship. What is compared to a sailing ship?

_____

_____

_____

_____

_____

INFER

Lines 28–49 of Sandburg's poem quote Longfellow's poem (which is titled "The Building of the Ship"). Sandburg wrote this poem during the early years of World War II. Why do you think he includes these lines by Longfellow here?

_____

_____

_____

_____

_____

_____

_____

_____

_____

_____

25   "Thou, too, sail on, O Ship of State!

        Sail on, O Union, strong and great!"

Noah Brooks, remembering more of the poem, speaks:

        "Thou, too, sail on, O Ship of State!

        Sail on, O Union, strong and great!

30   Humanity with all its fears,

        With all the hopes of future years,

        Is hanging breathless on thy fate!

        We know what Master laid thy keel,

        What workmen wrought thy ribs of steel,

35   Who made each mast, and sail, and rope,

        What anvils rang, what hammers beat,

        In what a forge and what a heat

        Were shaped the anchors of thy hope!

        Fear not each sudden sound and shock,

40   'Tis of the wave and not the rock;

        'Tis but the flapping of the sail,

        And not a rent made by the gale!

        In spite of rock and tempest's roar,

        In spite of false lights on the shore,

45   Sail on, nor fear to breast the sea!

        Our hearts, our hopes, are all with thee,

        Our hearts, our hopes, our prayers, our tears,

        Our faith triumphant o'er our fears,

        Are all with thee—are all with thee!"

50   Noah Brooks sees Lincoln's eyes filled with tears,

        the cheeks wet.

They sit quiet a little while, then Lincoln saying:

"It is a wonderful gift to be able to stir men like that."

Mr. Longfellow—and his boy sitting propped up in a

        chair—

55 with a bullet wound a foot long in his shoulders—
    would have liked to hear President Lincoln saying
        those words.

    Now Mr. Longfellow is gone far away, his boy, too,
        gone far away,
60 and they never dreamed how seventy-eight years later
    the living President of the United States, in the White
        House at Washington,
    takes a pen, writes with his own hand on a sheet of paper
    about the Union Ship of State sailing on and on—
        never going down—
65 how the President hands that sheet of paper
    to a citizen soon riding high in the air, high over salt water,
    high in the rain and the sun and the mist over
        the Atlantic Ocean,
    riding, pounding, flying, everything under control,
70 crossing the deep, wide Atlantic in a day and a night,
    coming to London on the Thames in England,
    standing before the First Minister of the United Kingdom
    so the whole English-language world
    from England across North America to Australia and
75   New Zealand
    can never forget Mr. Longfellow's lines:
        "Thou, too, sail on, O Ship of State!
        Sail on, O Union, strong and great!"
                    [*Collier's*, June 14, 1941]

INTERPRET

The date at the bottom of the poem tells us that the poem was published in 1941, when Franklin Delano Roosevelt was president. Where have Longfellow and his boy "gone" (lines 58–59)?

_____

_____

_____

_____

_____

INFER

The paper (line 65) President Roosevelt sent to London was a commitment by the United States to aid England in World War II. Why do you think Roosevelt wanted England to remember Longfellow's lines?

_____

_____

_____

_____

_____

_____

FLUENCY

Sandburg noted that this poem is meant to be read aloud. Do so, reading once aloud for practice and once to someone else, for fun.

Lincoln Monument: Washington /
Mr. Longfellow and His Boy

SKILLS FOCUS

Literary Skills
Analyze lyric
and narrative
poetry.

Stanzas Chart   In many poems, **stanzas**—groupings of lines—function as paragraphs in prose do: They deliver units of meaning. Analyze the stanzas in "Lincoln Monument: Washington" and "Mr. Longfellow and His Boy" by filling in the chart below.

"Lincoln Monument: Washington"	"Mr. Longfellow and His Boy"
Stanza 1	Stanza 1
	Stanza 2
Stanza 2	Stanza 3
	Stanza 4
Stanza 3	Stanza 5

Lincoln Monument: Washington/
Mr. Longfellow and His Boy

COMPREHENSION

Reading Comprehension   Answer each question below.

1. In "Lincoln Monument: Washington," lines 2 and 3 are almost the same. What word has been added in line 3? Why might the poet have added that word?

_____

_____

2. Why do you think the poet exaggerates how many years have passed in 4–5?

_____

_____

3. How can a marble monument be a "voice forever"?

_____

_____

4. Who is described in stanza 1 of "Mr. Longfellow and His Boy"?

_____

_____

5. Who was Noah Brooks? What special moment did he and Lincoln share?

_____

_____

6. Who quotes Longfellow's poem years later? Why is the poem appropriate on that occasion?

_____

_____

Literary Criticism: A Biographical Approach

Man Reading by Josef Scharl.
© Christie's Images/CORBIS.

Academic Vocabulary for Collection 7

These are the terms you should know
as you read and analyze the selections in this collection.

————

Fiction A prose account that is made-up rather than true. The term *fiction* usually refers to novels and short stories.

Biographical approach Considering an author's life experiences as you respond to his or her literary works.

Biographical criticism Evaluating how an author's life is evident in what he or she writes.

● ● ●

Speaker The person who is telling you the story or talking to you in a poem. The speaker is not always the writer of the story or poem.

Theme A truth or insight about life revealed in a literary work. A theme makes a comment about the topic of a work. For example: "Dogs are more than just pets" or "Friends make life worthwhile."

● ● ●

Idiom An expression peculiar to a particular region. An idiom means something different from the literal meaning of its words. For example: A "cool cat" is not a cold feline; it is a hip or savvy person.

The Treasure of Lemon Brown

by Walter Dean Myers

LITERARY FOCUS: THE WRITER'S BACKGROUND

Writers often use aspects of their own life experiences to create fiction. The **setting** may be based on memories of a special place. The **characters** may be based on people they know. The **plot** may include events from their own lives. The **theme** might involve issues that have been important to them.

The setting of "The Treasure of Lemon Brown" is Harlem, a neighborhood in New York City where Walter Dean Myers grew up in the 1940s. Myers once said, "Harlem was a place of affirmation. The excitement of city living exploded in the teeming streets." Keep that description in mind as you read the story.

READING SKILLS: RETELLING

Any time you describe to friends what happened to you in real life or what happened in a movie or book, you are using the skill of **retelling.** You can also retell events to yourself, to check your understanding of what has happened. To make sure that you understand what you are reading, stop from time to time and retell what has happened. You can jot down your retelling notes in a reading notebook or journal.

SKILLS FOCUS

Literary Skills
Understand a biographical approach to literary criticism.

Reading Skills
Retell the story.

Vocabulary Skills
Clarify word meanings by using context.

VOCABULARY DEVELOPMENT

PREVIEW SELECTION VOCABULARY

These are words you should get to know before you read "The Treasure of Lemon Brown."

impromptu (im·prämp′tōō′) *adj.:* unplanned.

> *Greg's friends had an impromptu checkers tournament.*

tentatively (ten′tə·tiv·lē) *adv.:* in an uncertain or hesitant way.

> *Greg pushed tentatively on the tenement door.*

intently (in·tent′lē) *adv.:* with close attention.

> *Greg listened intently to the sounds in the room.*

brittle (brit″l) *adj.:* having a sharp, hard quality; ready to break.

> *The man's voice sounded high and brittle.*

ominous (äm′ə·nəs) *adj.:* threatening.

> *After the crash, Greg heard only an ominous silence.*

CLARIFYING WORD MEANINGS: CONTEXT

Many words in English have more than one meaning. *Brittle,* for example, can mean "having a sharp, hard quality" or "unbending." You can clarify the way a word is being used by looking at its **context,** the words and sentences surrounding it. There are four basic types of **context clues:** definition, restatement, example, and contrast. In these examples the italicized passages provide context clues for the boldface word.

DEFINITION: Something that is **brittle** *is hard and easily broken.*

RESTATEMENT: That old photograph is **brittle.** It is *very fragile.*

EXAMPLE: The old photograph was **brittle.** *It broke into pieces* when we took it out of the photo album.

CONTRAST: *Unlike the soft flexible boughs* of a young tree, this tree's branches were old and **brittle.**

The Treasure of Lemon Brown

Walter Dean Myers

IDENTIFY

Which two characters do you meet in the first two paragraphs? Underline the text that tells you.

INFER

Pause at line 24. Why is it important to Greg's father that Greg study instead of play basketball?

The dark sky, filled with angry, swirling clouds, reflected Greg Ridley's mood as he sat on the stoop of his building. His father's voice came to him again, first reading the letter the principal had sent to the house, then lecturing endlessly about his poor efforts in math.

"I had to leave school when I was thirteen," his father had said; "that's a year younger than you are now. If I'd had half the chances that you have, I'd . . ."

Greg had sat in the small, pale-green kitchen listening, knowing the lecture would end with his father saying he couldn't play ball with the Scorpions. He had asked his father the week before, and his father had said it depended on his next report card. It wasn't often the Scorpions took on new players, especially fourteen-year-olds, and this was a chance of a lifetime for Greg. He hadn't been allowed to play high school ball, which he had really wanted to do, but playing for the Community Center team was the next best thing. Report cards were due in a week, and Greg had been hoping for the best. But the principal had ended the suspense early when she sent that letter saying Greg would probably fail math if he didn't spend more time studying.

"And you want to play *basketball*?" His father's brows knitted over deep-brown eyes. "That must be some kind of a joke. Now you just get into your room and hit those books."

That had been two nights before. His father's words, like the distant thunder that now echoed through the streets of Harlem, still rumbled softly in his ears.

"The Treasure of Lemon Brown" by Walter Dean Myers from *Face to Face: A Collection of Stories by Celebrated Soviet and American Writers,* edited by Thomas Pettepiece and Anatoly Aleksin. Copyright © 1983 by Walter Dean Myers. Reproduced by permission of **Miriam Altshuler Literary Agency, on behalf of Walter Dean Myers.**

© Bettmann/CORBIS.

INFER

What does Greg's decision to walk down the street instead of study say about him (lines 33–34)?

It was beginning to cool. Gusts of wind made bits of paper dance between the parked cars. There was a flash of
30 nearby lightning, and soon large drops of rain splashed onto his jeans. He stood to go upstairs, thought of the lecture that probably awaited him if he did anything except shut himself in his room with his math book, and started walking down the street instead. Down the block there was an old tenement that had been abandoned for some months. Some of the guys had held an **impromptu** checkers tournament there the week before, and Greg had noticed that the door, once boarded over, had been slightly ajar.

Pulling his collar up as high as he could, he checked
40 for traffic and made a dash across the street. He reached the house just as another flash of lightning changed the night to day for an instant, then returned the graffiti-scarred building to the grim shadows. He vaulted over the outer stairs and pushed **tentatively** on the door. It was open, and he let himself in.

VOCABULARY

impromptu (im·prämp′tōō′) *adj.*: unplanned; made or done without preparation.

tentatively (ten′tə·tiv·lē) *adv.*: in an uncertain or hesitant way.

Copyright © by Holt, Rinehart and Winston. All rights reserved.

The inside of the building was dark except for the dim light that filtered through the dirty windows from the street lamps. There was a room a few feet from the door, and from where he stood at the entrance, Greg could see a squarish
50 patch of light on the floor. He entered the room, frowning at the musty smell. It was a large room that might have been someone's parlor at one time. Squinting, Greg could see an old table on its side against one wall, what looked like a pile of rags or a torn mattress in the corner, and a couch, with one side broken, in front of the window.

He went to the couch. The side that wasn't broken was comfortable enough, though a little creaky. From this spot he could see the blinking neon sign over the bodega[1] on the corner. He sat awhile, watching the sign blink first green,
60 then red, allowing his mind to drift to the Scorpions, then to his father. His father had been a postal worker for all Greg's life and was proud of it, often telling Greg how hard he had worked to pass the test. Greg had heard the story too many times to be interested now.

For a moment Greg thought he heard something that sounded like a scraping against the wall. He listened carefully, but it was gone.

Outside, the wind had picked up, sending the rain against the window with a force that shook the glass in its
70 frame. A car passed, its tires hissing over the wet street and its red taillights glowing in the darkness.

Greg thought he heard the noise again. His stomach tightened as he held himself still and listened **intently**. There weren't any more scraping noises, but he was sure he had heard something in the darkness—something breathing!

He tried to figure out just where the breathing was coming from; he knew it was in the room with him. Slowly

---

1. **bodega** (bō·dä′gə) n.: small grocery store.

he stood, tensing. As he turned, a flash of lightning lit up the room, frightening him with its sudden brilliance. He

80 saw nothing, just the overturned table, the pile of rags, and an old newspaper on the floor. Could he have been imagining the sounds? He continued listening, but heard nothing and thought that it might have just been rats. Still, he thought, as soon as the rain let up he would leave. He went to the window and was about to look out when he heard a voice behind him.

"Don't try nothin', 'cause I got a razor here sharp enough to cut a week into nine days!"

Greg, except for an involuntary tremor in his knees,

90 stood stock-still. The voice was high and **brittle,** like dry twigs being broken, surely not one he had ever heard before. There was a shuffling sound as the person who had been speaking moved a step closer. Greg turned, holding his breath, his eyes straining to see in the dark room.

The upper part of the figure before him was still in darkness. The lower half was in the dim rectangle of light that fell unevenly from the window. There were two feet, in cracked, dirty shoes from which rose legs that were wrapped in rags.

100 "Who are you?" Greg hardly recognized his own voice.

"I'm Lemon Brown," came the answer. "Who're you?"

"Greg Ridley."

"What you doing here?" The figure shuffled forward again, and Greg took a small step backward.

"It's raining," Greg said.

"I can see that," the figure said.

The person who called himself Lemon Brown peered forward, and Greg could see him clearly. He was an old man. His black, heavily wrinkled face was surrounded by a halo

110 of crinkly white hair and whiskers that seemed to separate

IDENTIFY

Pause at line 81. Go back to line 65, and circle the details that increase the suspense.

VOCABULARY

brittle (brit″l) *adj.:* having a sharp, hard quality. *Brittle* also means "touchy" or "unbending."

INFER

Pause at line 104. How might Greg be feeling at this point in the story? Why?

Pause at line 118. Why does Greg conclude that Lemon Brown is harmless?

_____

_____

_____

_____

_____

_____

_____

_____

_____

_____

_____

_____

_____

Dialect is a way of speaking that is characteristic of a group of people or a geographic area. In lines 120–125, underline words and phrases in Greg and Lemon Brown's conversation that show their dialect is different from standard English.

© Elizabeth Young/CORBIS.

his head from the layers of dirty coats piled on his smallish frame. His pants were bagged to the knee, where they were met with rags that went down to the old shoes. The rags were held on with strings, and there was a rope around his middle. Greg relaxed. He had seen the man before, picking through the trash on the corner and pulling clothes out of a Salvation Army box. There was no sign of the razor that could "cut a week into nine days."

"What are you doing here?" Greg asked.

120 "This is where I'm staying," Lemon Brown said. "What you here for?"

"Told you it was raining out," Greg said, leaning against the back of the couch until he felt it give slightly.

"Ain't you got no home?"

"I got a home," Greg answered.

"You ain't one of them bad boys looking for my treasure, is you?" Lemon Brown cocked his head to one side and squinted one eye. "Because I told you I got me a razor."

"I'm not looking for your treasure," Greg answered,
130   smiling. "*If* you have one."

"What you mean, *if* I have one," Lemon Brown said.
"Every man got a treasure. You don't know that, you must
be a fool!"

"Sure," Greg said as he sat on the sofa and put one leg
over the back. "What do you have, gold coins?"

"Don't worry none about what I got," Lemon Brown
said. "You know who I am?"

"You told me your name was orange or lemon or
something like that."

140   "Lemon Brown," the old man said, pulling back his
shoulders as he did so, "they used to call me Sweet Lemon
Brown."

"Sweet Lemon?" Greg asked.

"Yessir. Sweet Lemon Brown. They used to say I sung
the blues so sweet that if I sang at a funeral, the dead would
commence to rocking with the beat. Used to travel all over
Mississippi and as far as Monroe, Louisiana, and east on
over to Macon, Georgia. You mean you ain't never heard
of Sweet Lemon Brown?"

150   "Afraid not," Greg said. "What . . . what happened
to you?"

"Hard times, boy. Hard times always after a poor man.
One day I got tired, sat down to rest a spell and felt a tap on
my shoulder. Hard times caught up with me."

"Sorry about that."

"What you doing here? How come you didn't go on
home when the rain come? Rain don't bother you young
folks none."

"Just didn't." Greg looked away.

160   "I used to have a knotty-headed boy just like you."
Lemon Brown had half walked, half shuffled back to the

PREDICT

Pause at line 133. What
might Lemon Brown's
treasure be?

_____

_____

_____

_____

INTERPRET

Lemon Brown pulls back his
shoulders as he repeats his
name (lines 140–142), even
after Greg seems to make
fun of it. What does Lemon
Brown's action reveal about
him?

_____

_____

_____

_____

_____

_____

_____

_____

_____

_____

_____

_____

IDENTIFY

Pause at line 171. Go back to line 144 on page 235. Underline four details you've learned about Lemon Brown's life from what he's said to Greg.

PREDICT

Pause at line 188. What do you think will happen next? Explain.

_____

_____

_____

_____

_____

_____

_____

_____

_____

INFER

Who is referred to as "Ragman" in line 191?

_____

_____

_____

_____

_____

_____

_____

corner and sat down against the wall. "Had them big eyes like you got. I used to call them moon eyes. Look into them moon eyes and see anything you want."

"How come you gave up singing the blues?" Greg asked.

"Didn't give it up," Lemon Brown said. "You don't give up the blues; they give you up. After a while you do good for yourself, and it ain't nothing but foolishness singing

170 about how hard you got it. Ain't that right?"

"I guess so."

"What's that noise?" Lemon Brown asked, suddenly sitting upright.

Greg listened, and he heard a noise outside. He looked at Lemon Brown and saw the old man was pointing toward the window.

Greg went to the window and saw three men, neighborhood thugs, on the stoop. One was carrying a length of pipe. Greg looked back toward Lemon Brown, who moved

180 quietly across the room to the window. The old man looked out, then beckoned frantically for Greg to follow him. For a moment Greg couldn't move. Then he found himself following Lemon Brown into the hallway and up darkened stairs. Greg followed as closely as he could. They reached the top of the stairs, and Greg felt Lemon Brown's hand first lying on his shoulder, then probing down his arm until he finally took Greg's hand into his own as they crouched in the darkness.

"They's bad men," Lemon Brown whispered. His breath

190 was warm against Greg's skin.

"Hey! Ragman!" a voice called. "We know you in here. What you got up under them rags? You got any money?"

Silence.

"We don't want to have to come in and hurt you, old man, but we don't mind if we have to."

Lemon Brown squeezed Greg's hand in his own hard, gnarled fist.

There was a banging downstairs and a light as the men entered. They banged around noisily, calling for the ragman.

200 "We heard you talking about your treasure." The voice was slurred. "We just want to see it, that's all."

"You sure he's here?" One voice seemed to come from the room with the sofa.

"Yeah, he stays here every night."

"There's another room over there; I'm going to take a look. You got that flashlight?"

"Yeah, here, take the pipe too."

Greg opened his mouth to quiet the sound of his breath as he sucked it in uneasily. A beam of light hit the wall a

210 few feet opposite him, then went out.

"Ain't nobody in that room," a voice said. "You think he gone or something?"

"I don't know," came the answer. "All I know is that I heard him talking about some kind of treasure. You know they found that shopping-bag lady with that money in her bags."

"Yeah. You think he's upstairs?"

"HEY, OLD MAN, ARE YOU UP THERE?"

Silence.

220 "Watch my back, I'm going up."

There was a footstep on the stairs, and the beam from the flashlight danced crazily along the peeling wallpaper. Greg held his breath. There was another step and a loud crashing noise as the man banged the pipe against the wooden banister. Greg could feel his temples throb as the man slowly neared them. Greg thought about the pipe,

INFER

Pause at line 201. Why have the men come looking for Lemon Brown?

_____

_____

_____

PREDICT

Pause at line 219. What might happen if the men find Lemon Brown and Greg? What do you think is going to happen next?

_____

_____

_____

RETELL

Pause at line 220. Retell the story from line 144 up to this point.

_____

_____

_____

_____

_____

_____

_____

_____

_____

Why does Lemon Brown draw attention to himself (lines 234–236)?

_____

_____

_____

_____

_____

_____

_____

Circle the details that show what is happening in lines 250–255. What happens to the three thugs?

_____

_____

_____

_____

_____

_____

ominous (ăm′ə·nəs) *adj.:* threatening; seeming to indicate that something bad will happen.

wondering what he would do when the man reached them—what he *could* do.

Then Lemon Brown released his hand and moved toward the top of the stairs. Greg looked around and saw stairs going up to the next floor. He tried waving to Lemon Brown, hoping the old man would see him in the dim light and follow him to the next floor. Maybe, Greg thought, the man wouldn't follow them up there. Suddenly, though, Lemon Brown stood at the top of the stairs, both arms raised high above his head.

"There he is!" a voice cried from below.

"Throw down your money, old man, so I won't have to bash your head in!"

Lemon Brown didn't move. Greg felt himself near panic. The steps came closer, and still Lemon Brown didn't move. He was an eerie sight, a bundle of rags standing at the top of the stairs, his shadow on the wall looming over him. Maybe, the thought came to Greg, the scene could be even eerier.

Greg wet his lips, put his hands to his mouth, and tried to make a sound. Nothing came out. He swallowed hard, wet his lips once more, and howled as evenly as he could.

"*What's that?*"

As Greg howled, the light moved away from Lemon Brown, but not before Greg saw him hurl his body down the stairs at the men who had come to take his treasure. There was a crashing noise, and then footsteps. A rush of warm air came in as the downstairs door opened; then there was only an **ominous** silence.

Greg stood on the landing. He listened, and after a while there was another sound on the staircase.

"Mr. Brown?" he called.

"Yeah, it's me," came the answer. "I got their flashlight."

260   Greg exhaled in relief as Lemon Brown made his way slowly back up the stairs.

"You ok?"

"Few bumps and bruises," Lemon Brown said.

"I think I'd better be going," Greg said, his breath returning to normal. "You'd better leave, too, before they come back."

"They may hang around outside for a while," Lemon Brown said, "but they ain't getting their nerve up to come in here again. Not with crazy old ragmen and howling
270 spooks. Best you stay awhile till the coast is clear. I'm heading out west tomorrow, out to East St. Louis."

"They were talking about treasures," Greg said. "You *really* have a treasure?"

"What I tell you? Didn't I tell you every man got a treasure?" Lemon Brown said. "You want to see mine?"

"If you want to show it to me," Greg shrugged.

"Let's look out the window first, see what them scoundrels be doing," Lemon Brown said.

They followed the oval beam of the flashlight into one
280 of the rooms and looked out the window. They saw the men who had tried to take the treasure sitting on the curb near the corner. One of them had his pants leg up, looking at his knee.

"You sure you're not hurt?" Greg asked Lemon Brown.

"Nothing that ain't been hurt before," Lemon Brown said. "When you get as old as me, all you say when something hurts is, 'Howdy, Mr. Pain, sees you back again.' Then when Mr. Pain see he can't worry you none, he go on mess with somebody else."

Greg smiled.

290   "Here, you hold this." Lemon Brown gave Greg the flashlight.

RETELL

Pause at line 266. Briefly retell in your own words the important events that have happened since Greg first encountered Lemon Brown (page 233, line 87).

CLARIFY

Re-read lines 292–296. What is Lemon Brown's treasure?

_____

_____

_____

_____

_____

_____

_____

_____

_____

_____

He sat on the floor near Greg and carefully untied the strings that held the rags on his right leg. When he took the rags away, Greg saw a piece of plastic. The old man carefully took off the plastic and unfolded it. He revealed some yellowed newspaper clippings and a battered harmonica.

"There it be," he said, nodding his head. "There it be."

Greg looked at the old man, saw the distant look in his eye, then turned to the clippings. They told of Sweet
300 Lemon Brown, a blues singer and harmonica player who was appearing at different theaters in the South. One of the clippings said he had been the hit of the show, although not the headliner. All of the clippings were reviews of shows Lemon Brown had been in more than fifty years ago. Greg looked at the harmonica. It was dented badly on one side, with the reed holes on one end nearly closed.

"I used to travel around and make money for to feed my wife and Jesse—that's my boy's name. Used to feed them good, too. Then his mama died, and he stayed with his mama's sister. He growed up to be a man, and when the war come, he saw fit to go off and fight in it. I didn't have nothing to give him except these things that told him who I was, and what he come from. If you know your pappy did something, you know you can do something too.

"Anyway, he went off to war, and I went off still playing and singing. 'Course by then I wasn't as much as I used to be, not without somebody to make it worth the while. You know what I mean?"

"Yeah," Greg nodded, not quite really knowing.

"I traveled around, and one time I come home, and there was this letter saying Jesse got killed in the war. Broke my heart, it truly did.

"They sent back what he had with him over there, and what it was is this old mouth fiddle and these clippings. Him carrying it around with him like that told me it meant something to him. That was my treasure, and when I give it to him, he treated it just like that, a treasure. Ain't that something?"

"Yeah, I guess so," Greg said.

"You *guess* so?" Lemon Brown's voice rose an octave[2] as he started to put his treasure back into the plastic. "Well, you got to guess, 'cause you sure don't know nothing. Don't know enough to get home when it's raining."

"I guess . . . I mean, you're right."

"You ok for a youngster," the old man said as he tied the strings around his leg, "better than those scalawags what come here looking for my treasure. That's for sure."

"You really think that treasure of yours was worth fighting for?" Greg asked. "Against a pipe?"

---

2. **octave** (ăk′tiv) *n.*: eight tones on a musical scale.

IDENTIFY

Pause at line 322. What happened to Lemon Brown's son?

_____

_____

_____

_____

_____

FLUENCY

Read the boxed passage aloud twice. Focus the first time on the meaning of each sentence. Then, strive to capture the feelings of pride and sorrow that the old man expresses.

INFER

Pause at line 328. Why did Lemon Brown's son consider the newspaper clippings and the harmonica to be treasures?

_____

_____

_____

_____

_____

_____

_____

_____

_____

"What else a man got 'cepting what he can pass on to his son, or his daughter, if she be his oldest?" Lemon Brown said. "For a big-headed boy, you sure do ask the foolishest questions."

Lemon Brown got up after patting his rags in place and looked out the window again.

"Looks like they're gone. You get on out of here and get yourself home. I'll be watching from the window, so you'll be all right."

Lemon Brown went down the stairs behind Greg. When they reached the front door, the old man looked out first, saw the street was clear, and told Greg to scoot on home.

"You sure you'll be ok?" Greg asked.

"Now, didn't I tell you I was going to East St. Louis in the morning?" Lemon Brown asked. "Don't that sound ok to you?"

"Sure it does," Greg said. "Sure it does. And you take care of that treasure of yours."

"That I'll do," Lemon said, the wrinkles about his eyes suggesting a smile. "That I'll do."

The night had warmed and the rain had stopped, leaving puddles at the curbs. Greg didn't even want to think how late it was. He thought ahead of what his father would say and wondered if he should tell him about Lemon Brown. He thought about it until he reached his stoop, and decided against it. Lemon Brown would be ok, Greg thought, with his memories and his treasure.

Greg pushed the button over the bell marked "Ridley," thought of the lecture he knew his father would give him, and smiled.

EVALUATE

Greg questions whether Lemon Brown's treasure was worth fighting for (lines 338–339). What do you think? Why was it—or was it not—worth a fight?

_____

_____

_____

_____

_____

_____

_____

_____

_____

INTERPRET

How has Greg changed since the beginning of the story? Circle the detail in the last paragraph that helps reveal the change.

_____

_____

_____

_____

_____

_____

_____

_____

The Treasure of Lemon Brown

Story Map   Fill out the story map below for "The Treasure of Lemon Brown." Then, answer the question about how the story might reflect the writer's heritage, attitudes, and beliefs.

SKILLS FOCUS

Literary Skills
Analyze the writer's background.

Basic Situation: Greg Ridley, a fourteen-year-old, is at odds with his father because of Greg's disappointing efforts in math. If Greg's next report card doesn't improve, his father won't let him join the basketball team.

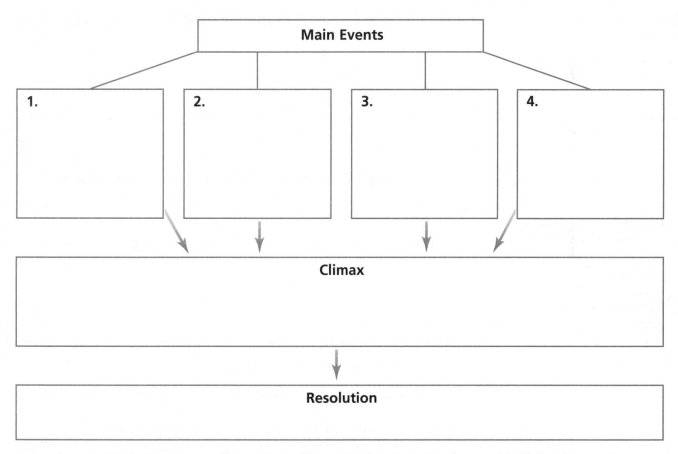

Main Events

1.

2.

3.

4.

Climax

Resolution

How do you think the story reflects the author's heritage, attitudes, and beliefs? (Note: See page 739 of *Elements of Literature* for more information about Walter Dean Myers.)

_____

_____

_____

Skills Review

The Treasure of Lemon Brown

VOCABULARY AND COMPREHENSION

A. Clarifying Word Meanings: Context Read each item below. Write the correct word from the Word Bank on each line. Use context clues to help you.

1. Mathilde's mom wasn't sure if she would be able to take the last week of August off. Their vacation plans were made _____.

2. Sidney had not prepared at all for the graduation ceremony. His speech was _____.

3. No one was surprised when the dried rose crumbled to pieces. Dried flowers are very _____.

4. Clouds loomed and thunder rumbled ever closer. The weather had turned _____.

5. Simon and Jan were well prepared for the upcoming test. They had studied _____ for days.

B. Reading Comprehension Number the sentences to show the order of events in "The Treasure of Lemon Brown."

_____ Three men come after Lemon Brown, looking for his treasure.

_____ Mr. Ridley reads a letter about his son's poor grades.

_____ Greg meets Lemon Brown and learns he was a blues singer.

_____ Greg finally sees Lemon Brown's treasure and learns about his son.

_____ Lemon Brown and Greg scare the men away.

SKILLS FOCUS

Vocabulary Skills
Clarify word meanings by using context.

Before You Read

SHORT STORY

This selection also
◆ appears in *Elements
of Literature.*

A Smart Cookie by Sandra Cisneros

LITERARY FOCUS: THEMES CROSS CULTURES

A **theme** reveals some truth or basic insight into life. Some themes are
universal: They cross barriers of culture, tradition, and time. One theme
that occurs in literature all over the world is that parents want their
children to have better opportunities than they had. As you read "A
Smart Cookie," look for clues that help reveal its theme. It helps to know
that the name *Esperanza,* the speaker's name, means "hope" in Spanish.

READING SKILLS: UNDERSTANDING IDIOMS

An **idiom** is an expression that means something different from the
literal meaning of the words. The title of Sandra Cisneros's story "A
Smart Cookie" is an idiom, an expression peculiar to American English.
It refers to a person who is very alert and intelligent.

Here are some common idioms along with their meanings. Can you
think of more to add to the chart?

Idiom	Meaning
shake a leg	hurry up
burn one's bridges	sever ties or friendships in a particular place you are leaving
off the top of one's head	without thinking
sleep like a log	sleep soundly
go to the dogs	neglect oneself; disregard normal standards of conduct and decency

**SKILLS
FOCUS**

Literary Skills
Understand
universal themes.

Reading Skills
Understand
idioms.

A Smart Cookie

Sandra Cisneros

BACKGROUND: Literature and Culture

In this character sketch, the speaker is Esperanza, the young girl who narrates all the stories in Sandra Cisneros's book *The House on Mango Street*. In this sketch, Esperanza lets her mother do a lot of the talking.

Esperanza's mother refers to the tragic opera *Madama Butterfly* by Giacomo Puccini. Butterfly, the heroine of that opera, is a young Japanese woman who falls deeply in love with a U.S. naval officer and marries him. Shortly after their marriage her husband returns to America. Butterfly waits for years and years for him to come back to her and their child. When he does finally return, he has an American wife with him. Butterfly, in despair, gives them her beloved child and then takes her own life.

IDENTIFY

Re-read lines 1–6. Underline the details revealing that Esperanza's mother is intelligent and talented.

INFER

Pause at line 12. What have you learned so far about Esperanza's mother?

_____

_____

_____

_____

_____

I could've been somebody, you know? my mother says and sighs. She has lived in this city her whole life. She can speak two languages. She can sing an opera. She knows how to fix a TV. But she doesn't know which subway train to take to get downtown. I hold her hand very tight while we wait for the right train to arrive.

She used to draw when she had time. Now she draws with a needle and thread, little knotted rosebuds, tulips made of silk thread. Someday she would like to go to the
10   ballet. Someday she would like to see a play. She borrows opera records from the public library and sings with velvety lungs powerful as morning glories.

Today while cooking oatmeal she is Madame Butterfly until she sighs and points the wooden spoon at me. I could've been somebody, you know? Esperanza, you go to school. Study hard. That Madame Butterfly was a fool. She stirs the oatmeal. Look at my comadres.° She means Izaura whose husband left and Yolanda whose husband is dead. Got to take care all your own, she says shaking her head.

20   Then out of nowhere:

Shame is a bad thing, you know. It keeps you down. You want to know why I quit school? Because I didn't have nice clothes. No clothes, but I had brains.

Yup, she says disgusted, stirring again. I was a smart cookie then.

© Royalty-Free/CORBIS.

INFER

Re-read lines 15–19. What does the mother think about her closest friends?

_____

_____

_____

CLARIFY

Re-read lines 21–25 carefully. Why does Esperanza's mother say that shame is a bad thing?

_____

_____

_____

INTERPRET

Is Esperanza's mother sincere when she says she was "a smart cookie"? Explain.

_____

_____

_____

FLUENCY

Read the boxed passage aloud several times. Use your voice to indicate which lines are spoken by Esperanza and which are spoken by her mother.

° **comadres** (kô·mä′dräs) *n.:* Spanish for "close female friends" (literally, a child's mother and godmother).

A Smart Cookie

Literary Skills
Analyze themes.

"Most Important Word" Chart   **Theme** is what a story or poem or play reveals to us about our lives. Theme is usually not stated directly. You have to read a selection carefully, look for important passages and important words, and then come up with a general statement saying what you think the text tells you about life. Try a strategy called "Most Important Word" to identify the theme of "A Smart Cookie."

• Look for a word that has an impact on you as you read the story. Look for a word that is repeated or a word that is used at the beginning or end of the story and seems important to you.

• Think about how the word relates to the story's characters and to what happens to them. Fill in your ideas on the chart below.

• Reflect on what you have written. Then, make a generalization about the theme that all of those comments seem to support.

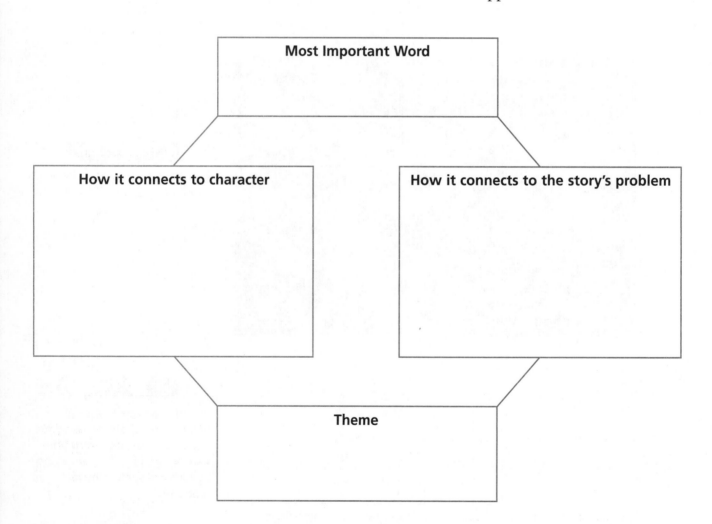

Most Important Word

How it connects to character

How it connects to the story's problem

Theme

Skills Review

A Smart Cookie

COMPREHENSION

A. Idioms   Match each idiom, shown in boldface, with its meaning. Use context clues to help you.

_____ 1. The rowdy class **clammed up** when the principal came in.

a. understand

_____ 2. Liu couldn't **get a handle** on his math assignment. It was too hard for him.

b. got quiet

_____ 3. Our plans for a vacation **went down the tubes** when the hurricane hit.

c. were cancelled

B. Reading Comprehension   Read the following statements about "A Smart Cookie." In the space provided, write T for True and F for False.

_____ 1. Esperanza is aware of her mother's talent.

_____ 2. Esperanza's mother has lived in the city for many years.

_____ 3. Opera is important to Esperanza's mother.

_____ 4. Esperanza's mother left school because she was bored.

_____ 5. Esperanza's mother believes that a woman's chief goal should be to raise a family.

SKILLS FOCUS

Reading Skills
Analyze idioms.

The Buried Treasure *retold by* Laurence Yep

LITERARY FOCUS: FOLK TALES

A **folk tale** is a story with no known author. Folk tales, like myths, were originally passed from one generation to another by word of mouth. Unlike myths, however, which are about gods and heroes, folk tales are usually about ordinary people or about animals that act like people. Folk tales in different cultures often share similar **motifs**—characters, images, or story lines. The **trickster** figure, for example, appears as Anansi, the Spider, in African folklore; as Raven in Inuit tales; and as Coyote in the folklore of the Zuni people.

"The Buried Treasure" is an old Chinese folk tale that has been retold by Laurence Yep. Like most folk tales, Yep's stories are full of magic and supernatural events. Yep is especially interested in stories that help young people live between two cultures.

READING SKILLS: READING FOR DETAILS

Although writers don't always agree with their characters' statements and choices, writers sometimes express their attitudes and beliefs in the stories they tell. Often, however, the writer's attitudes are only **implied,** or suggested. The reader infers the writer's attitudes and beliefs by reading between the lines.

As you read "The Buried Treasure," guess at Laurence Yep's attitudes toward life by paying attention to the details in the story that describe the characters' actions, beliefs, and attitudes.

SKILLS FOCUS

Literary Skills
Understand the characteristics of folk tales; understand a writer's beliefs.

Reading Skills
Read for details.

Vocabulary Skills
Understand synonyms.

VOCABULARY DEVELOPMENT

PREVIEW SELECTION VOCABULARY

Before you read "The Buried Treasure," get to know these words from the story.

summoned (sum′ənd) *v.:* called or sent for.

> *The old man summoned his sons to his bedside.*

tenants (ten′ənts) *n.:* people who pay rent to use land or a building.

> *The tenants were farmers who rented the fields and payed the rent with crops they grew.*

bewildered (bē·wil′dərd) *adj.:* hopelessly confused.

> *The older brother was bewildered by the contents of the jar.*

SYNONYMS

A **synonym** is a word that shares a meaning with another word. *Intelligent* and *smart,* for example, are synonyms. When you learn a new word, it helps to also learn its synonyms. Following are sentences using the Vocabulary words above. A synonym for each Vocabulary word appears in parentheses.

- I was **summoned** (sent for) by the school principal.
- The apartment was empty because the **tenants** (renters) had moved away.
- The poorly written directions had us all **bewildered** (confused).

The Buried Treasure

a Chinese folk tale, retold by Laurence Yep

Illustration by Mou-Sien Tseng.

COMPARE & CONTRAST

Pause at line 15. How do Old Jarhead's two sons differ?

There was once a rich man who heard that there was no lock that could not be picked. So he put his money into jars and buried them in secret places. In fact, the whole town nicknamed him "Old Jarhead."

Now, Jarhead had two sons. The older son, Yuè Cang, already managed the family's lands and properties. However, the younger son, Yuè Shêng, cared neither for books nor for business. Old Jarhead scolded and begged him to change, and each time the young man promised

10 to behave. However, he never remembered his promise.

Since Yuè Shêng was also a friendly fellow, he never turned a guest away from his door. Often he had to provide meals for three or even four guests a day. Everyone took advantage of him. As a result, his money poured through his hands like water.

One day when Old Jarhead fell sick, he **summoned** his sons to his bedside and told them the contents of his will. To the older son, he left everything. His younger son, Yuè Shêng, would receive nothing.

VOCABULARY

summoned (sum′ənd) *v.*: called or sent for.

From *Tree of Dreams: Ten Tales from the Garden of Night* by Laurence Yep. Copyright © 1995 by Laurence Yep. Published and reproduced by permission of **Troll Associates, LLC.**

20   Hurt, Yuè Shêng sighed. "Well, it isn't as if you didn't warn me."

    Alarmed, Old Jarhead tried to sit up but could not. "I'm not trying to punish you," he wheezed. "I have money set aside for you. But if I gave it to you now, you'd spend it all. You'll get it when you've learned the value of hard work."

    Despite his faults, Yuè Shêng was a good son. Bowing his head, he said, "Father, may the day of your death never come. May you live a thousand years."

    However, Old Jarhead grew steadily worse and died
30 shortly after that. Yuè Shêng wept until his eyes were purple, for he truly loved his father, though he had not listened to him. His older brother hardly shed a tear, for he had loved their father's wealth more than their father. When Yuè Shêng asked his brother about the burial, his brother replied, "I'm too busy. You handle it." So Yuè Shêng organized everything by himself.

    Old Jarhead had been an important man in town. Yuè Shêng was determined that he should have a proper funeral. He ordered an elaborate coffin and then asked a
40 priest to name a good date on which to bury his father.

    On the appointed day, Yuè Shêng hired a band of musicians and scattered lots of glittering ghost money. Ghosts were too stupid to tell the shiny paper money from real money. They would be so busy trying to pick it up that they would leave Old Jarhead's ghost alone. At the grave-side, Yuè Shêng set out a banquet for his father's spirit. At home, he put out yet another feast for the many mourners. He even let his father's tenant farmers have seats, though his older brother protested.

50   Everyone in town said the elaborate funeral was fitting for someone as important as Old Jarhead. Although Yuè Shêng had arranged everything, his older brother took all the credit.

IDENTIFY

Read lines 23–25 carefully. When will the younger son get his money? Circle the words that tell you.

CLARIFY

Re-read lines 41–45. What is "ghost money"? Why does Yuè Shêng scatter it on his father's grave?

_____

_____

_____

_____

_____

_____

IDENTIFY

Underline details in lines 37–49 that tell you about Chinese burial traditions.

IDENTIFY

By the time you get to line 53, the **conflict** in the story is clear. What is the problem in the story?

_____

_____

_____

_____

INFER

Why does the younger brother lose his home *and* his friends (line 60)?

_____

_____

_____

_____

_____

_____

_____

_____

IDENTIFY

Pause at line 69. In what way does the older son show disrespect for his heritage?

_____

_____

_____

_____

_____

VOCABULARY

tenants (ten′ənts) *n.:* people who pay rent to use land or a building.

Circle the definition provided in the context of the previous sentence.

Yet when the bills came due, the older brother passed them on to Yuè Shêng. "I would never have ordered anything so extravagant," Yuè Cang said. "This is much too wasteful. I refuse to pay."

The funeral had indeed been very expensive, so Yuè Shêng sold everything he owned to settle the debt. But when Yuè Shêng lost his house, he lost his friends. None of them would give him so much as a bowl of rice.

Naturally, Yuè Shêng went to his brother to borrow some money. He found Yuè Cang tearing down their father's old house. That upset Yuè Shêng very much.

"Why are you destroying all of our memories?" Yuè Shêng demanded.

"This old pile is riddled with[1] termites," his older brother explained, "and I've found a much better place to build. I'm very busy, brother. What do you want?"

When Yuè Shêng asked for help, his brother sniffed. "Humph, I'm not going to feed every moocher in town. You're still much too wasteful." He gave Yuè Shêng only a few copper coins. "These will keep you from starving if you're careful. I have expenses of my own."

After this, Yuè Shêng went down to his brother's fields. Yuè Cang rented the fields to farmers who paid him with a share of their crops.

The **tenants** were surprised to see Yuè Shêng there.

"Please show me what to do," Yuè Shêng humbly begged them. "If I don't work, I'll starve."

One of the tenants, a fellow named Turnip Nose, grunted. "So your brother's so small-hearted that he turned his back on you. Well, your father was a nice gent. For his sake, I'll give you part of my share. But you'll have to work very hard."

---

1. **riddled with:** full of.

"I'm not afraid to use my hands," Yuè Shêng said.

Each season, then, Turnip Nose told him what to do. In the spring, Yuè Shêng pulled the plow himself to turn up the soil. Next, he planted seed and weeded the rice plants and tended them. When the crops ripened, he harvested them, and Turnip Nose gave him a small part of what they had grown. If Yuè Shêng was careful, it would be just enough rice to live on.

As year followed year, Yuè Shêng became lean and tough as wood. One day when he was washing up, he saw his reflection in the bucket and thought, If Father could see me, he would laugh. I certainly know all about hard work now.

That night, Yuè Shêng dreamed that he was walking on their old estate. He passed by two pine trees growing from the same trunk. Behind them was an old well that had been filled in. Next to it were the ruins of an old brick wall. Right at the corner, he dug beneath the foundation. And there in the dirt was a jar of gold.

As soon as Yuè Shêng awoke the next morning, he jumped up. Trembling, he went back to the site of his father's house. The walls had all been torn down, but the twin pine trees still grew. Beyond them, he found the well that his brother's men had filled in. Then he traced the remains of the wall until he came to the corner. With his hoe, Yuè Shêng began to dig.

Notes _____

PREDICT

Pause at line 98. What do you predict is going to become of Yuè Shêng?

Illustration by Mou-Sien Tseng.

IDENTIFY

Pause at line 115. Folk tales often include dreams that guide the hero. What does this dream lead Yuè Shêng to?

_____

_____

_____

_____

_____

_____

_____

_____

IDENTIFY

Pause at line 121. What conflict has the gold caused for Yuè Shêng?

_____

_____

_____

_____

_____

_____

_____

_____

_____

_____

When he reached the foundation, he heard a clink. Falling to his knees, he scrabbled in the dirt. Gradually, he uncovered a jar. With shaking fingers, he unsealed the lid. The jar was crammed with gleaming gold ingots.[2]

Yuè Shêng lifted some of the heavy ingots into his hands. The sun shone from their sides. "This is the gold Father intended for me when I learned what work meant," he said aloud. Yet as he stared at them, he felt guilty. "But

120 father left the house to my older brother. By rights, the jar still belongs to him."

The honest man put back the gold ingots and covered the jar again. Then he went to his brother's house. However, the gatekeeper would not let him inside. "I'm sorry, young master, but your brother has ordered me not to let you in. He doesn't want to see you anymore. Please don't beg."

So Yuè Shêng asked for ink and paper to write a note. In it, he told his brother where the treasure was. Folding it

130 up, he asked the gatekeeper to take it to his brother.

At first, Yuè Cang was just going to tear the note up without reading it. However, his wife scolded him, saying, "Your brother could be very sick. Imagine what people would say if we let him die?"

Reluctantly, the older brother read the note. As soon as he finished, he jumped up and called for his servants. "What's wrong?" his wife asked.

The older brother rushed from the room, bellowing to his servants. Some brought his sedan chair;[3] others

140 snatched up shovels and hoes. Cursing and shouting, the older brother guided everyone to the ruins of the old house. Getting out of his sedan chair, he went to the spot described in the note and commanded his men to dig there.

---

2. **ingots** (iŋ'gəts) _n.:_ bars of cast metal; here, of gold.
3. **sedan chair:** covered portable chair used for carrying a person, with horizontal poles that rest on the shoulders of the carriers.

When they had uncovered the jar, Yuè Cang told them to stand back. Then he knelt and lifted the lid. Immediately, he fell backward with a scream. When the curious servants peeked inside, they saw the jar was full of snakes. After the older brother had recovered himself, he straightened his robes and dusted himself off. "This is not a funny prank at all," he said sternly.

150

Getting back into his sedan chair, Yuè Cang ordered his servants to take him and the jar to his brother's hut. Yuè Shêng was sitting outside, eating a simple meal of rice with a few salted vegetables.

When Yuè Shêng saw the jar in a servant's arms, he set down his bowl and stood up. "What are you doing here?"

His brother glared from his sedan chair. "I'm returning your jar to you."

"But Father gave the house to you. The jar is yours," Yuè Shêng protested.

160

"No. It's all yours," his brother said, then gestured to his servants. As they all marched forward, one threw the jar at Yuè Shêng's feet. When it shattered, shining gold ingots spilled around his ankles.

"Where are the snakes?" the older brother asked, **bewildered.**

"There was only gold in the jar when I looked," Yuè Shêng explained.

Then Yuè Cang understood. "It's a sign from our father that this gold is destined only for you," he said. "This is the

170

share he always meant to give you."

Although Yuè Shêng offered him the gold again, his brother refused to take even a share. So Yuè Shêng used the money to buy a house and fields of his own. But he was always careful with his money, for he knew his father was not likely to send him another dream.

IDENTIFY

Folk tales often include supernatural events. What fantastic event has happened in line 147?

_____

_____

_____

IDENTIFY

What magical change has happened in lines 163–164? Read on, and circle Yuè Cang's explanation for this strange event.

VOCABULARY

bewildered (bē·wil′dərd) *adj.:* hopelessly confused.

FLUENCY

It can be fun to act out this folk tale. Read the boxed passage aloud until you can read it smoothly. Then, act out the dialogue with a partner.

INTERPRET

What moral lesson does this folk tale teach?

_____

_____

_____

_____

_____

The Buried Treasure

Story-Attitude Chart   Writers sometimes express their attitudes through what their characters say and do. (Writers, however, don't always agree with all their characters' statements and choices.) Often the writer's attitudes are only implied, or suggested. The reader infers the writer's attitudes by reading between the lines. Guess at Lawrence Yep's attitudes toward life by filling in the following chart.

In the Story . . .	Possible Writer's Attitude
Yuè Shêng is humble enough to take work as a laborer.	
Yuè Cang is careful with his money, but he does not show any generosity.	
Yuè Shêng spends money, but he does not worship it. He is rewarded at the end.	

Skills Review

The Buried Treasure

VOCABULARY AND COMPREHENSION

A. Synonyms Replace each boldface word with the Word Bank word that is its synonym. Write the synonym on the line within the parentheses.

Word Bank

summoned
tenants
bewildered

1. The property had to be vacated by its **renters** (_____)

   within thirty days.

2. We found ourselves **confused** (_____) by the changes

   in the new computer software.

3. When I was **called** (_____) to the stage I got a little

   nervous.

B. Reading Comprehension Answer each question below.

1. In what ways are Yuè Cang and Yuè Shêng different? _____

   _____

   _____

2. What does Yuè Shêng do when his father dies? _____

   _____

3. What happens to Yuè Shêng after his father's funeral? _____

   _____

4. Why does Yuè Shêng offer the jar of gold to his brother? _____

   _____

   _____

5. What lessons do the two brothers learn? _____

   _____

   _____

SKILLS FOCUS

Vocabulary Skills
Use synonyms.

Reading for Life

© David Hanover/Getty Images.

Academic Vocabulary for Collection 8

These are the terms you should know
as you read the documents in this collection.

Workplace Documents Workplace documents serve two basic functions: communication and instruction. E-mail, memos, and reports are all types of communication. Employee manuals and project guidelines, for example, provide instructions.

Consumer Documents A consumer is someone who buys goods or services. Consumer documents are documents that inform the consumer. Instruction manuals, warranties, and product recalls are examples of consumer documents.

Public Documents Informational documents that inform the public. They tell people what is happening in their community, city, state, or nation. Examples of public documents include voter registration packets, brochures about national monuments, directories of community services, and so on.

Before You Read

This selection also appears in *Elements of Literature.* ◆

Leash-Free Dog Run Documents

by Sheri Henderson

READING FOCUS: USING DOCUMENTS TO SOLVE A PROBLEM

You will often need to use information from a variety of documents to explain a situation, make a decision, or solve a problem. The documents that follow relate to a proposal for a place where dogs can run unleashed. These documents are in the form of two Web pages and a business letter. Web pages may have text, graphics, photographs, sound, and videoclips. When you read a Web page, take note of heads, lists, diagrams, and illustrations.

As you read the documents, pretend you are a member of the community working on the leash issue.

READING SKILL: TIPS FOR READING INFORMATIONAL TEXTS

- **Numbered steps** indicate that directions must be followed in a specific order.
- **Subheads** tell you what ideas are being discussed.
- The use of **boldface** signals something important.
- **Graphics** such as maps and charts convey information visually.

SKILLS FOCUS

Reading Skills
Use information from documents to solve a problem.

Leash-Free Dog Run Documents

Sheri Henderson

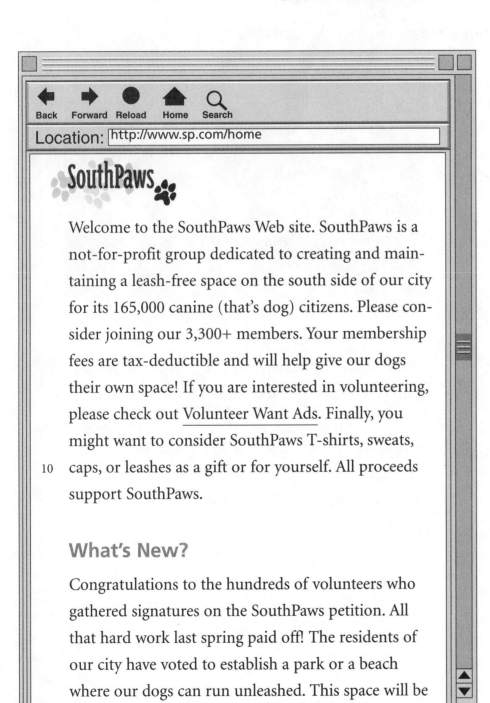

Location: http://www.sp.com/home

SouthPaws

Welcome to the SouthPaws Web site. SouthPaws is a not-for-profit group dedicated to creating and maintaining a leash-free space on the south side of our city for its 165,000 canine (that's dog) citizens. Please consider joining our 3,300+ members. Your membership fees are tax-deductible and will help give our dogs their own space! If you are interested in volunteering, please check out Volunteer Want Ads. Finally, you might want to consider SouthPaws T-shirts, sweats,
10 caps, or leashes as a gift or for yourself. All proceeds support SouthPaws.

What's New?

Congratulations to the hundreds of volunteers who gathered signatures on the SouthPaws petition. All that hard work last spring paid off! The residents of our city have voted to establish a park or a beach where our dogs can run unleashed. This space will be

ANALYZE

Why is Volunteer Want Ads underlined (line 8)?

_____

_____

_____

_____

IDENTIFY

In the first paragraph, underline the sentence that describes the type of Web site SouthPaws is. Circle the items SouthPaws sells. Why does SouthPaws sell these things?

_____

_____

_____

INFER

What issue does the SouthPaws petition address? Underline the information in lines 12–24 that supports your **inference.**

_____

_____

_____

Back   Forward   Reload   Home   Search

Location: http://www.sp.com/home

Cameron Davidson/Getty Images.

jointly funded by the city and SouthPaws donations. SouthPaws volunteers will supervise the space during daylight hours and will be empowered to ticket dog owners who do not observe cleanup and safety rules. We will have one trial year after the space officially opens to prove that the idea works. Now we need your help more than ever.

20

We are working with the city Parks and Recreation Department to choose a location. These are the most likely locations:

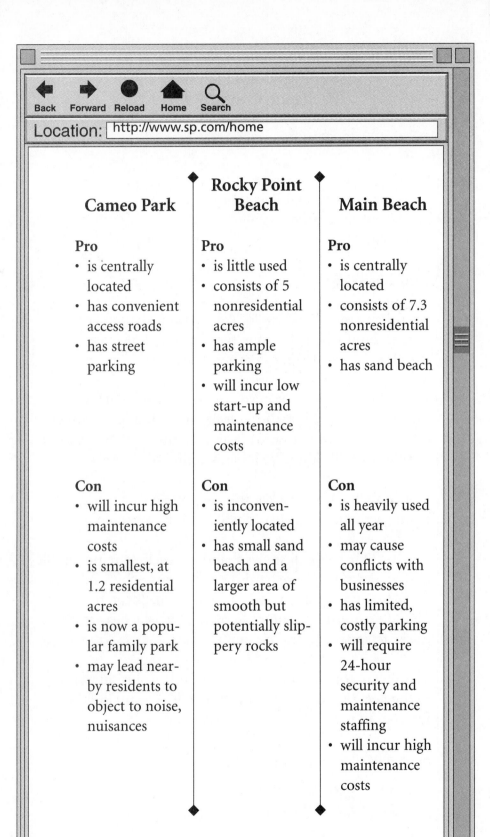

Cameo Park

Pro
- is centrally located
- has convenient access roads
- has street parking

Con
- will incur high maintenance costs
- is smallest, at 1.2 residential acres
- is now a popular family park
- may lead nearby residents to object to noise, nuisances

Rocky Point Beach

Pro
- is little used
- consists of 5 nonresidential acres
- has ample parking
- will incur low start-up and maintenance costs

Con
- is inconveniently located
- has small sand beach and a larger area of smooth but potentially slippery rocks

Main Beach

Pro
- is centrally located
- consists of 7.3 nonresidential acres
- has sand beach

Con
- is heavily used all year
- may cause conflicts with businesses
- has limited, costly parking
- will require 24-hour security and maintenance staffing
- will incur high maintenance costs

Pick a Site

Click here to cast your vote in our survey.

Location: http://www.sp.com/home

Back   Forward   Reload   Home   Search

MAKE A JUDGMENT

Which site is the best choice for the "unleashed" location? Underline the "pros," and circle the "cons" that lead you to make that decision.

SouthPaws

SouthPaws • 1111 South P Street • South City, CA • 90123

December 12, 2004

Ms. T. Wagger
Director of Parks and Recreation
2222 Central Avenue
South City, CA 90123

Dear Ms. Wagger,

SouthPaws members would like you to take their concerns into account when choosing the site of the proposed dog run. Here they are, in order of importance:

10

1. **Space.** Healthy dogs need ample space in which to run. The park needs to be large enough for a fair number of dogs to run around in it without colliding with one another. Ample size will minimize the possibility of dogfights.

2. **Conflicts.** A site that is already popular for sports, family activities, or tourism will likely be a problem.

3. **Site.** Our research shows that dog beaches are preferable to dog parks. Dogs are hard on park grass, which quickly turns to mud in rainy weather. Sand or shells can be brushed off a dog, but mud requires a bath. Dog beaches are also

20

easier to supervise and clean.

Thank you for working with us to find a solution that is in the best interests of the most people. We are looking forward to meeting with you next week.

Sincerely,

A. K. Nine

A. K. Nine
Chairperson
SouthPaws Site Committee

Location: http://www.sp.com/home

Did You Know?

- In our city there are 165,000 licensed dogs.
- The city devotes a total of 10 acres to leash-free dog areas.
- The city devotes 1,050 acres to softball, 1,040 acres to golf, 287 acres to tennis.
- Eastside Leash-Free Dog Park accommodates 2,000 dogs per week on its 1-acre site.

SouthPaws Membership Information

10 **Annual Tax-Deductible Membership Fees**

Basic: $15 per year; entitles you to newsletter and voting rights

Deluxe: $25 per year; entitles you to the above plus one T-shirt or cap

Sponsor: $100 per year; entitles you to all of the above plus discounted dog-obedience classes and merchandise from local merchants

Angel: $250 per year; entitles you to all of the above plus your name on our Wall of Fame

---

EVALUATE

Review the statistics in lines 1–8. Is the city a dog-friendly place? Circle the reasons that support your evaluation.

_____

_____

_____

_____

_____

_____

_____

IDENTIFY

Examine the list in lines 9–19. How is the list organized?

_____

_____

_____

_____

_____

_____

_____

IDENTIFY

Circle the items you would receive if you were to join SouthPaws as an "angel" (lines 18–19).

Location: http://www.sp.com/home

20 **New!**

Help SouthPaws while you tell the world about your
best friend. Buy a brick in the new Dog Walk of
Fame. Your pet's name and a short message will be
inscribed. Be sure to provide your pet's name, your
name, and your message (up to 45 letter spaces).
(Available to SouthPaws members only; $50 per pet's
name.)

Membership in SouthPaws makes a great gift. Print
out a membership application, complete it, and mail
30 it with your donation. Don't want to join? Then how
about making a donation? We appreciate contribu-
tions in any amount.

CONNECT

Imagine you are buying a
brick for your dog in the new
"Dog Walk of Fame" (lines
22–23). What message would
you write? Remember, your
message can only be 45 letter spaces long.

_____

_____

_____

_____

_____

_____

_____

_____

Robert Bossi/Getty Images.

Leash-Free Dog Run Documents

Business Letter Template   Imagine that you are T. Wagger, Director of Parks and Recreation. You want to respond to the chairperson of the Site Committee of SouthPaws. To do this, use this business-letter template. State your preferred site on the line provided. Then, write your reasons on the lines labeled "Space," "Conflicts," and "Type of Area."

SKILLS FOCUS

Reading Skills
Analyze information from documents to solve a problem.

2222 Central Avenue
Central City, CA 90123

December 14, 2004

A. K. Nine
Chairperson, Site Committee
SouthPaws
1111 South P. Street
South City, CA 90123

Dear A. K. Nine:

Thank you for your letter of December 12. It is important for us to work with the community in deciding where to put the dog park. Therefore, I would like to inform you that we favor the site at _____. Our reasons, in order of importance, are as follows:

1. Space: _____

_____

2. Conflicts: _____

_____

3. Type of Area: _____

_____

Thank you for continuing to work with us on this issue. I look forward to seeing you at the upcoming meeting.

Sincerely,

T. Wagger
Director, Parks and Recreation

Leash-Free Dog Run Documents

COMPREHENSION

Reading Comprehension   Answer the following questions.

1. What issue is the SouthPaws Web site concerned with?

   _____

   _____

   _____

2. What three sites does SouthPaws discuss developing?

   _____

   _____

   _____

3. Which proposed site addresses most of SouthPaws' concerns? Explain.

   _____

   _____

   _____

4. What three major concerns about a dog run do SouthPaws members have?

   _____

   _____

   _____

5. How much does it cost to buy a brick on the Dog Walk of Fame?

   _____

   _____

   _____

SKILLS FOCUS

Reading Skills
Analyze
information
from documents.

Passports: Don't Leave Home Without One by Carolyn Liberatore Lavine

READING FOCUS: ANALYZING A DOCUMENT

When you read informational materials, you should read carefully and slowly. Here are some pointers for getting the most out of an informational document. Use these pointers as you read the instructions and tips for getting a passport in the article that follows.

- **Identify your purpose for reading the informational materials.** For example, are you looking for instruction on how to make something, or are you trying to find out whom to contact for more information?
- **Skim the text, and notice its features.** Take note of heads, lists, and special features.
- **Read carefully, and absorb what the text has to say.** Refer to diagrams and illustrations for guidance. If a glossary or footnotes have been provided, use them.
- **If any information is confusing, re-read to clarify.**

SKILLS FOCUS

Reading Skills
Understand informational documents.

Vocabulary Skills
Recognize word roots.

VOCABULARY DEVELOPMENT

PREVIEW SELECTION VOCABULARY

Before you read the next selection, get to know these words.

ambassador (am·bas′ə·dər) *n.*: person who formally represents his or her nation while living in another nation.

An ambassador is a special diplomat appointed by a country.

obtain (əb·tān′) *v.*: get.

Before you can apply for a passport, you must obtain a certified copy of your birth certificate.

official (ə·fish′əl) *adj.*: having to do with a recognized authority, such as a government office.

A photocopy of a birth certificate is not an official copy.

affirm (ə·fʉrm′) *v.*: say that something is true; agree.

The passport clerk will ask you to affirm that everything on your application is accurate.

embassy (em′bə·sē) *n.*: offices of an ambassador and the ambassador's staff.

If you need help when you are traveling abroad, you can call the American embassy.

consulate (kän′səl·it) *n.*: office of the consul, the person appointed by a government to aid and serve its citizens.

The consulate will help citizens when they travel in a foreign city.

CLARIFYING WORD MEANINGS: WORD ROOTS

The **root** of a word is its basic element, before any affixes are added. The root of the word *consulate* is *consul*. A consul is a person appointed to serve a government's citizens in a foreign city or nation. If we add the suffix *–ship* to *consul*, we get another word: *consulship*, which refers to a consul's term of office. Here are some more word roots:

Word Root	Meaning	Related Vocabulary Word
ambactus	"vassal" or "servant"	ambassador; embassy
tenere	"to hold"	obtain
officium	"office"	official
firmus	"firm"	affirm

from Cobblestone, *December 1994*

Passports: Don't Leave Home Without One

Carolyn Liberatore Lavine

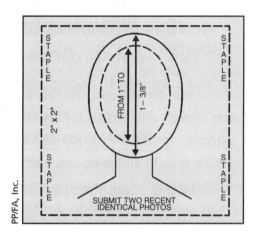

PP/FA, Inc.

2" x 2"

FROM 1" TO 1 – 3/8"

STAPLE

STAPLE

STAPLE

STAPLE

SUBMIT TWO RECENT IDENTICAL PHOTOS

If you decide that you would like to study art in Europe, pursue a career as a foreign diplomat, or simply travel abroad, you will need a passport. A passport is an official document used by both foreign countries and your birth country as proof of your identity and citizenship. It is a good idea to apply for a passport the minute you even suspect that you might be traveling abroad. You will want to take off at a moment's notice when your appointment comes through as **ambassador** to Greece! Here is how to

10 get a passport:

1. Get a passport application form. This form is available at some post offices and most county office buildings from the clerk of court. You also can get a form by writing to the U.S. Department of State, Bureau of Consular Affairs, Passport Services, 1425 K Street N.W., Washington, D.C. 20524.

IDENTIFY

What does the illustration show you? Is it drawn to actual size? Use a ruler to find out.

_____

_____

_____

VOCABULARY

ambassador (am·bas′ə·dər) *n.:* person who represents a nation while living in another nation.

DECODING TIP

In "K Street N.W.," the *N.W.* stands for "Northwest" (line 15).

2. Carefully fill out the one-page form. Type or print clearly and answer *all* the questions. Ask a parent to double-check them. If you do not have a Social Security number, fill in that box with zeros.

3. Obtain an official copy of your birth certificate. Visit or write to the county office building in the county in which you were born. You must have a *certified copy* of your birth certificate (one with a raised seal on it) to get a passport. A photocopy of the original will not be accepted.

4. Have two identical photographs taken of yourself alone. Check the yellow pages under "Photographers—Passport" for a photographer who knows all the rules about passport photos. Expect to pay ten to fifteen dollars for two photos. Remember to smile!

5. Take the completed application, official birth certificate, and photos to the county office that sent you the form. If you are under eighteen, a parent or guardian must accompany you. Your parent or guardian must show his or her driver's license or photo ID to the county clerk. If the person's last name is different from yours, he or she must provide a certified copy of his or her marriage license or divorce papers and proof of his or her citizenship. (A passport can be used for this.)

6. Swear or affirm to the clerk that everything on your application is true—including that the photograph attached is really you. Most passport photos are notoriously unflattering.

7. Sign your name on the application form and pay the passport fee. If you are under eighteen, the fee is thirty dollars. Have a check or money order made payable to "Passport Office." Be prepared to pay a ten-dollar "execution fee" in cash to the county.

You can expect your passport in the mail four to six weeks
50   later. . . . A passport for children under eighteen years of
age is valid for five years. After that, a passport can be
renewed for fifty-five dollars plus the ten-dollar execution
fee. It is valid for ten years.

If you do travel abroad, you will want to find out
about visas, too. A visa is an official document that is issued
by the country to which you are traveling. It sets some
limitations on the amount of time you can spend in the
country. Students who go abroad to study usually must
have a visa. Call the **embassy** or **consulate** of the country
60   you plan to visit to find out more.

CORBIS.

embassy (em'bə·sē) *n.:*
offices of an ambassador
and the ambassador's staff.

consulate (kän'səl·it) *n.:* office
of the consul, the person
appointed by a government
to aid and serve its citizens.

**COMPARE &
CONTRAST**

How is the information in
the passage beginning on
line 49 different from the
information presented
in the list?

_____

_____

_____

_____

_____

_____

CONNECT

If you were to go get a
passport, what information
in this article would you
re-read?

_____

_____

_____

_____

_____

Passports: Don't Leave Home Without One

SKILLS FOCUS

Reading Skills
Analyze informational documents.

Passport Application   Fill out all the information on this sample passport application.

After you practice filling out this form, you might want to get a real passport for yourself. Re-read the article to find out where to get the application and a photograph. You might also try to find out how to get a passport application online.

UNITED STATES DEPARTMENT OF STATE
APPLICATION FOR ☐ PASSPORT ☐ REGISTRATION
(Type or print all capital letters in blue or black ink in white areas only)

Sample

1. NAME (First and Middle)

LAST

2. MAIL PASSPORT TO: STREET / RFD # OR P.O. BOX   APT. #

☐ 5 Yr.   ☐ 10 Yr.   Issue Date _____

CITY   **STATE**   R   D   O   DP

ZIP CODE   **COUNTRY / IN CARE OF (if applicable)**   End. # _____   Exp. _____

3. SEX   **4. PLACE OF BIRTH** (City & State or City & Country)   **5. DATE OF BIRTH** Month Day Year   **6. SOCIAL SECURITY NUMBER** (SEE FEDERAL TAX LAW NOTICE ON PAGE 2)
☐ M ☐ F

7. HEIGHT Feet Inches   **8. HAIR COLOR**   **9. EYE COLOR**   **10. HOME TELEPHONE** ( )   **11. BUSINESS TELEPHONE** ( )   **12. OCCUPATION**

13. PERMANENT ADDRESS (DO NOT LIST P.O. BOX)   STREET/RFD #   CITY   STATE   ZIP CODE

14. FATHER'S FULL NAME Last First   BIRTHPLACE   BIRTHDATE   U.S. CITIZEN ☐ Yes ☐ No   **15. MOTHER'S FULL MAIDEN NAME** Last First   BIRTHPLACE   BIRTHDATE   U.S. CITIZEN ☐ Yes ☐ No

16. HAVE YOU EVER BEEN MARRIED? ☐ Yes ☐ No   SPOUSE'S OR FORMER SPOUSE'S FULL NAME AT BIRTH Last First   BIRTHPLACE   BIRTHDATE   U.S. CITIZEN ☐ Yes ☐ No

DATE OF MOST RECENT MARRIAGE Month Day Year   WIDOWED/DIVORCED? ☐ Yes Give Date Month Day Year ☐ No   **17. OTHER NAMES YOU HAVE USED** (1)   (2)

18. HAVE YOU EVER BEEN ISSUED A U.S. PASSPORT? ☐ Yes ☐ No   IF YES, COMPLETE NEXT LINE AND SUBMIT PASSPORT IF AVAILABLE.   DISPOSITION
NAME IN WHICH ISSUED   MOST RECENT PASSPORT NUMBER   APPROXIMATE ISSUE DATE Month Day Year   ☐ Submitted ☐ Stolen ☐ Lost ☐ Other _____

It is necessary to submit a statement with an application for a new passport when a previous valid or potentially valid passport cannot be presented. The statement must set forth in detail why the previous passport cannot be presented. Use Form DSP-64.

S T A P L E   S T A P L E
FROM 1" TO 1 – 3/8"
2" x 2"
S T A P L E   S T A P L E
SUBMIT TWO RECENT IDENTICAL PHOTOS

19. EMERGENCY CONTACT. If you wish, you may supply the name, address and telephone number of a person not traveling with you to be contacted in case of emergency.

NAME

STREET

CITY   STATE   ZIP CODE

TELEPHONE ( )   RELATIONSHIP

20. TRAVEL PLANS (not mandatory)   Month Day Year
Date of Trip
Length of Trip
COUNTRIES TO BE VISITED

21. STOP. DO NOT SIGN APPLICATION UNTIL REQUESTED TO DO SO BY PERSON ADMINISTERING OATH.
I have not, since acquiring United States citizenship, performed any of the acts listed under "Acts or Conditions" on the reverse of this application form (unless explanatory statement is attached). I solemnly swear (or affirm) that the statements made on this application are true and the photograph attached is a true likeness of me.

X _____   X _____
Parent's/Legal Guardian's Signature if identifying minor child   **Applicant's Signature - age 13 or older**

PP/FA, Inc.

Skills Review

Passports: Don't Leave Home Without One

VOCABULARY AND COMPREHENSION

A. Clarifying Word Meanings: Word Roots   Match the Word Bank words with their roots. (Two Word Bank words share a word root.) Write the correct letter on the line.

_____ **1.** official

_____ **2.** consulate

_____ **3.** affirm

_____ **4.** obtain

_____ **5.** ambassador/
        embassy

a. *tenere,* "to hold"

b. *officium,* "office"

c. *firmus,* "firm"

d. *ambactus,* "vassal"

e. *consul,* "person who serves his or her country while living in a foreign country"

> ### Word Bank
> ambassador
> obtain
> official
> affirm
> embassy
> consulate

B. Reading Comprehension   Answer each question below.

1. What are three reasons for getting a passport? _____

_____

_____

2. Where can you get an application for a passport? _____

_____

3. How will the identification of your parent or guardian be checked?

_____

_____

4. For how long is a passport valid? _____

_____

5. How is a visa different from a passport? _____

_____

_____

SKILLS FOCUS

Vocabulary Skills
Recognize word roots.

Part Two

Reading Informational Texts

Academic Vocabulary for Part Two

These are the terms you should know
as you read and analyze the informational selections in this section.

———

Proposition Important idea or opinion offered for discussion.

Support Evidence that suggests that a statement is true.

Main Idea The most important point in a text or section of text.

Summary A brief restatement of the main events or ideas in a text.

Biased Treatment One-sided treatment of a subject.

Objective Treatment Discussing all sides of a subject, allowing readers
to draw their own conclusions.

Inference An educated guess, based on facts or details in a text.

Unsupported Inference An inference, or guess, that isn't supported
by evidence.

Comparison Description of how two or more things are alike.

Contrast Description of how two or more things are different.

Logic Sound or correct reasoning, based on reasons, evidence, and
examples.

Coherence Text that is easily understood and that flows naturally
from one idea to the next has coherence.

● ● ●

Text Features Special type, such as boldface, italics, capitals, and
bullets that call attention to important information.

Headings Words or phrases that are used to break up a text into
sections.

Illustrations Drawings, photos, art, graphs, maps, or other visuals
that explain or enrich a text.

Captions Brief explanations of art, illustrations, charts, or maps. A
caption usually appears below or next to the visual it describes.

Footnotes Definitions and/or examples of difficult terms within the
text. Footnotes are numbered and usually appear at the bottom
of the text page.

ARTICLE

Music from the Start

by Patricia Hunt-Jones

READING SKILLS: ANALYZING PROPOSITION AND SUPPORT

When you propose, or suggest, a course of action or reveal an idea or belief, you are making a **proposition**. In many informational texts the writer offers one or more propositions for you to consider. A proposition is usually followed by reasons that **support** it. These reasons may take the form of statistics, examples, anecdotes, and expert opinions.

As you read "Music from the Start," keep track of the writer's propositions and support in a chart like this one:

Proposition:			
Support:	Support:	Support:	Support:

VOCABULARY DEVELOPMENT: PREVIEW SELECTION VOCABULARY

Preview these vocabulary words before you begin to read.

archaeologists (är′kē·äl′ə·jists) *n.:* scientists who study ancient people and their culture.

Archaeologists recently discovered flutes that are about 9,000 years old.

representation (rep′ri·zen·tā′shən) *n.:* image or likeness.

The stone tablet had a representation of people playing music etched on it.

transformed (trans·fôrmd′) *v.:* changed the form or appearance of.

Egyptian musicians transformed the harp; they changed it from a three-string instrument into a 20-string instrument.

harmonious (här·mō′nē·əs) *adj.:* having musical tones combined to give a pleasing effect.

The double-pipe flute made a pleasing, harmonious sound.

accompaniment (ə·kum′pə·nə·mənt) *n.:* something that goes with, or accompanies, something else.

An instrumental accompaniment is often played when someone sings a melody.

SKILLS FOCUS

Reading Skills
Analyze proposition and support.

from Archaeology's dig, June/July 2000

Music from the Start

Patricia Hunt-Jones

© Tom Grill/CORBIS.

And I've often wondered how did it all start?
Who found out that nothing can capture a heart,
Like a melody can? Well, whoever it was, I'm a fan.

—from the song "Thank You for the Music"
by the 1970s rock-and-roll group ABBA

When you're hanging out in your room listening to the
sounds of 'N Sync, Britney Spears, or Fresh Prince, did you
ever wonder when people started making music? Well, hold
onto your headphones because, believe it or not, people
10   have been playing musical instruments for more than
10,000 years. In fact, **archaeologists** recently discovered
flutes in China that are around 9,000 years BMTV (Before
Music Television), making them among the oldest playable
multinote musical instruments ever found.

But the story of how people developed music is about
more than the discovery of old instruments. Through

TEXT STRUCTURE

In this informational article the writer presents a **proposition,** an important idea or opinion, and supports the proposition with reasons. Circle the proposition in the first paragraph of this article.

TEXT STRUCTURE

Propositions are supported with statistics and other facts, examples, anecdotes, and expert opinions. Underline a detail in lines 6–14 that supports the proposition.

VOCABULARY

archaeologists
(är′kē·äl′ə·jists) *n.:* scientists who study ancient people and their culture.

representation
(rep′ri·zen·tā′shən) *n.:* image
or likeness.

Like many long words, *representation* is built upon a base
word plus a prefix and suffix.
What is the prefix? What is
the suffix? What is the base
word? Divide the word to
show the three parts.

_____

_____

_____

_____

_____

_____

_____

_____

_____

_____

_____

_____

_____

_____

The English word *lyre* (line 28)
comes from the Greek word
lyra, "stringed instrument."

A related word, *lyric*,
describes a poem that does
not tell a story but instead
expresses the speaker's
thoughts or feelings. *Lyrics*
are the words to a song.

sculpture, paintings, writing on tablets and tombs, and
even Bible stories, archaeologists have learned how
people of ancient cultures created and improved the
20 music they loved.

Ancient Music Makers

The earliest **representation** of people playing musical
instruments appeared on Sumerian writing tablets in
Mesopotamia (now modern Iraq) around 3000 B.C.
Sumerian music was first played on drums and bird-bone
flutes (both of which archaeologists have found in the
area). The Sumerians later developed stringed instruments
such as lutes, harps, and lyres. As the centuries passed,
Sumerian kings paid musicians to write and play music for
30 festivals and religious holidays.

© Amy Butler/Getty Images.

The History of Music BMTV (Before Music Television)	
9000 B.C.	The Chinese invent a flute out of hollow bird bones. It is among the first multinote, playable musical instruments.
3000 B.C.	The first stringed instruments, such as harps, lutes, and lyres, are developed in Sumer, a city in Mesopotamia.
2134–1600 B.C.	Portable harps are invented in Egypt. Priests and dancers play them at festivals and religious ceremonies.
1550–1080 B.C.	Many new kinds of instruments are created in Egypt including pipes, trumpets, drums, and tambourines. These folks knew how to party.
8th Century B.C.	The famous Greek poet Homer describes many instruments and songs in his famous poems, the *Iliad* and the *Odyssey*.
600 B.C.	As described in the Bible, a golden statue of the Assyrian king Nebuchadnezzar is dedicated as a full orchestra plays.
427–322 B.C.	In their writings, the famous Greek philosophers Plato and Aristotle say music is important in the education of Greek citizens.
50 B.C.	The water organ is invented by the Romans using old cows' stomachs to hold the water.

40

50

60

(continued)

TEXT STRUCTURE

How many years does this time line span?

_____

_____

_____

_____

_____

_____

_____

_____

_____

_____

IDENTIFY

Skim through the time line. In which two times and places were many instruments created?

_____

_____

_____

_____

_____

_____

_____

_____

_____

Read the top entry of the chart on this page. What can you infer about Carinus from these details?

_____

_____

_____

_____

The History of Music BMTV *(continued)*	
A.D. 284	The Roman emperor Carinus throws a huge party with an orchestra of 200 flutes, 100 harps, and 100 trumpets.
A.D. 1000–1500	The Aztecs in Mexico play percussion instruments and horns, primarily during religious ceremonies.

VOCABULARY

transformed (trans·fôrmd′) *v.*: changed the form or appearance of.

The prefix *trans–* is from a Latin word meaning "over, on the other side of, through, or across." What is a *transformer*? a *transfusion*? *transportation*?

_____

_____

_____

_____

_____

_____

_____

IDENTIFY

Underline the details in lines 74–91 that support the writer's **proposition** that people have played musical instruments for thousands of years.

Appreciation for the sound of Sumerian stringed instruments carried over to ancient Egypt. During the next 1,000 years, Egyptian musicians **transformed** the harp, originally a three-string instrument, into a 20-string instrument.

While we have a lot of information about Egyptian music, musicians, and instruments, we have no idea how their music sounded. We do know that the ancient Egyptians so enjoyed music that their cow-goddess, Hathor, ruled over love, joy, and—you guessed it—music. Paintings and reliefs in royal tombs show Egyptians—from the wives of pharaohs to the lowliest slaves—playing music as far back as 2600 B.C. In Egypt, music was mostly played during religious ceremonies, great festivals, and large parades. Even divorcing Egyptian couples would fight over who owned the rights to instruments, written music, and musicians (who were slaves).

Besides stringed instruments, Egyptian musicians also played pipes and trumpets. In fact, two trumpets, one of bronze and gold, the other silver, were found in the tomb of the boy king, Tutankhamen. They are now in the Cairo Museum, as is the mummified body of Harmosis, ancient Egypt's greatest musician.

The Greek Beat

The ancient Greeks weren't the first culture to develop *mousike* (their word for music) and instruments, but they made the biggest contribution to the art of Western music as we know it today. The instruments found in Greece were similar to those in Sumer and Egypt. How do we know this? Herodotus, a 5th-century B.C. Greek historian, writes about Greeks traveling to Sumer and Egypt to study and

100 borrow their instrument-making skills and musicology (the science of writing and creating music). Pythagoras, the 6th-century mathematician, also went to Sumer to study the science of music. He would eventually develop the octave, the group of eight notes—do, re, mi, etc.—that became the foundation for modern Western music.

Which instruments made the Greeks get up and boogie? Ancient writings tell of how audiences loved the *aulos,* which was a double-pipe flute. The two pipes were

© Bettmann/CORBIS.

WORD STUDY

Underline the definition of the word *musicology* (line 100).

The suffix *-logy* is from a Greek word meaning "word" or "study of" or "theory of." What is *biology? psychology? theology?*

_____

_____

_____

_____

_____

_____

_____

_____

WORD STUDY

What does *octave* mean (line 104)? How do you know?

_____

_____

_____

_____

_____

_____

_____

_____

_____

played at the same time, and archaeologists believe this
created a **harmonious** sound. We don't know which pipe
carried the melody (main music line) and which carried
the harmony (complementary music line), or even how
they sounded together. We do know that the flute players
had to wear a head harness (much like a retainer) to hold
the pipes to their lips.

The ancient Greeks also developed the *phorminx,* a
seven-string lyre, and the cithara, which was a popular
instrument used in local concerts. They also created one
of the first organs. The organ player would move a lever
which would drive air into a pipe using water pressure to
create a sound.

In Greece, music was so popular that it was played as
accompaniment to everyday chores and during battle
training for soldiers. During concerts, audiences shoved
and pushed each other for the best seats. Musicians
performed and composed original music, wore fancy
costumes, made tons of money, and were worshiped by
adoring fans. The Greeks might also be the first Western
culture that put words to music. They would recite their
historical or romantic poetry while instruments played in
the background. And we have the Greeks to thank for many
of our modern music words, such as *chorus, choir,
orchestra,* and *harmony.*

Music from the Start

Proposition-and-Support Chart   An important idea or opinion is called a **proposition.** In most cases, writers support their propositions with a variety of reasons. Look back through "Music from the Start" and any notes you took. Then, use the chart below to identify one of the writer's propositions plus the reasons the writer gives to support the proposition.

SKILLS FOCUS

Reading Skills
Analyze proposition and support.

Support:

Support:

Proposition:

Support:

Support:

Skills Review

Music from the Start

VOCABULARY AND COMPREHENSION

A. Selection Vocabulary   Write the Word Bank words on the blanks to complete this paragraph. Use each word only once.

A group of (1) _____ discovered a beautiful picture of musicians from ancient Greece. It was a(n) (2) _____ of flute and lyre players and a singer at a feast. The picture suggested that the instruments provided (3) _____ to the singer's voice. In one corner was the image of a creature that had been (4) _____ into a man with the head of a bull. Even it was singing happily to the (5) _____ music.

B. Reading Comprehension   Answer each question below.

1. What are some of the oldest instruments ever found? _____

   _____

2. When were the first stringed instruments thought to be developed? Where were they developed? _____

   _____

3. For what purpose did the Aztecs play musical instruments? What kinds of instruments did they play? _____

   _____

4. What ancient culture made the greatest contribution to Western music as we know it today? _____

   _____

5. Who developed the octave, the group of eight notes that became the foundation for modern Western music? _____

   _____

ARTICLES

The Cook Legacy by John Robson
An Air of Duty and Discipline
by Barbara Krasner-Khait

READING SKILLS: COMPARING AND CONTRASTING TEXTS

Imagine that you're researching a topic, such as the Bermuda Triangle. Although you will find lots of essays and articles on that topic, the treatment of the topic will vary a lot. Writing that covers many aspects of a topic has a **broad scope.** Writing that covers only one or two aspects of a topic has a **limited scope.** In addition to variations in scope, some articles contain bias, whereas others are objective. **Bias** is a one-sided treatment of a subject and does not present an accurate picture of a topic or issue. An **objective** treatment, on the other hand, discusses many aspects of a subject, allowing you to draw your own conclusions.

As you read the two selections about Captain Cook, ask:
- How are the selections similar in their scope and treatment of ideas?
- Is there evidence of bias, or is each treatment balanced and objective?

VOCABULARY DEVELOPMENT: PREVIEW SELECTION VOCABULARY

Preview these words before you begin reading.

replica (rep′li·kə) *n.:* copy; reproduction.

A replica of Cook's ship draws huge numbers of visitors every year.

specimens (spes′ə·mənz) *n.:* samples; examples.

Cook brought important plant specimens back to Europe after his voyages.

culprits (kul′prits) *n.:* people who have committed crimes.

Cook did not tolerate theft, either from members of his crew or natives.

reluctantly (ri·luk′tənt·lē) *adv.:* with hesitation; unwillingly.

Cook's men didn't always agree with him, but they reluctantly followed his orders.

entreaties (en·trēt′ēz) *n.:* pleas; sincere requests.

Once Cook issued his orders, no amount of entreaties would sway his decision.

SKILLS FOCUS

Reading Skills
Compare and contrast texts.

The Cook Legacy

John Robson

James Cook (1728–1779), the most famous and widely traveled of English explorers.

© CORBIS.

IDENTIFY

Re-read lines 1–9. What is the topic of the first paragraph?

_____

_____

_____

_____

_____

_____

VOCABULARY

replica (rep′li·kə) *n.:* copy; reproduction.

Captain James Cook is a name known and recognized throughout the world. Like Christopher Columbus and Marco Polo, Cook was an explorer whose fame continued long after his death. Almost every year, new books celebrate his voyages and achievements. A **replica** of the *Endeavour* sails to international ports, drawing huge numbers of visitors, while museums in various countries house collections of materials associated with his voyages and host exhibits celebrating his achievements.

10   Surely one of the greatest explorers, sailors, surveyors, and mapmakers of all time, James Cook raised the art of marine exploration to a new level. When he sailed into the Pacific Ocean in 1769, that vast expanse of water was only

partly known. Nevertheless, using the knowledge he gained from crisscrossing its waters many times over the next twelve years, Cook produced a map that we can recognize today. Unlike earlier sailors, Cook knew exactly where he was and skillfully and quickly made charts that showed where he had been. He also had a knack for finding islands in the vast ocean. Like someone playing pinball, Cook seemed to bounce from tiny island to tiny island.

Of equal interest is what he did not find. To disprove the existence of a great southern continent, Cook sailed farther south than any of his predecessors. The first to cross the Antarctic Circle, he sailed in extreme cold among the icebergs and in dense fog. In doing so, he showed that the continent, if it existed at all, would be too harsh to inhabit.

On his third voyage, Cook helped prove that a Northwest Passage through the North American continent, south of 65 degrees north, was not possible. The cold and ice north of Alaska and Canada had finally stopped Cook as he sailed north through the Bering Strait, and it would take ships that were larger and stronger than his to get through this area.

© Bettmann/CORBIS.

INTERPRET

Re-read lines 10–34. Does the author show **bias** in favor of Cook? Explain.

WORD STUDY

Predecessors (pred'ə·ses'ərz), in line 24, means "ones who have gone before."

specimens (spes'ə·mənz) *n.:* samples; examples.

Re-read lines 46–50. Does the writer show any **bias** here? Explain.

_____

_____

_____

_____

_____

_____

_____

_____

_____

_____

Read the boxed passage aloud several times. As you read, strive for a clear and smooth presentation. Be sure to pause when you come to a comma.

The noun *advocate* (ad'və·kit), line 56, means "supporter." It comes from the Latin *advocatus,* meaning "counselor." *Advocate* can also be a verb (ad'və·kāt') that means "give support."

Cook's three voyages can be regarded as the first scientific voyages. The work of the naturalists (Joseph Banks, Daniel Solander, and Johann and Georg Forster), the astronomers (Charles Green, William Wales, and William Bayly), the artists (Sydney Parkinson, Herman Sporing, William

40   Hodges, and John Webber), and Cook himself ensured that the voyages would be remembered for more than just the sailing. The **specimens** brought back to Europe, the collection of charts, drawings, and paintings, and the descriptions of people, places, and events combined to produce a treasury of information still being used today.

> Cook's dealings with the people of the Pacific were good, but not perfect. Sadly, he died in Hawaii after one confrontation. Until that time, however, relations had been friendly, and Cook genuinely regretted every death that
> 50   resulted from contact with visiting Europeans. Cook's descriptions, and those of his colleagues, provide us with great insight into the lives of Pacific Islanders who had had no previous contact with foreigners.

In dealing with his own men, Cook was strict but fair. Their health was a major concern, and Cook was an early advocate of a good diet and cleanliness. His insistence on fresh food at every opportunity and on making sure that the crew washed both their clothes and themselves ensured that few men became sick or died. Cook set standards that

60   others soon followed.

In the early 1800s, a Russian explorer named a group of scattered islands in the Pacific after Cook. Nearly 200 years later, the people of the Cook Islands voted to retain that name and not replace it with a Polynesian one. Similarly, mountains, towns, inlets, and other geographical features around the world have been named for him.

In the 1990s, the United States government recognized the role of Cook in the history of exploration by naming two space shuttles for ships that he took to the Pacific. The
70 *Discovery* and the *Endeavour* shuttles are two additional examples of how the achievements of Captain James Cook continue to be celebrated throughout the world.

Volunteers paint the hull of the replica of Captain Cook's ship *Endeavour*.

Re-read lines 67–72. What two pieces of evidence support the writer's **proposition** that Cook's achievements are still recognized?

_____

_____

_____

_____

_____

_____

An Air of Duty and Discipline

Barbara Krasner-Khait

COMPARE & CONTRAST

Re-read lines 1–5. Now, go back and read the first paragraph of the first selection. Is the **scope** of this selection broader or more limited than the scope of the first selection? Explain.

_____

_____

_____

_____

VOCABULARY

culprits (kul′prits) *n.:* people who have committed crimes.

INTERPRET

Pause at line 22. Does the writer approve of Cook's methods of discipline? Explain, using details from the text to support your ideas.

_____

_____

_____

_____

_____

Captain James Cook made the importance of discipline clear to his men. As crew members of the *Endeavour* prepared to sail in August 1768, he read them the 36 clauses of the Articles of War, many of which dealt with discipline and punishment.

If any man disobeyed Cook's orders, he would be subjected to a dozen lashes with a whip for each violation. Crew members were forced to witness the punishment so they would not make the same mistake.

10 Cook's insistence on duty and discipline served the voyage well in time of crisis. When the *Endeavour* sustained heavy damage on Australia's Great Barrier Reef in June 1770, botanist Joseph Banks was impressed by the men's cheerfulness as they banded together to preserve the ship. He was also surprised that given the grueling work they had to do, they did not disobey. Banks attributed this to the "cool and steady conduct of the officers," no doubt a tribute to Cook's style of leadership.

Cook did not tolerate theft, whether the **culprits** were 20 members of his own crew or natives. Once, for example, when some food was stolen on board, Cook cut the crew's meat allowance in half until the thief came forward.

Cook's disciplinary actions changed noticeably on the third voyage, however. Some could not understand his new policies, but perhaps the long voyages were taking their toll.

Cook had fallen ill on both his second and his third voyages and showed signs of tiredness. As a result, his relationship with his men and with Pacific Islanders seems to have been affected. On one occasion, at Moorea°, natives stole a goat

30 from the ship. Cook's officers and men **reluctantly** followed disciplinary orders. According to midshipman Gilbert, they "burnt in all 20 Houses & 18 large War Canoes . . ." and ". . . neither tears nor **entreaties** could move Cook. He seem'd to be very rigid in the performance of his order . . . I can't well account for Capt Cook's proceedings on this occasion; as they were so very different from his conduct in like cases in his former voyages."

Although Cook ran a tight ship and was stern while at sea, he would sometimes relax and talk with his men while

40 on shore, forgetting for a time that he was their commander. Some men loved him for the hard discipline; others did not. Some adored him and considered him a father figure; others considered him a tyrant. There is no doubt, however, that the air of duty and discipline aboard Cook's ships contributed to the success of the voyages.

° **Moorea:** island in French Polynesia, located twelve miles from Tahiti.

© Dave Bartruff/CORBIS.

Captain Cook.

IDENTIFY

Place a check mark next to information in lines 23–45 that shows the writer is giving an **objective** treatment of her subject.

VOCABULARY

reluctantly (ri·luk'tənt·lē) *adv.:* with hesitation; unwillingly.

entreaties (en·trēt'·ēz) *n.:* pleas; sincere requests.

COMPARE & CONTRAST

Re-read lines 38–45. Then, go back and read the last paragraph of the first selection. Based on these two closing paragraphs, which selection do you think gives a more **objective** treatment of the topic? Explain.

_____

_____

_____

_____

_____

_____

_____

_____

_____

_____

_____

_____

The Cook Legacy / An Air of Duty and Discipline

SKILLS FOCUS

Reading Skills
Compare and contrast texts.

Comparison-and-Contrast Chart   Compare and contrast information from the two texts you just read by completing the chart below. Look through each selection, and decide whether each has a broad or limited scope. Check the appropriate box. Then, list three pieces of information from each article. Finally, check the boxes in the last row to indicate whether the selections are biased (one-sided) or objective. Provide a brief explanation of why you answered as you did.

The Cook Legacy	An Air of Duty and Discipline
Broad scope? ☐ Limited scope? ☐	Broad scope? ☐ Limited scope? ☐
Informative details 1) 2) 3)	Informative details 1) 2) 3)
Biased? ☐ Objective? ☐	Biased? ☐ Objective? ☐

Skills Review

The Cook Legacy / An Air of Duty and Discipline

VOCABULARY AND COMPREHENSION

A. Selection Vocabulary   Write the Word Bank words on the blanks to complete this paragraph. Use each word only once.

The museum had a great collection of (1) _____ from Cook's voyages. I didn't want to spend a day of our vacation in a museum, but I (2) _____ agreed after my brother's tearful (3) _____. A man at the museum said they used to have a miniature (4) _____ of one of Cook's ships, but it was stolen in a burglary. Unfortunately, the police haven't found the (5) _____ who took it.

Word Bank

replica
specimens
culprits
reluctantly
entreaties

B. Reading Comprehension   Answer each question below.

1. Who was Captain James Cook? _____

_____

2. Why are Cook's voyages still famous? _____

_____

3. In what way has Cook's role in exploration been recognized by the

   United States government? _____

_____

4. According to the second selection, what does Cook order his men to

   do when a goat is stolen from their ship? Were these orders consistent

   with Cook's previous actions? _____

_____

5. Did all of Cook's men feel the same way about him? Explain. _____

_____

_____

Birth of a Legend by Stephen Lyons

READING SKILLS: UNDERSTANDING TEXT STRUCTURES

Text structures help you find and understand information in articles and books. Read about the different kinds of text structures below, and think about the kinds of information they might help you find. Then, look for how these text structures are used in "Birth of a Legend."

- **Main headings and subheadings**   Words or short phrases that give the main idea of the text that follows.
- **Displayed quotations**   Quotations set apart from the text that hint at the topic.
- **Interview format**   At the beginning of a sentence or passage, a boldface word followed by a colon identifies the speaker. This text structure is often used with interviews.
- **Captions**   Descriptions of art, illustrations, charts, or maps. A caption usually appears below or next to the visual it describes.
- **Footnotes**   Definitions and/or examples of difficult terms. Footnotes are numbered and usually appear at the bottom of the text page.
- **Illustrations**   Art, photographs, drawings, charts, or maps that accompany a text.

VOCABULARY DEVELOPMENT: PREVIEW SELECTION VOCABULARY

Take some time to preview the words below.

complied (kəm·plīd′) *v.:* agreed; went along with.

> *When the man commanded the Loch Ness Monster to leave the swimmer alone, the beast complied; it turned and swam away.*

protruding (prō·trōōd′iŋ) *v.* used as *adj.:* jutting out.

> *The creature's hump was protruding above the surface of the water.*

submerged (səb·murjd′) *v.:* plunged into water; sank.

> *Each time we spotted the monster, it submerged again beneath the water.*

predominant (prē·däm′ə·nənt) *adj.:* having superior strength or influence.

> *Occasional breezes stirred from several directions, but the predominant wind was blowing from the southwest.*

nonchalant (nän′shə·länt′) *adj.:* matter-of-fact; showing no concern.

> *I tried to act nonchalant when the big monster appeared, but I was scared.*

SKILLS FOCUS

Reading Skills
Understand text structures.

from NOVA Online

Birth of a Legend

Stephen Lyons

BACKGROUND: Informational Text and Legend

This article about the world's most famous monster is from a Web site called *NOVA Online.* In Scotland and Ireland a lough, or loch (läk), is a lake. Loch Ness is a lake in Scotland that has earned fame from a monster that might not really live there at all. The search for the monster has gone on for years.

"Many a man has been hanged on less evidence than there is for the Loch Ness Monster."

—G. K. Chesterton

When the Romans first came to northern Scotland in the first century A.D., they found the Highlands occupied by fierce, tattoo-covered tribes they called the Picts, or painted people. From the carved, standing stones still found in the region around Loch Ness, it is clear the Picts were fascinated by animals and careful to render them with great fidelity. All

10 the animals depicted on the Pictish stones are lifelike and easily recognizable—all but one. The exception is a strange beast with an elongated beak or muzzle, a head locket or spout, and flippers instead of feet. Described by some scholars as a swimming elephant, the Pictish beast is the earliest known evidence for an idea that has held sway in the Scottish Highlands for at least 1,500 years—that Loch Ness is home to a mysterious aquatic animal.

TEXT STRUCTURE

Circle the quotation of G. K. Chesterton. A clever quotation at the beginning of an article can grab our attention and focus our thinking on the article's topic.

Does Chesterton believe in the monster? Explain.

_____

_____

_____

_____

_____

_____

WORD STUDY

The words *beak* and *locket* (line 12) are defined in context by restatement. Underline the two restatements.

To be *malevolent*
(mə·lev'ə·lənt) means "wish-
ing someone harm" (line 22).
Even if you didn't know the
definition of *malevolent,* the
context would give you a
clue about the word's meaning. The description of what
the water horse does to children should tell you that
whatever *malevolent* means,
it isn't very good.

The Latin prefix *mal–* means
"wrong or bad." What does
maladjusted mean?

_____

_____

_____

_____

_____

_____

complied (kəm·plīd') *v.:*
agreed; went along with.

How does the context
tell you what the word
complied means?

_____

_____

_____

_____

_____

_____

Residents at the coast of Loch Ness.

In Scottish folklore, large animals have been associated
with many bodies of water, from small streams to the
largest lakes, often labeled Loch-na-Beistie on old maps.
These water-horses, or water-kelpies, are said to have
magical powers and malevolent intentions. According to
one version of the legend, the water-horse lures small
children into the water by offering them rides on its back.
Once the children are aboard, their hands become stuck
to the beast and they are dragged to a watery death, their
livers washing ashore the following day.

The earliest written reference linking such creatures to
Loch Ness is in the biography of Saint Columba, the man
credited with introducing Christianity to Scotland. In A.D.
565, according to this account, Columba was on his way to
visit a Pictish king when he stopped along the shore of
Loch Ness. Seeing a large beast about to attack a man who
was swimming in the lake, Columba raised his hand,
invoking the name of God and commanding the monster
to "go back with all speed." The beast **complied,** and the
swimmer was saved.

When Nicholas Witchell, a future BBC correspondent, researched the history of the legend for his 1974 book *The Loch Ness Story,* he found about a dozen pre-20th-century references to large animals in Loch Ness, gradually shifting in character from these clearly mythical accounts to something more like eyewitness descriptions.

But the modern legend of Loch Ness dates from 1933, when a new road was completed along the shore, offering the first clear views of the loch from the northern side. One April afternoon, a local couple was driving home along this road when they spotted "an enormous animal rolling and plunging on the surface." Their account was written up by a correspondent for the *Inverness Courier,* whose editor used the word "monster" to describe the animal. The Loch Ness Monster has been a media phenomenon ever since.

Public interest built gradually during the spring of 1933, then picked up sharply after a couple reported seeing one of the creatures on land, lumbering across the shore road. By October, several London newspapers had sent correspondents to Scotland, and radio programs were being interrupted to bring listeners the latest news from the loch. A British circus offered a reward of £20,000 for the capture of the beast. Hundreds of Boy Scouts and outdoorsmen arrived, some venturing out in small boats, others setting up deck chairs and waiting expectantly for the monster to appear.

The excitement over the monster reached a fever pitch in December, when the *London Daily Mail* hired an actor, film director, and big-game hunter named Marmaduke Wetherell to track down the beast. After only a few days at the loch, Wetherell reported finding the fresh footprints of a large, four-toed animal. He estimated it to be 20 feet long. With great fanfare, Wetherell made plaster casts of the footprints and, just before Christmas, sent them off to the Natural History Museum in London for analysis. While the world waited for the museum zoologists to return from holiday, legions of monster hunters descended on Loch Ness, filling the local hotels. Inverness was floodlit for the occasion, and traffic jammed the shoreline roads in both directions.

The bubble burst in early January, when museum zoologists announced that the footprints were those of a
80 hippopotamus. They had been made with a stuffed hippo foot—the base of an umbrella stand or ashtray. It wasn't clear whether Wetherell was the perpetrator of the hoax or its gullible victim. Either way, the incident tainted the image of the Loch Ness Monster and discouraged serious investigation of the phenomenon. For the next three decades, most scientists scornfully dismissed reports of strange animals in the loch. Those sightings that weren't outright hoaxes, they said, were the result of optical illusions caused by boat wakes, wind slicks, floating logs,
90 otters, ducks, or swimming deer.

Saw Something, They Did

Nevertheless, eyewitnesses continued to come forward with accounts of their sightings—more than 4,000 of them, according to Witchell's estimate. Most of the witnesses described a large creature with one or more humps **protruding** above the surface like the hull of an upturned boat. Others reported seeing a long neck or flippers. What was most remarkable, however, was that many of the eyewitnesses were sober, level-headed people:
100 lawyers and priests, scientists and schoolteachers, policemen and fishermen—even a Nobel Prize winner.

Keystone/Hulton Archive Picture Collection.

Is this the Loch Ness Monster?

WORD STUDY

An *anecdote* (an′ik·dōt′) is a short, entertaining story used to make a point. Anecdotes are often personal. What would you say *anecdotal evidence* is (line 104)?

_____

_____

_____

_____

_____

_____

_____

_____

Eyewitness Accounts

While no hard evidence for the existence of the Loch Ness Monster has yet turned up, heaps of anecdotal evidence exist. Although such eyewitness accounts are of little value scientifically, they can be compelling nevertheless. Below, lend an ear to several native Scots who swear they saw something in the loch. These tales were collected by the producers of the NOVA film *The Beast of Loch Ness.*

TEXT STRUCTURE

Circle the subheading for the first eyewitness account. What purpose does this heading have?

_____

_____

_____

_____

110   *"I saw it, and nothing can take that away."*

Well, we're talking about an incident that happened approximately 32 years ago, almost to the very day— mid-summer, June 1965. I, along with a friend, was on the south shore of Loch Ness, fishing for brown trout, looking almost directly into Urquhart Bay, when I saw something break the surface of the water. I glanced there, and I saw it, and then it wasn't there, it had disappeared.

TEXT STRUCTURE

Who is speaking now? Turn to the next page to find out.

_____

_____

_____

submerged (səb·mʉrjd′) *v.*: plunged into water; sank.

predominant (prē·däm′ə·nənt) *adj.*: having superior strength or influence.

TEXT STRUCTURE

Why do you think a description of the eyewitness is included at the end of this anecdote? (See line 140.)

_____

_____

_____

_____

_____

TEXT STRUCTURE

Who is talking now (line 145)? Where can you find out?

_____

_____

_____

WORD STUDY

Gobsmacked (line 145) is British slang. What do you guess it means?

_____

_____

But while watching, keeping an eye, and fishing gently, I saw an object surface. It was a large, black object—a whale-like object, going from infinity up, and came round onto a block end—and it **submerged,** to reappear a matter of seconds later. But on this occasion, the block end, which had been on my right, was now on my left, so I realized immediately that while in the process of surfacing, as it may, it had rotated. And with the **predominant** wind, the south-west wind, it appeared to be, I would say, at that stage drifting easily across.

So I called to my friend Willie Frazer, who incidentally had a sighting of an object on the loch almost a year ago to the very day. I called him, and he come up and joined me. We realized that it was drifting towards us, and, in fact, it came to within I would say about 250, 300 yards.

In no way am I even attempting to convert anybody to the religion of the object of Loch Ness. I mean, they can believe it, but it doesn't upset me if they don't believe it. Because I would question very much if I hadn't the extraordinary experience of seeing this object. If I hadn't seen it I would have without question given a lot of skepticism to what it was. But I saw it, and nothing can take that away.

—Ian Cameron, a retired superintendent of the Northern Police Force, lives with his wife Jessie in Inverness, Scotland, at the head of the loch. A keen angler, he is an authority on the Atlantic salmon.

"I'm gobsmacked . . . I just didn't know what it was."

Right, I'm driving along the loch side, glancing out of the window. You can see the rock formation, I was just down on the road there, it just rises. I saw this boiling in the water. I thought, "No, it can't be anything," and I carried on

150 a wee bit. Then I looked again, and I saw three black
humps. I mean, you know, there's the chance, I've seen
something in the water. But what is it?

So I'm gobsmacked, I'm looking out the window, I
just didn't know what it was. Then the people came
behind me, and they obviously wanted me to move. But I
didn't want to lose sight of this thing. So I just pulled over
to the side, grabbed my camera, and I thought I was being
very cool and very **nonchalant** and took two or three
photos. In fact, as I say, I had taken nine or ten, without
160 realizing, I just punched the button. It was just a pity it
was a small camera.

NOVA: Did anybody else see anything?

WHITE: Yeah, the other two people who were there—
I was just so excited I didn't get their name and address or
anything—they saw it exactly the same as me. Because the
wee wifey, who would have been a lady in her fifties, on
holiday, she was Scottish, she said to me, "I've not been in
the bar this morning!" And her husband said, "Ach, it's an
eel! It's an eel!" And I said, "There's no eels that big!" And

Wide view of Loch Ness.

VOCABULARY

nonchalant (nän′shə·länt′)
adj.: matter-of-fact; showing
no concern or worry.

How can you tell from the
sentence the meaning of the
word *nonchalant* (line 158)?

_____

_____

_____

_____

_____

_____

_____

_____

_____

TEXT STRUCTURE

Circle the words *NOVA* and
WHITE in lines 162 and 163.
What does this text format
indicate?

_____

_____

_____

_____

_____

_____

170   he said, "Ach, it's otters!" And I said, "You don't get otters swimming out like that!"

I saw what I saw, and I'm not going to be dissuaded. It wasn't just an imagination. I'm a sane guy, and I've got no ax to grind. As I say I sell pet food! What use to me is the Loch Ness Monster? Unless I can invent a food called, I don't know, Monster Munchies perhaps?

—Richard White lives in the village of Muir of Ord, north of Inverness. He runs his own business selling pet food.

Submarine used in the search for the Loch Ness Monster.

Keystone/Hulton Archive Picture Collection.

Birth of a Legend

Text Structures Chart Text structures help you find and understand information in articles and books. Read through "Birth of a Legend," and fill in the chart below with examples of the types of text structures you found in the article.

SKILLS FOCUS

Reading Skills
Analyze text structures.

Article Title:

_____

_____

_____

Illustrations & Captions:

_____

_____

_____

_____

_____

_____

_____

Main Idea of Article:

_____

_____

_____

_____

_____

_____

Headings (What Are They?):

_____

_____

_____

_____

Skills Review

Birth of a Legend

VOCABULARY AND COMPREHENSION

A. Selection Vocabulary   Write the Word Bank words on the blanks to complete this paragraph. Not all words will be used.

We had no choice in the matter—we simply (1) _____ with the captain's orders. Even in our cabins, though, we could see what looked like the head of a giant lizard. We caught only a glimpse of this strange creature before it (2) _____ again. I looked around to see if the other passengers were nervous, but they appeared (3) _____. As a result, I, too, made an effort to look unconcerned.

B. Reading Comprehension   Answer each question below.

1. Where is Loch Ness? What is the earliest known evidence for the idea of the Loch Ness Monster? _____

_____

2. Who was Saint Columba? According to this article, what did he do that was special? _____

_____

3. What year did the modern legend of Loch Ness begin? Why is that date important? _____

_____

4. Who was Marmaduke Wetherell? _____

_____

5. What do most scientists think of the sightings at Loch Ness? _____

_____

Before You Read

An Anne Frank Scrapbook

READING SKILLS: FINDING THE MAIN IDEA

A topic and a main idea are two different things. A **topic** is simply what a text is about. A **main idea** is the most important idea that is revealed about the topic. In the chart below, a single topic, baseball, is treated two different ways. Notice how the details in each piece add up to a different main idea.

Topic: Baseball	
Detail: Children as young as age three play baseball ↓	Detail: The speed of play teaches patience ↓
Detail: Corporate teams play throughout the summer ↓	Detail: Team sports like baseball build spirit of cooperation ↓
Detail: Local senior citizens have organized summertime baseball ↓	Detail: Winning and losing teaches us all about realities of life ↓
Main Idea: Baseball can be enjoyed by people of all ages	**Main Idea:** Playing baseball builds character

VOCABULARY DEVELOPMENT: PREVIEW SELECTION VOCABULARY

Before reading "An Anne Frank Scrapbook," preview these words.

tolerance (tăl′ər·əns) *n.:* respect for views different from your own.

> *Anne and her older sister, Margot, were raised in Germany in an atmosphere of tolerance; the Franks had friends of many faiths and nationalities.*

haven (hā′vən) *n.:* safe place; refuge.

> *The Franks thought Amsterdam would be a safe haven, but they were again forced to live under Nazi rule when Germany invaded the Netherlands.*

debilitated (dē·bil′ə·tāt′əd) *adj.:* weakened; made feeble.

> *Anne and Margot, already debilitated, contracted typhus and grew even sicker.*

SKILLS FOCUS

Reading Skills
Find main ideas.

An Anne Frank Scrapbook

Frankfurt, Germany ■ 1929–1933

Anne Frank, born on June 12, 1929, was the second daughter of Otto and Edith Frank, both from respected German-Jewish families.

Otto Frank could trace his family heritage in Frankfurt back to the seventeenth century, and Edith Hollander Frank came from a prominent Aachen family.

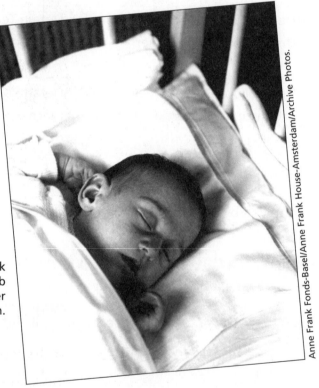

Anneliese Frank sleeping in a crib shortly after her birth.

Anne and her older sister, Margot, were raised in Germany in an atmosphere of **tolerance;** the Franks had friends

10 of many faiths and nationalities. Otto Frank served honorably as an officer in the German army during World War I.

Anne Frank Fonds-Basel/Anne Frank House-Amsterdam/Archive Photos.

Anne and her sister, Margot, with their father before their move to Amsterdam.

VOCABULARY

tolerance (täl'ər·əns) *n.:* respect for views different from your own.

Underline the detail that reveals the Franks' views on tolerance.

INTERPRET

Pause at line 12. What is ironic about Otto Frank's having served in the German army?

_____

_____

_____

_____

_____

_____

_____

_____

_____

_____

_____

_____

_____

_____

_____

_____

_____

_____

The Move to Amsterdam ■ 1933–1940

However, the circumstances of the early 1930s dramatically altered the situation for the Frank family. In the summer of 1933, Otto Frank left Frankfurt for Amsterdam to set up a branch of his brother's company called the Dutch Opekta Company.

Less than a year later, Edith, Margot, and Anne (four years
20   old) joined Otto in Amsterdam.

Anne, her mother, and Margot hold hands in Frankfurt before their move.

A portrait of Anne taken in a photo booth. The date and her weight in kilograms are printed on the border. (A kilogram is about 2.2 pounds.)

By the mid-1930s, the Franks were settling into a normal routine in their apartment at 37 Merwedeplein: The girls were attending school, the family took vacations at the beach, and their circle of Jewish and non-Jewish friends grew.

A page from Anne's photo album, with portraits and beach scenes.

IDENTIFY

Re-read the paragraph to the left. What detail tells you that the Franks enjoyed living in a tolerant society?

_____

_____

_____

_____

_____

_____

_____

_____

_____

_____

_____

_____

_____

_____

_____

_____

_____

_____

_____

_____

_____

_____

haven (hā′vən) *n.:* safe place, refuge.

What clue word helps you with the meaning of *haven*? Circle it.

_____

_____

_____

_____

_____

_____

_____

_____

_____

_____

_____

_____

_____

_____

_____

_____

_____

_____

_____

_____

In 1938, Otto expanded his business, going into partnership with a merchant, Hermann van Pels, also a Jewish refugee from Nazi Germany.

Living Under Nazi Rule ▪ 1940–1942

30   Unfortunately, the Frank's belief that Amsterdam offered them a safe **haven** from Nazism was shattered when, in May 1940, Germany invaded the Netherlands and the Franks were once again forced to live under Nazi rule.

Anne Frank attended the local Montessori school, but after summer recess in 1941, the Nazi authorities forbade Jews to attend school with non-Jews.

Anne Frank Fonds-Basel/Anne Frank House-Amsterdam/Archive Photos.

In the first few years of the occupation, Anne and Margot continued to socialize with their friends and attend school.

But the Nazi administration, in conjunction with the Dutch Nazi Party and civil service, began issuing anti-Jewish decrees.

In May 1942, all Jews aged six and older were required to wear a yellow Star of David on their clothes. This was to set them apart from non-Jews.

Gabriel Hackett/Archive Photos.

WORD STUDY

The word *mandatory*, in the first line under the heading, means "forced." It means that the Jews were handed over to authorities and forced to work in the camps.

The word is based on *manus*, Latin for "hand." How is *manus* used in *manufacture*, *manual*, and *manuscript*?

_____

_____

_____

_____

_____

_____

_____

_____

_____

_____

_____

_____

_____

_____

_____

All Jews had to register their businesses and, later,
40   surrender them to non-Jews. Fortunately, Otto Frank, in anticipation of this decree, had already turned his business over to his non-Jewish colleagues Victor Kugler and Johannes Kleiman.

The Franks Plan to Go into Hiding ▪ 1942

By 1942, mass arrests of Jews and mandatory service in German "work camps" were becoming routine. Fearful for their lives, the Frank family began to prepare to go into hiding.

They already had a place in mind—an annex of rooms
50   above Otto Frank's office at 263 Prinsengracht in Amsterdam.

In addition, people on the office staff in the Dutch Opekta Company had agreed to help them. Besides Kugler and Kleiman, there were Miep and Jan Gies, Bep Voskuijl, and Bep's father—all considered to be trustworthy.

IDENTIFY

Re-read lines 39–48. Underline details that reveal how the Franks' normal life was shattered under the Nazi administration.

WORD STUDY

The word *implying* (line 69) means "suggesting." *Imply* and *infer* are closely linked. Speakers or writers imply; listeners and readers infer.

The people reading the notes would *infer*, or guess, that the Franks had left the country.

CLARIFY

Re-read lines 63–71. What caused the Frank family to flee to a hiding place?

_____

_____

_____

_____

_____

_____

_____

IDENTIFY

Pause at line 71. Why did the Franks feel that going into hiding was the only way to be safe?

_____

_____

_____

_____

_____

_____

The Frank family in Amsterdam.

Anne Frank Fonds-Basel/Anne Frank House-Amsterdam/ Archive Photos.

These friends and employees not only agreed to keep the business operating in their employer's absence; they agreed to risk their lives to help the Frank family survive.

Mr. Frank also made arrangements for his business partner,
60   Hermann van Pels, along with his wife, Auguste, and their son, Peter, to share the Prinsengracht hideaway.

The Secret Annex ■ 1942–1944

While these preparations were secretly under way, Anne celebrated her thirteenth birthday on June 12, 1942. On July 5, 1942, her sister, Margot, received a call-up notice to be deported to a Nazi "work camp."

Even though the hiding place was not yet ready, the Frank family realized that they had to move right away. They hurriedly packed their belongings and left notes implying
70   that they had left the country. On the evening of July 6, they moved into their hiding place.

Anne Frank Fonds-Basel/Anne Frank House-Amsterdam/ Archive Photos.

Less than two months after this photo was taken, Anne and her family went into hiding.

A week later, on July 13, the van Pels family joined the Franks. On November 16, 1942, the seven residents of the Secret Annex were joined by its eighth and final resident, Fritz Pfeffer.

For two years the Franks were part of an extended family in the Annex, sharing a confined space and living under constant dread of detection and arrest by the Nazis and their Dutch sympathizers.

80

Arrest and Deportation ■ 1944

At approximately 10 A.M., August 4, 1944, the Frank family's greatest fear came true. A Nazi policeman and several Dutch collaborators appeared at 263 Prinsengracht, having received an anonymous phone call about Jews hiding there. They charged straight for the bookcase leading to the Secret Annex.

EVALUATE

Re-read lines 72–79. Were the Franks truly safe? Explain.

WORD STUDY

A *collaborator* (kə·lab'ə·rā·tər) in this context (line 83) is someone who works with the enemy. Collaborators can also be people who work together on projects.

An Anne Frank Scrapbook   317

INTERPRET

Re-read the last sentence on this page. What powerful **irony** does this sentence convey—that is, a sense that we know something that the people involved do not know?

Karl Joseph Silberbauer, an Austrian Nazi, forced the residents to turn over all valuables. When he found out that Otto Frank had been a lieutenant in the German

90 army during World War I, he was a little less hostile. The residents were taken from the house, forced into a covered truck, taken to the Central Office for Jewish Emigration, and then to Weteringschans Prison.

Two of the helpers, Victor Kugler and Johannes Kleiman, were also imprisoned for their role in hiding the family. Miep Gies and Bep Voskuijl were not arrested, although Miep was brought in for questioning by the police.

A hinged bookcase at the rear of the office wall was all that separated the Secret Annex from the outside world.

Wolfgang Kaehler/CORBIS.

On August 8, 1944, after a brief stay in Weteringschans Prison, the residents of the Secret Annex were moved to

100 Westerbork transit camp. They remained there for nearly a month, until September 3, when they were transported to the Auschwitz death camp in Poland. It was the last Auschwitz-bound transport ever to leave Westerbork.

In October 1944, Anne and Margot were transported from Auschwitz to the Bergen-Belsen concentration camp in Germany. Thousands died from planned starvation and epidemics at Bergen-Belsen, which was without food, heat, medicine, or elementary sanitary conditions.

CORBIS.

Hundreds of women and children were packed into one room at the Bergen-Belsen concentration camp. Bergen-Belsen became overcrowded with prisoners as the Nazis retreated from the Eastern Front.

110   Anne and Margot, already **debilitated,** contracted typhus and grew even sicker. Margot, nineteen years old, and Anne, fifteen years old, died in February and March, 1945.

After the War

Otto Frank was the only resident of the Annex to survive the Holocaust. He found it difficult to settle permanently in Amsterdam with its constant reminders of his lost family.

He and his second wife, Elfried Geiringer, also an Auschwitz survivor, moved to Basel, Switzerland, in 1953. Otto Frank died on August 19, 1980; he was ninety-one.

VOCABULARY

debilitated (dē·bil′ə·tāt′əd) *adj.*: weakened; made feeble.

Circle the words that help you figure out the meaning of *debilitated*.

INTERPRET

Read back through the text, and look at the details given about the Frank family's views on tolerance compared with the actions of the Nazi forces. What **main idea** do these details add up to?

_____

_____

_____

_____

_____

_____

CONNECT

This Web site reveals what one family—the Franks—experienced during World War II. Where might you look to find other sources on the topic of World War II?

_____

_____

_____

_____

_____

An Anne Frank Scrapbook

Main-Idea Chart   Jot down key details from "An Anne Frank Scrapbook" in the chart below. Then, in the space provided, describe its main idea.

Topic: Anne Frank's Family

Detail
↓

Detail
↓

Detail
↓

Detail
↓

Detail
↓

Main Idea

Skills Review

An Anne Frank Scrapbook

VOCABULARY AND COMPREHENSION

A. Selection Vocabulary   Write words from the Word Bank on the blanks to complete the paragraph below.

> **Word Bank**
>
> tolerance
> haven
> debilitated

In my (1) _____ state, there was nothing I could do but dream of a happier future. I imagined finding a (2) _____ where we could be safe. There we would live with others in a spirit of (3) _____. It would be a place where people with different beliefs would live together peacefully.

B. Reading Comprehension   Answer each question below.

1. Where and when was Anne Frank born? _____

   _____

2. In 1942, why did the Franks go into hiding in Amsterdam? Where did they hide? _____

   _____

3. How long did the Franks stay in hiding in Amsterdam? How were they finally arrested? _____

   _____

4. How, when, and where did Anne die? _____

   _____

5. Which member of the Frank family survived the Holocaust? When did he or she die? _____

   _____

from **Beyond the Grave**

by Troy Taylor

READING SKILLS: SUPPORTED AND UNSUPPORTED INFERENCES

In the yard a cat meows suddenly, races into the house, and dives under the sofa. Outside you can hear the furious barking of a large dog. Do you infer that—

(A) the cat is eager for his nap, or

(B) the cat has been frightened by a large dog?

If you chose A, your inference, or guess, is unsupported: The facts don't indicate that the cat is tired or that the cat likes to nap under the sofa. If you chose B, your inference *is* supported: The facts given seem to add up to that conclusion.

As you read the excerpt from *Beyond the Grave,* check to see if the writer's inferences about the mysterious visitor to Edgar Allan Poe's grave are supported or unsupported.

VOCABULARY DEVELOPMENT: PREVIEW SELECTION VOCABULARY

Spend a few minutes getting to know these words before you read from *Beyond the Grave.*

compelling (kəm·pel′iŋ) *adj.:* irresistibly interesting; captivating.

> *One of the most compelling cemeteries on the East Coast is located in Baltimore, although many people are unaware that a portion of it even exists.*

tangible (tan′jə·bəl) *adj.:* able to be touched; actual or real.

> *Unlike a ghost, the man visiting the grave seems to be quite tangible.*

ritual (rich′o͞o·əl) *n.:* ceremony.

> *The man carries out an odd ritual, leaving roses and cognac at the grave every January 19.*

elusive (ē·lo͞o′siv) *adj.:* hard to capture or get hold of.

> *The mysterious man remains elusive. He was photographed once in 1990, but his face was shadowed by his black hat.*

SKILLS FOCUS

Reading Skills
Analyze supported and unsupported inferences.

from Beyond the Grave

Troy Taylor

One of the most **compelling** cemeteries on the East Coast is located in Baltimore, although many people are unaware that a portion of it even exists. It is called the Old Western Burial Ground, and it holds the remains of people such as Edgar Allan Poe, the son of Francis Scott Key, the grandfather of President James Buchanan, five former mayors of Baltimore, and fifteen generals from the Revolutionary War and the War of 1812.

Not all of the cemetery is easy to find, for the
10   Westminster Presbyterian Church (now Westminster Hall) was built over a large portion of the cemetery. These graves and tombs date back to a century before the church was built. Much of the cemetery, where Poe is buried, is still accessible above ground in the churchyard, but a large portion of the graveyard can only be reached by way of the catacombs underneath the building. It is here where the ghosts of this eerie graveyard are said to walk. Strangely though, these restless spirits are not the most enduring mystery of the Western Burial Ground.

20   This famous and unsolved mystery involves a man who has been seen in the graveyard for more than fifty years. Whoever this strange figure may be, he is always described in the same way. Dressed completely in black, including a black fedora and a black scarf to hide his face, he carries a walking stick and strolls into the cemetery every year on January 19, the birth date of Edgar Allan Poe. On every occasion, he has left behind a bottle of cognac

From "The Mystery of Edgar Allan Poe & the Haunted Catacombs" from *Beyond the Grave* by Troy Taylor. Copyright © 2001 by **Troy Taylor**. Reproduced by permission of the author.

Notes _____

_____

_____

_____

_____

_____

_____

_____

> ### VOCABULARY
>
> **compelling** (kəm·pel′iŋ) *adj.:* irresistibly interesting; captivating.

> ### WORD STUDY
>
> Catacombs (line 16) are a series of vaults or galleries in an underground burial place.

> ### WORD STUDY
>
> A fedora (line 24) is a type of hat.

> ### IDENTIFY
>
> Pause at line 26. How is the mysterious visitor described? Circle the words that people use to describe him.

and three red roses on the gravesite of the late author. After
placing these items with care, he then stands, tips his hat,
30 and walks away. The offerings always remain on the grave.
One year, they were accompanied by a note, bearing no
signature, which read: "Edgar, I haven't forgotten you."

There have been many stories that claim the ghost
of Edgar Allan Poe haunts his gravesite, but the man in
black seems to be quite **tangible,** although who he is
remains a riddle. In addition, scholars and curiosity seekers
remain puzzled by the odd **ritual** he carries out and the
significance of the items he leaves behind. The roses and
cognac have been brought to the cemetery every January
40 since 1949, and yet no clue has been offered as to the origin
or true meaning of the offerings.

The identity of the man has been an intriguing
mystery for years. Many people, including Jeff Jerome, the
curator of the nearby Edgar Allan Poe house, believe that
there may be more than one person leaving the tributes.
Jerome himself has seen a white-haired man while other

© Lee Snider/CORBIS.

observers have reported a man with black hair. Possibly, the second person may be the son of the man who originated the ritual. Regardless, Jerome has been quoted as saying that if he has his way, the man's identity will never be known. This is something that most Baltimore residents agree with. Jerome has received numerous telephone calls from people requesting that no attempt ever be made to approach the man.

For some time, rumors persisted that Jerome was the mysterious man in black, so in 1983, he invited 70 people to gather at the graveyard at midnight on January 19. They had a celebration in honor of the author's birthday with a glass of amontillado, a Spanish sherry featured in one of Poe's horror tales, and readings from the author's works. At about an hour past midnight, the celebrants were startled to see a man run through the cemetery in a black frock coat. He was fair-haired and carrying a walking stick and quickly disappeared around the cemetery's east wall. The roses and cognac were found on Poe's grave as usual.

Not in an effort to solve the mystery, but merely to enhance it, Jerome allowed a photographer to try and capture the **elusive** man on film. The photographer was backed by *Life* magazine and was equipped with rented infrared night-vision photo equipment. A radio signal triggered the camera so that the photographer could remain out of sight. The picture appeared in the July 1990 issue of *Life* and showed the back of a heavyset man kneeling at Poe's grave. His face cannot really be seen because it was shadowed by his black hat. No one else has ever been able to photograph the mysterious man again.

INFER

Pause at line 54. Why might Jerome wish the visitor's identity to remain a secret?

VOCABULARY

elusive (ē·lōō′siv) *adj.:* hard to capture or get hold of.

ANALYZE

In the final sentence of the text, the writer appears to be stating a fact. Re-read the final section of the text, and explain whether or not you think the statement is, indeed, a fact.

from Beyond the Grave

Inferences Chart   In the excerpt from *Beyond the Grave,* the writer makes a lot of inferences about who pays annual visits to Poe's grave. In the chart below, record some of the writer's inferences. Then, indicate whether each inference is supported or unsupported in the right-hand column.

Writer's Inference	Supported by Facts?

Skills Review

from Beyond the Grave

VOCABULARY AND COMPREHENSION

A. Selection Vocabulary   Write words from the Word Bank on the blanks to complete the paragraph below.

> **Word Bank**
>
> compelling
> tangible
> ritual
> elusive

The mystery was so (1) _____ that I could not get it out of my mind. I decided I couldn't rest until I had found some (2) _____ evidence that would finally reveal the identity of the mysterious visitor. However, such evidence was proving maddeningly (3) _____. Would we never have an explanation for this strange (4) _____ that took place each year?

B. Reading Comprehension   Answer each question below.

1. Where is Edgar Allan Poe buried? Is his gravesite in the churchyard or in catacombs beneath the building? _____

   _____

2. What does the mysterious visitor leave at Poe's grave every year on Poe's birthday? How does the visitor dress? _____

   _____

3. For how many years have the offerings been left at Poe's grave?

   _____

4. Why does Jeff Jerome invite people to Poe's grave on January 19, 1983, at midnight? What do the guests see? _____

   _____

5. Why does Jerome allow a photographer to try to get a photograph of the mysterious visitor? _____

   _____

Petals by Pat Mora
Petals: A Summary

READING SKILLS: WHAT GOES INTO A SUMMARY

If you asked a friend what he did over the weekend, would you expect him to say he brushed his teeth and ate lunch? Probably not. You'd expect only the highlights or important details. In a text summary, **critical details** are the details that are necessary for a summary to make sense. If a critical detail is left out, the summary falls apart or is not logical.

Here is a checklist of what a good summary contains:
- **Author** and **title** of the work.
- A **summary of a story** should identify the main characters, the main problem or conflict, the main events in the order they happen, and the resolution of the problem.
- A **summary of a poem** should capture the essence of the poem and describe its form and any rhyme and rhythm.
- A work's **theme**—its insight about life—should also be revealed in a summary.

As you read "Petals" and "Petals: A Summary," notice the details in the summary, and think about how the summary helps you understand the poem.

SKILLS FOCUS

Reading Skills
Understand summaries.

Petals

Pat Mora

have calloused her hands,
brightly colored crepe paper: turquoise,
yellow, magenta, which she shapes
into large blooms for bargain-hunting tourists
5   who see her flowers, her puppets, her baskets,
but not her—small, gray-haired woman
wearing a white apron, who hides behind
blossoms in her stall at the market,
who sits and remembers collecting wildflowers
10 as a girl, climbing rocky Mexican hills
to fill a straw hat with soft blooms
which she'd stroke gently, over and over again
with her smooth fingertips.

© Royalty-Free/CORBIS.

Flower in stained-glass window (detail).

CLARIFY

Line 1 seems to begin in the middle of a sentence, but it's really a continuation of the thought that begins in the poem's title. What has caused the callouses on the woman's hands?

IDENTIFY

Re-read the poem carefully, and underline the details that seem important to you.

INTERPRET

What **theme** is hinted at in the woman's memories of collecting wildflowers in lines 9–13?

_____

_____

_____

_____

FLUENCY

Read the poem aloud a few times, speaking as clearly and smoothly as you can. Remember that the poem's title is part of the poem. Think about which words you will emphasize and about where you will slow down for dramatic effect.

Petals: A SUMMARY

"Petals" is a poem by Pat Mora. The poem is a single sentence, and the title is its first word. In it, an old woman sits in a Mexican market selling colorful flowers that she has fashioned from crepe paper. Almost invisible to her customers, she hides behind the huge paper blossoms and remembers collecting wildflowers in the hills as a girl. Though short, this poem has many themes. One is that the beauty of nature is unforgettable.

Petals / Petals: A Summary

Summary Worksheet   When you analyze a summary, you check to see if the **critical details** and important elements of the text are included in the summary. Re-read "Petals" and "Petals: A Summary," which is also printed below. Locate and underline all of the critical details in the summary printed below.

SKILLS FOCUS

Reading Skills
Analyze a summary.

"Petals: A Summary"

"Petals" is a poem by Pat Mora. The poem is a single sentence, and the

title is its first word. In it, an old woman sits in a Mexican market selling

colorful flowers that she has fashioned from crepe paper. Almost invisible

to her customers, she hides behind the huge paper blossoms and

remembers collecting wildflowers in the hills as a girl. Though short, this

poem has many themes. One is that the beauty of nature is unforgettable.

Skills Review

Petals / Petals: A Summary

COMPREHENSION

Reading Comprehension   Answer each question below.

1. Why does the woman have calloused hands?

   _____

   _____

   _____

2. To whom does the woman sell her crafts?

   _____

   _____

   _____

3. What does the woman remember as she sits in her stall at the market?

   _____

   _____

   _____

4. Besides details from the poem, what additional information is provided in "Petals: A Summary"?

   _____

   _____

   _____

   _____

   _____

   _____

The Mane Story by Fiona Sunquist

READING SKILLS: LOGIC, COHERENCE, AND CONSISTENCY

What if a newspaper sports story started by summarizing a baseball game and suddenly shifted to a discussion about a highly paid basketball star? You'd probably be pretty confused. In order for a text to make sense and to hold together, it should be logical and coherent.

Logic is simply correct reasoning. A statement is logical if it is supported by reasons, evidence, and examples. For a text to be logical, it must also have **coherence.** A coherent text is easily understood and flows naturally from one idea to the next. One way writers make a text coherent is by using **transitional words** to connect ideas. A text that is both logical and coherent has **internal consistency.** That means that all of its parts work together and make sense.

As you read "The Mane Story," notice the transitional words the writer uses to give the text coherence. The list below shows how transitional words are used and gives examples of words used in each situation.

Type of Transition	Words Used
Connecting ideas in time sequence, or **chronologically**	first, next, before, then, when, while, meanwhile, at last
Connecting things in **space**	above, across, among, before, below, here, in, near, there, under, next to
Connecting ideas in **order of importance**	first, mainly, more important, to begin with, then, last
Comparing ideas	also, and, another, just as, like, similarly
Contrasting ideas	although, but, however, still, yet, on the other hand

SKILLS FOCUS

Reading Skills
Understand logic, coherence, and consistency.

THE MANE STORY
The Surprising Truth About This Cat's Big Hair

Fiona Sunquist

© Royalty-Free/CORBIS.

IDENTIFY

Circle the word that connects the two ideas in lines 5–7.

IDENTIFY

What **transitional word** is used in line 8? What type of transition is this?

_____

_____

_____

If the lion is the "king of beasts," his mane is his crown. Male lions are the only cats with manes, and they use them to win and defend territory. What does a big hairy head have to do with keeping a kingdom? It's all about a "look." A mane makes a male lion look bigger than he is, both from the side and head on. And in the lion's world, bigger is better.

When a male lion meets another lion, he does what researchers call a "lion strut." He raises his body as high as

10　possible on stiffly stretched legs, tucks his chin into his chest, and arches his black-tufted tail high in the air over his back. Along with his mane, the strut makes him look more threatening.

In a fight with another male over females or territory, a lion's mane also comes in handy as a neck protector. The dense mat of hair absorbs blows as the lions whack each other with their front paws. Sometimes one lion's claws get caught in the other's mane, leaving him tangled and vulnerable.

20 One of the signs of a strong and healthy lion is a mane that is in good shape. "The condition of the mane reflects the condition of the lion," says Karyl Whitman, a biologist who studies lions in the wild. "If a lion is seriously injured, he will sometimes lose his mane entirely."

Some scientists think that big manes make male lions more attractive to females. "A healthy mane indicates that a lion is probably a good protector and will help provide for the females and their cubs," Whitman explains.

But while manes may be useful for impressing the lionesses, they can be a major disadvantage to the males 30 when it comes to hunting. All that fluff makes it difficult to sneak up on prey. In a pride, or group, lionesses do most of the hunting.

African lions live on grassy plains, in open woodlands, and in scrub forests south of the Sahara in the areas shown in dark gray on the map above.

FLUENCY

Read lines 8–13 aloud several times. Strive to read the passage as clearly and smoothly as you can. Think about how you might emphasize the description of the "lion strut" for dramatic effect.

IDENTIFY

Underline the **evidence** in lines 19–23 that supports the first sentence of the paragraph.

IDENTIFY

Skim through lines 8–32. Circle the word *mane* each time it appears. What does this repetition tell you about the article's coherence and consistency?

Re-read lines 33–40. How does having a dark mane benefit older lions?

_____

_____

_____

_____

_____

_____

_____

_____

_____

Examine the chart at the right. Why do you think the writer chose to present this information in this format?

_____

_____

_____

_____

_____

_____

_____

_____

_____

A lion's mane usually gets darker as he gets older. A big, dark mane on a resident lion (a male that protects a lion pride) makes him very visible from a distance. Nomad lions (wandering males without a pride) can probably spot a resident lion in time to avoid his territory—and a battle. "Lions don't fight unless they have to," says Whitman. Just as a lion's strut can avoid an all-out fight, visibility also helps keep peace in the kingdom.

Now you know one way a lion maintains power: He
40 makes sure that no day is a bad hair day!

By the Numbers

3 is the number of cubs in a typical litter of lions.

5 miles is the distance the sound of a lion's roar can carry.

15 pounds of meat is a typical meal for an adult male lion.

20 hours is how long some lions spend resting each day.

36 miles an hour is a lion's top running speed.

430 pounds is a male lion's average weight.

2,200 pounds is the top weight of prey a pride can kill.

The Mane Story

Logic-and-Coherence Chart   Use the chart below to analyze the logic and coherence of "The Mane Story." In the left-hand column, list several statements the writer makes, along with the support she uses to show that the statements are logical. In the right-hand column, list examples of transitional words the writer uses, and identify the type of transition. HINT: Refer to the chart on page 333 for types of transitions.

Reading Skills
Analyze a text for logic and coherence.

Statement: Support:	Transitional Word: Type of Transition:
Statement: Support:	Transitional Word: Type of Transition:
Statement: Support:	Transitional Word: Type of Transition:

Skills Review

The Mane Story

COMPREHENSION

Reading Comprehension   Answer each question below.

1. What is the topic of the article?

   _____

   _____

2. How is a lion's mane useful in a fight with another lion?

   _____

   _____

   _____

3. In what way can manes be a disadvantage to lions?

   _____

   _____

   _____

4. What does a dark mane indicate?

   _____

   _____

   _____

5. About how much meat does an adult male lion eat in a typical meal? What is the average weight of a male lion?

   _____

   _____

   _____

Before You Read

ARTICLE

Earth-Friendly Products?

READING SKILLS: ELEMENTS AND FEATURES OF CONSUMER MATERIALS

How much long-distance time do I get with this cell-phone contract? How do I install this new computer game? Can I put these plastic boxes in the recycling bin? Answers to questions like these are found in consumer materials. Examples of **consumer materials** include contracts, instruction manuals, and product information.

It's important to analyze consumer materials carefully, especially when reading product information. Something that sounds very good at first glance may not be exactly what you expected. In "Earth-Friendly Products?", which is written for consumers, you'll learn how to avoid being misled by product labels.

VOCABULARY DEVELOPMENT: PREVIEW SELECTION VOCABULARY

Take some time to preview these words before you read "Earth-Friendly Products?"

biodegradable (bī′ō·di·grā′də·bəl) *adj.:* able to be broken down by the action of living organisms (such as bacteria).

The package claimed the bags were biodegradable, but our science teacher said it would take many years for bacteria to break them down.

skeptical (skep′ti·kəl) *adj.:* doubtful; having reservations about something.

I'm sometimes skeptical about claims on product packaging because the goal of the packaging is to persuade you to buy the product.

reclaimed (rē′klāmd′) *v.:* rescued; recovered for use.

I try to buy paper products that have been reclaimed from the trash and recycled into new products.

decomposition (dē·käm′pə·zish′ən) *n.:* decay; the breaking down of a substance into simple substances.

If decomposition of a product takes many years, a claim that the product is biodegradable doesn't seem to mean much.

SKILLS
FOCUS

Reading Skills
Understand
consumer
materials.

from Zillions, April/May 1992

Earth-Friendly Products?

PREDICT

Identify and circle the question that precedes the first paragraph of the article. Based on what it says, do you think the article will be on the side of the businesses that produce trash or on the side of the environment?

_____

_____

_____

_____

VOCABULARY

biodegradable
(bi′ō·di·grā′də·bəl) *adj.:* able to be broken down by the action of living organisms (such as bacteria).

skeptical (skep′ti·kəl) *adj.:* doubtful; having reservations about something.

INTERPRET

Locate and circle the subheads within the article. How are the subheads alike?

_____

_____

_____

_____

_____

Can the People Who Bring You All That Trash Be Nice to Nature?

Eric is seriously Earth-friendly, and not just around his house. He tries to stay Earth-friendly when he shops, too. "When I buy something that I can recycle," he says, "I'm glad."

These days, it's easy to find products that make Eric feel good. More and more products claim they're
10 "recyclable," "recycled," "**biodegradable,**" or otherwise neat for the environment. Brian is **skeptical.** He believes many of the claims are phony. Lauren feels the same way: "I don't always trust them."

Are these *Zillions* readers right to be suspicious? Should Eric trust the claims made by many products?

Recyclable?

Advertisers can say almost anything they want when it comes to "Earth-friendliness." There are no official government rules, for instance, about what can or can't be called
20 "recyclable."

Consider the juice box. You could tote your apple juice in a thermos, but "juice boxes are convenient, easier to carry than a thermos, and don't spill like cans," says Lauren. They also add up to a lot of garbage, say environmentalists. The four billion juice boxes sold in 1990 equaled about

80,000 tons of trash. Because they are made of several materials—six layers of paper, plastic, and aluminum foil—they are costly to recycle into useful stuff. Yet some ads claimed the boxes were "as easy to recycle" as newspaper.

30   "*I* can't find where to recycle them," says juice-box fan Lauren. No wonder—there are only a handful of places to do it. Most are in school programs partly paid for by the juice-box companies. For most of us, it's impossible to recycle the boxes.

     "Recyclable" claims on many plastic containers are baloney, and not the kind you eat. One yogurt tub states: "This is a recyclable container." Its lid *is* made from a plastic that's easily recycled, but the tub itself isn't. It's made from a different plastic that's much harder to recycle. 40 Most plastic food containers are never recycled.

     Another plastic that is rarely recycled is polystyrene (often referred to as Styrofoam). Maybe your school cafeteria has polystyrene trays or plates like the ones at RHAM Middle School, in Hebron, Connecticut. The kids there are helping their school explore whether the cafeteria should switch to another kind of tray. "We're looking into cardboard or permanent trays," says Jessica. "Every kind has good and bad points."

     The reality of any "recyclable" claim always depends on 50 your local recycling programs. "Before you buy, check whether the product can be recycled in your area," suggests Anthony. A product can be covered with "recyclable" labels. But if there's no place for *you* to recycle it, it's not recyclable. This may be true even for items like plastic milk jugs, made of one of the few plastics easy to recycle. Lauren's community doesn't collect them. Anthony's does.

IDENTIFY

According to this article, why are juice boxes difficult to recycle? Underline details that support your response.

_____

_____

_____

_____

_____

_____

DECODING TIP

Divide *polystyrene* (line 41) into syllables to help you pronounce this chemical's name.

IDENTIFY

Pause at line 56. What does the writer suggest you do before making your purchase?

_____

_____

_____

_____

_____

_____

Gary Buss/FPG International LLC.

VOCABULARY

reclaimed (rē′klāmd′) *v.*: rescued; recovered for use.

The prefix *re–* means "again." Think of at least five other words that use the prefix *re–*.

_____

_____

_____

_____

_____

_____

IDENTIFY

The author makes a claim in lines 58–61 that not all things labeled "recycled" have been reclaimed from trash. Read on, and underline examples she gives to support her claim.

Recycled?

Maybe you think a "recycled" product is made of stuff that has been used, then **reclaimed** from the trash, like old
60   newspapers. That's sometimes true. But often these items are made from material that's never been used at all. It can be trimmings left over at the factory or items that could not be sold.

   For example, suppose a company makes too many large rolls of paper and can't sell them all. It can grind up the leftover paper, mix it with new paper, and sell it as "recycled" paper. That's true for much of the recycled paper we buy. This sort of re-use has been going on for many years. Suddenly, however, these products have acquired a
70   "recycled" label, so people like Eric will feel good about buying them.

Real wastepaper is often used in making cereal boxes and other kinds of cardboard. To tell if your favorite cereal brand uses recycled paper, just cut through a box. If it's gray or brown under the coating, it's probably made from wastepaper. White all the way through? It's fresh from the tree.

Biodegradable?

A truly biodegradable product is something like an apple
80 core. Once it's thrown away, it breaks down (rather quickly) into substances that aren't harmful to the Earth. People purchased one company's trash bags and another company's disposable diapers because ads made them think these products were better for the environment. But most trash bags and diapers end up in landfills where they are covered with piles of garbage. They are never exposed to the air, sunlight, and moisture that could make them break down.

We found a new wrinkle in environmental ad talk on a box of trash bags, which claims to be "Fighting Pollution."
90 The label boasts that these bags "will not release harmful products of **decomposition** that can contaminate underground water supplies." That's trying to get some mileage out of the fact these bags are *not* biodegradable!

Buys 'R' Us?

Finding out what's *really* better for the environment has even the experts confused. And since companies can claim almost anything, you'd have to be a wizard at environmental ad games to know what to believe. To make less garbage, just follow the three Rs:
100 **Reduce:** This is the most important of the three. If you don't need it, don't buy it. Or use it. Lauren bought

DECODING TIP

Draw a vertical line between the syllables of *landfills* (line 85). What two words make up this word? What can you guess the word means?

_____

_____

_____

_____

WORD STUDY

The **idiom** found in line 88 makes no sense if it is translated literally. Underline the idiom. Based on its context, what do you guess the idiom means?

_____

_____

_____

_____

_____

_____

_____

VOCABULARY

decomposition
(dē·käm′pə·zish′ən) *n.:* decay; the breaking down of a substance into simple substances.

Composition, decomposition, and related words, such as *compose,* come from the Latin *componere,* meaning "put together."

a teeny hairclip, but the clerk gave her a humongous bag. "I gave it back."

Re-use: Choose products (and packages) that can be used more than once. Avoid anything used just once and thrown away, like a juice box.

Recycle: Think of this as a last resort. According to one expert: "We're recycling products we probably shouldn't be using in the first place." Make the effort to find out what can be recycled in your area. (The information on the next page can help you understand plastic codes.) If you're not sure, swallow a product's environmental claims with a grain of salt. Or swallow the product. One of the world's most Earth-friendly containers is an ice-cream cone.

110

Plastics Decoded

If you turn over most plastic containers, you'll see a number from 1 to 7. What does it mean? It's a code for the type of plastic used. Jessica knew that plastics with higher numbers aren't very recyclable:

Code 1: Used for soft-drink bottles; often recycled.

Code 2: Used for milk and detergent jugs; often recycled.

Code 3: Used for shampoos and similar products; rarely recycled—produces toxic gases when burned.

Code 4: Used for plastic wrap; rarely recycled.

Code 5: Used for food containers; rarely recycled.

Code 6: Used for Styrofoam, fast-food containers, trays, cups, plates; sometimes recycled from schools and restaurants.

Code 7: All other types of plastic; rarely recycled.

CORBIS.

IDENTIFY

What kind of information is the consumer given in the list on this page?

Earth-Friendly Products?

Consumer-Materials Chart   In "Earth-Friendly Products?" you learned how important it is to analyze product packaging. Fill in the chart below with examples from the selection that show how labels can be misleading.

Recyclable?	Recycled?	Biodegradable?
Product Claims:	Product Claims:	Product Claims:
Possible Problems:	Possible Problems:	Possible Problems:

Skills Review

Earth-Friendly Products?

VOCABULARY AND COMPREHENSION

A. Selection Vocabulary   Write words from the Word Bank on the blanks to complete the paragraph below.

When shopping for groceries, be (1) _____ of the claims you see on every product. Many companies announce boldly that their products are (2) _____, but often the claim is false. Other companies claim that purchasers can recycle the packaging, but often only one or two of its components can be (3) _____. In a landfill, only a small percentage of containers can be broken down through (4) _____.

B. Reading Comprehension   Answer each question below.

1. Why can advertisers make almost any "earth-friendly" claims they want about their products? _____

   _____

2. Is everything labeled "recyclable" really recyclable? Explain.

   _____

3. Is a recycled product always made from materials reclaimed from trash? Explain. _____

   _____

4. What are the "three Rs" of making less garbage? _____

   _____

5. Would a plastic product be more likely to be recycled if it had a recycling code of 1 or of 7? Explain. _____

   _____

Index of Authors and Titles

Vocabulary Development

Pronunciation guides, in parentheses, are provided for the vocabulary words in this book. The following key will help you use those pronunciation guides.

As a practice in using a pronunciation guide, sound out the words used as examples in the list that follows. See if you can hear the way the same vowel might be sounded in different words. For example, say "at" and "ate" aloud. Can you hear the difference in the way "a" sounds?

The symbol ə is called a **schwa.** A schwa is used by many dictionaries to indicate a sort of weak sound like the "a" in "ago." Some people say the schwa sounds like "eh." A vowel sounded like a schwa is never accented.

The vocabulary words in this book are also provided with a part-of-speech label. The parts of speech are *n.* (noun), *v.* (verb), *pro.* (pronoun), *adj.* (adjective), *adv.* (adverb), *prep.* (preposition), *conj.* (conjunction), and *interj.* (interjection). To learn about the parts of speech, consult the *Holt Handbook.*

To learn more about the vocabulary words, consult your dictionary. You will find that many of the words defined here have several other meanings.

---

at, āte, cär; ten, ēve; is, īce; gō, hôrn, lŏok, tōol; oil, out; up, fʉr; ə *for unstressed vowels, as* a *in* ago, u *in* focus; ' *as in* Latin (lat''n); chin; she; zh *as in* azure (azh'ər); thin, *th*e; ŋ *as in* ring (riŋ)

Notes

Notes

Notes